Contemporary Economic Sociology

D1524187

- How are transnational processes re-making contemporary economies?
- Can capitalist globalisation be governed or resisted?
- Do class relations still shape people's social identities?
- How can we think about inequality in national and international contexts?

This text examines key contemporary issues in the sociology of economic life. Drawing on a range of critical perspectives, it analyses major trends in the restructuring of economy and society - from the politics and economics of globalisation to post-industrial economies, the 'end' of class and current patterns of inequality. The book is organised around three core themes: the globalisation of social and economic relations; shifts in the nature of products, production and work; changing class identities and economic inequalities.

Major changes in each of these spheres have re-shaped social and economic relations, structures of power and forms of identity. The book sets these changes in a transnational context, and examines critical frameworks for understanding such shifts. Drawing on arguments from economic sociology, politics and policy studies, political economy and critical geography, it analyses processes of social and economic restructuring over the last three decades. It includes discussions of globalisation and capitalist development; finance and information networks; structures of international economic governance; post-Fordism and the sign economy; the re-making of class; social exclusion and global inequalities. By making connections across wider fields of debate, the text both offers a critical survey of current concerns for the discipline of economic sociology, and sets out a broader sphere of interest for the social analysis of economic life.

This book provides an accessible and critical discussion of key issues in current social and economic analysis, in a context where readers are increasingly interested in the study of globalisation, international governance and economic power. Its international approach, together with its focus on wide-scale social and economic changes, gives the book considerable international appeal. The text will be particularly relevant to undergraduate and graduate students and scholars in the fields of economic and political sociology, politics and government, geography, economics and international relations.

Fran Tonkiss is Lecturer in Sociology at the London School of Economics and Political Science. She is the author of *Space, the City and Social Theory* (2005), the co-author of *Market Society* (2001), and the co-editor of *Trust and Civil Society* (2000).

Contemporary Economic Sociology

Globalisation, production, inequality

Fran Tonkiss

LONDON AND NEW YORK

First published 2006
by Routledge
2 Park Square, Milton Park, Abingdon, Oxon OX14 4RN

Simultaneously published in the USA and Canada
by Routledge
270 Madison Ave, New York, NY 10016

*Routledge is an imprint of the Taylor & Francis Group, an
informa business*

Typeset in Sabon by
RefineCatch Limited, Bungay, Suffolk
Printed and bound in Great Britain by
MPG Books Ltd, Bodmin

British Library Cataloguing in Publication Data
A catalogue record for this book is available from the British Library

Library of Congress Cataloging in Publication Data
A catalog record for this book has been requested

ISBN10: 0–415–30094–0 (pbk)
ISBN10: 0–415–30093–2 (hbk)
ISBN10: 0–203–97006–3 (ebk)

ISBN13: 978–0–415–30094–0 (pbk)
ISBN13: 978–0–415–30093–3 (hbk)
ISBN13: 978–0–203–97006–5 (ebk)

Contents

Introduction

This book examines economic changes in contemporary capitalist societies, and the ways in which social theorists have attempted to analyse them. It aims to set key issues within the sociology of economic life – capitalism, production, work, class, inequalities – in the context of increasingly international social and economic arrangements. The text is organised around three core themes: (1) capitalism and globalisation; (2) production; (3) class and inequality. Framed in this way, it rethinks central concepts in economic sociology in relation to recent processes of capitalist restructuring. This provides the basis for a critical analysis of such issues as economic globalisation; networks, power and resistance in the global economy; post-Fordism and post-industrialism; the economy of information and signs; class, insecurity and social exclusion.

Contemporary Economic Sociology builds on founding categories within the sociological tradition – such as capitalism, production and class – so as to address current socioeconomic problems. The title may look simple, but two basic qualifications still need to be made: quite what is meant by 'contemporary' in this context, and how to define the limits of economic sociology. In focusing on contemporary conditions, to take up the first question, I am concerned with broad processes of economic restructuring that can be traced from around the 1970s. The text in this way is engaged with the recent history of present conditions. This is partly to counter a tendency to see current arrangements as distinctly *new*, as is evident in certain debates over globalisation, in accounts of the 'immaterial' economy, or in statements about the death of class. It is also intended to chart a range of critical thinking about the intersection of economy and society which continues to inform debates today. The analytical frame for each part of the book, therefore, begins with arguments dating from the 1970s and 1980s which set up critical terms, identify substantive changes, and establish key points of reference. The first section on capitalism and globalisation opens with the perspective offered by world systems theory on the expansionary logic of capitalist accumulation. The accounts of changes in production in Part II start out from the work of the French regulation school on Fordism and post-Fordism, and from Daniel Bell's thesis on post-industrial society. The third section, on social identities and economic divisions, begins with neo-Marxist and Weberian debates over changing class structures. In general terms, this approach is designed to provide a critical context for current concerns, and to trace a contemporary history of debate over the dynamics and effects of social and economic restructuring.

This range of arguments, however, also raises the question of how economic sociology is to be defined. Thinking about the links between economic and social processes is not confined to sociologists in general, or to economic sociologists in particular. The text therefore draws on the interdisciplinary strengths of economic sociology to take in critical insights from the domains of politics, political economy, geography and anthropology. Economic sociology shares a border with each of these disciplines, but at times has seemed tentative about crossing them (see Swedberg 1991: 270). Beyond making links with relevant debates from elsewhere, the text also focuses on the work of sociologists who are not always closely associated with economic sociology as a distinct subdiscipline. Economic sociology may be defined by a diverse set of analytic concerns, including the study of firms and organisations; markets, hierarchies and networks; market structures; historical and comparative analysis of market forms; state policy in respect of markets; money, financial instruments and risk; economic behaviour and rationality; and cultures of economic life (see Block and Evans 2005; Carruthers and Babb 2000; Dodd 1994; Fevre 2003; Fligstein 2001; Holton 1992; Swedberg 1991; Trigilia 2002; Zelizer 1997; Zukin and DiMaggio 1990). This kind of diversity is a critical strength, although it can make it hard to work out just what counts as doing economic sociology. While attempts to demarcate the field might be important for staking out clear lines of enquiry and debate, they can also have the unintended effect of limiting sociology's engagement with economic issues to approved domains. The discussions that follow do not aim to set limits around economic sociology in any strict sense, nor to provide a survey of current approaches (for valuable overviews of the field, see Biggart 2003; Carruthers and Uzzi 2001; Dobbin 2004; Granovetter and Swedberg 2001; Guillen *et al.* 2002; Smelser and Swedberg 2005). Rather, they seek to add to economic sociology's critical range by bringing in perspectives from what might be considered the 'outside'. My point in adopting this approach is to underline the extent to which – after the critique of Marxism, after the end of class, after the cultural turn – sociologists in general (not just economic sociologists or even unrepentant Marxists, although a few of each will feature below) remain centrally concerned with economic problems. To draw some examples from across the text: the work of Wallerstein on the capitalist world economy, of Castells on network society, of Lash and Urry on the economy of signs, of Bourdieu on class and capital, all represent key interventions by sociologists on economic issues, but none of these authors would necessarily be identified with economic sociology as a narrow subdiscipline.

It follows that the book has a number of aims. Its primary concern is to highlight the contribution that sociological perspectives can make to the analysis of contemporary economic arrangements. It also emphasises the diversity of economic sociology's critical interests and its intersections with other fields of thought. And it sets itself against the notion that contemporary sociology has somehow become less bothered by, or less able to say anything useful about, economic problems and relations. The text does not focus on the central analytic objects of economic sociology – the formation of markets, the organisation and behaviour of firms, rationalities of economic behaviour – but rather examines substantive changes in the organisation of economic life through the lens of sociology and related disciplines. At the same time, the arguments developed below rest on two core precepts within economic sociology: that economic arrangements are *embedded* in social contexts, and *instituted* through formal and informal rules, conventions of conduct and exchange, systems of politics and regulation (see Granovetter 1985; Polanyi 1992). It seems particularly important in this context – although sometimes analytically difficult – to insist on the embedded and instituted character of economic processes which are increasingly international in character.

This points to the key problematic between economic sociology and contemporary economies: if a central argument in economic sociology concerns the embedded nature of economic life, how well does this argument fit with current capitalist arrangements? Globalising economic processes can appear radically disembedded from any local social and spatial contexts; therefore it may be even more crucial to press the claim, accepted by all economic sociologists and more than a few economists, that markets (even global ones) do not operate by themselves. The forms that markets take depends on the institutional – economic, social and political – arrangements that support them. Economic globalisation provides the frame for the first, and longest, section of the book. Globalisation is one of the most pervasive and least well defined concepts in contemporary social analysis. It is right for sociologists to be sceptical about such catch-all conceptions, and certainly to be sceptical about the kinds of totalising schemes that discourses of globalisation appear to offer. The contribution of economic sociology in this setting is to specify the socioeconomic agents and exchanges, the institutional and organisational forms, the regulatory conventions and networks, that can disappear into an abstract 'logic' of globalisation. This is also to say something about how economic sociology serves the discipline more generally. Issues of production, regulation, the analysis of capital, labour, work and inequality have been enduring themes within the sociology of economic life. The ways in which these phenomena have been reshaped only reinforce the fact that globalisation makes necessary a renewed attention to some central concerns within sociology. There is still an argument, in a mobile world, for pinning certain things down. Of course, this is not only a problem for economic sociologists. The discipline more broadly has been brought into question as too nation- or state-centred to be adequate to the analysis of new global realities. This more general problem for the discipline, however, has particular resonance for economic sociology, given that the restructuring of economic relations has been so crucial to the increasingly mobile character of objects, ideas, information, images and agents. *Contemporary Economic Sociology* therefore aims to contribute both to the analysis of transnational processes of social and economic restructuring, and to critical thinking about the nature and the analytic potential of sociological approaches to economic life.

Organisation of the book

Part I Economic globalisation

The concept of economic globalisation in general terms refers to how the exchange of goods, information, labour, money and images has come to operate on an increasingly international scale. Such globalising processes have been promoted by the growth and deregulation of finance markets since the 1970s, the development of new communications and transport technologies, and the extended reach of transnational corporations. This is to offer a very basic definition, but debates over globalisation are rarely confined to such bare-bones features. The perspectives considered in this first section go further in thinking about the social and political dimensions of economic globalisation, asking what these shifts entail for the organisation of social and economic power, how embedded they are in local contexts, and whether these processes can be controlled or resisted. The discussion divides into three chapters.

Capitalism and globalisation

Capitalism, as a social as well as an economic system, has been one of the central concerns within modern sociological analysis. The opening chapter examines how processes of globalisation have reshaped capitalist (and other) economies over time. It sets out the core features of economic globalisation – in respect of finance, production and technological changes – and assesses the extent to which global economic forms remain vulnerable to a critique of capital. The key theoretical focus is therefore on neo-Marxist approaches which stress the long-term historical and spatial development of capitalist economies, with particular emphasis on Immanuel Wallerstein's work in world systems theory, and David Harvey's work in critical geography. These thinkers treat globalisation as the intensification of capitalist accumulation processes on an international scale. While it can be argued that globalisation in itself is not necessarily or inevitably capitalist (see Castells 1999, 2000; Sklair 2002), current forms of globalisation are dominated by capitalist relations. It follows that the analysis of globalisation entails an analysis of capitalism.

A new global economy?

The critics considered in Chapter 1 take a long view of capitalist globalisation. Their accounts suggest that there is little that is 'new' about contemporary globalisation, however freshly minted some of the rhetoric that surrounds it. Chapter 2 takes up this issue of the novelty of current economic arrangements. It begins with perspectives that question the distinctiveness of recent trends towards internationalisation, focusing on Hirst and Thompson's critique of a globalisation 'myth'. The discussion goes on to consider alternative arguments that contemporary economies involve definite features which mark them off from earlier periods and which require new categories of analysis. Lash and Urry contend that recent economic changes have altered relations in time and space, referring to the 'speeding-up and stretching-out' – the temporal intensification and spatial extension – of social and economic processes. The chapter concludes with one of the most thoroughgoing accounts of a new international economy, represented by Manuel Castells' work on the emergence of a 'network society' that goes beyond established accounts of capitalist globalisation.

The politics of economic globalisation: governance and resistance

How is the global economy instituted through political and institutional measures? Chapter 3 offers a critical analysis of structures of control and tactics of resistance in the global economy. It looks at high-level strategies to govern global economic processes, considering the role of nation states and international institutions in such a project. The globalisation of social and economic relations produces acute problems of political regulation – what has been referred to as a 'crisis' of state sovereignty. The discussion turns from the putative 'crisis' of the nation state to the extended architecture of global governance which operates through international bodies, coalitions of nation states, non-governmental organisations and other civil actors. It concludes with an examination of current movements of global resistance. The politics of economic globalisation in this way works at different levels, mobilises different networks of actors, and seeks markedly different ends.

Part II Production

This section centres on a second key theme within sociological approaches to economic life: the process of production. Chapters 4 and 5 are concerned with changes in the organisation of production in contemporary economies, but also with changes in the nature of products themselves: that is, in both the form and the content of contemporary productive processes. These perspectives suggest that not only how we produce, but what we produce, has been transformed in recent decades. Such accounts go beyond production as a technical process to think about how this process is integrated into wider systems of regulation, consumption, class and culture.

Fordism and after

Chapter 4 considers approaches to production that see this as integral to social organisation. Theories of Fordism and accounts of post-Fordism each trace a complex of relations between production and consumption, production and social structure, the organisation of production and the organisation of space. The distinction between Fordism and post-Fordism is a highly schematic one, but it is very useful for thinking about how productive restructuring since the 1970s has been tied to wider changes in patterns of work and consumption, modes of political regulation, the spatial dispersal of economic processes, and the growth and differentiation of consumer markets. Fordism in this account represents a mode of mass production that corresponded not only to patterns of mass consumption, but to a political settlement between state, labour and capital. Economic organisation 'after' Fordism, in contrast, is characterised by smaller-scale and more flexible production, industrial deconcentration, customised products and niche marketing. It therefore configures a set of changes in production processes, in the spatial organisation of the economy, and in practices of consumption and social differentiation. The chapter begins with the classic statement on Fordism by Antonio Gramsci, and focuses in particular on the theorists of the French regulation school.

Knowledge, information, signs

Theories of post-Fordism imply that not only has the nature of production changed under advanced capitalism, but that what is produced increasingly takes the form of knowledge and information, images and services. Chapter 5 examines this shift to post-industrial modes of economic organisation, describing the expanding role of information, services and cultural goods in contemporary capitalist economies. It begins with Daniel Bell's work in the early 1970s on the transition to post-industrial society, and goes on to focus on Lash and Urry's account of 'reflexive accumulation' or the 'economy of signs'. Their approach looks to the role of non-material products in contemporary economies, and to the enhanced importance of knowledge and cultural content in the design, production, marketing and consumption of goods and services. Cultural or aesthetic questions, in this sense, are not confined to practices of consumption, but are bound up in the production and the positioning of both material and non-material commodities.

Part III Social identities and economic divisions

Class

Class is a foundational category for sociological analysis, but one that has been brought into question in recent years. Sociologists have become sceptical as to the salience of class as a means of explaining economic divisions and understanding social identities. Class, that is, has been criticised both as an objective economic category and as a subjective social category. This chapter considers reworkings and rejections of class analysis in the light of the socioeconomic changes described so far. The discussion begins with neo-Marxist and neo-Weberian approaches to the fragmentation of an industrial working class and the expansion of middle class groupings. In this sense, theories of post-industrialism and post-Fordism highlighted not only a shift in economic organisation at the level of production, but also changes in relations of social and economic power. Meanwhile, changing patterns of consumption, and the growing importance of consumption to social identities, have undermined notions of class-based relations of production and work. Although class categories may have been put into doubt in advanced capitalist economies, however, the systematic patterns of inequality with which class analysis has been engaged have not gone away. The critique of class therefore raises the question of how we are to analyse economic and social divisions 'after' class, particularly in the context of the brutal disparities that characterise the contemporary international economy. Chapter 6 ends with a discussion of class in an international context, where older class models may be hard to sustain, but where relations of economic inequality are starkly drawn and systematically reproduced.

Inequality

The discussion in the final chapter examines approaches to social and economic inequality that go beyond established class frameworks. It traces a shift away from the analysis of class, based on individuals' positions within an economic order, to notions of 'insecurity' or 'exclusion', as categories for analysing inequality wherein large numbers of people have only a precarious relation to economic membership. The argument here is that recent processes of socioeconomic change have produced pronounced, although not always especially new, patterns of inequality.

The latter part of this chapter is concerned with patterns of inequality in a global setting. Globalisation, like other forms of capitalist accumulation, is uneven and inequitable. The geographic dispersal of capital has been accompanied by the concentration of economic control in key sites, and by the radical exclusion of many places and people from economic resources and social opportunities. In a global social and economic system marked by extreme affluence at one end and severe poverty at the other, this concluding discussion considers the complex links between poverty, insecurity and inequality.

Part I
Economic globalisation

1 Capitalism and globalisation

Globalisation is now well established as a central theme in the social analysis of the economy. Over recent decades this broad concept has come to represent a general condition of economic life, as well as the key tendency driving diverse economic processes. It carries with it a certain sense of novelty, suggesting that current economic arrangements are distinctive in their form and unprecedented in their extent. A critical question therefore arises as to how far existing frameworks of socioeconomic analysis can account for the features and effects of globalisation. In particular, how does economic globalisation sit with sociology's long-standing concern with capitalism as a social and economic system? In a contemporary context, the study of capitalism has been somewhat subsumed within larger debates over globalisation. While the big idea of globalisation extends beyond economic relations to describe a range of political, cultural, military and technological factors (see Beck 2000a; Giddens 1990: 71; Held and McGrew 2003), my focus here is on economic globalisation – specifically in terms of its continuities with earlier capitalist arrangements. Can processes of globalisation be understood as the expression of a long-term capitalist logic? To what extent do global economic forms remain vulnerable to a critique of capital?

This chapter is therefore concerned with accounts that stress the capitalist nature of economic globalisation, and argue that it represents the extension and intensification of capitalist relations on an international scale. In particular, it takes up two of the perspectives with which Richard Swedberg (1991) once urged economic sociology to engage. The first is world systems theory, associated most notably with the work of the sociologist Immanuel Wallerstein. The second is neo-Marxism, represented here by the critical geography of David Harvey. Wallerstein and his colleagues offer a long historical view of the development of a capitalist world economy. Harvey analyses more recent processes of capitalist accumulation as these penetrate further and operate faster across geographical space. What these approaches share is the basic assumption that the logic of capital is to expand. Marx and Engels (1848: 224), of course, put it very simply: 'The need of a constantly expanding market for its products chases' capital, in the form of the bourgeoisie, 'over the whole surface of the globe. It must nestle everywhere, settle everywhere, establish connections everywhere.' From this simple conception of capital's restless tendencies, thinkers such as Wallerstein and Harvey develop complex analyses of capitalism's historical and geographical development. It is notable, however, that neither theorist tends much to use the language of globalisation. Wallerstein writes of the 'capitalist world-economy', while Harvey largely sticks with just 'capitalism', understood as an inherently expansionary process. Both contend, that is, that global economic processes can be understood via the analysis of capital. This is not to say there is nothing new about global economic processes or relations, but it does suggest there is nothing novel in itself about the fundamental logic of globalising capital: the tendency to extend, to seek new markets, to integrate distant actors, to colonise new spaces and sectors is all in accordance with what Harvey (1989: vii) calls the 'basic rules of capitalistic accumulation'.

The discussion that follows begins by outlining certain basic features of economic globalisation as a backdrop to these critical accounts. It then looks to world systems theory for an *historical* argument on the integration of a global capitalist system over several centuries. Harvey's work, in turn, offers a *spatial* analysis of capitalist processes of expansion and colonisation. I focus in particular on his recent treatment of contemporary global capital in terms of a 'new imperialism' of political and spatial domination (Harvey 2003). In making an argument about capitalism's relation to forms of imperialism, Harvey is concerned not only with the spatial expression but the historical antecedents of current capitalist arrangements, as well as with their political cladding. I return to this question of the politics of economic globalisation in more detail in Chapter 3.

Economic globalisation

Before taking up these critical accounts of capitalism's historical and geographical spread, it will be useful to set out certain basic conditions for, and features of, economic globalisation. The concept of globalisation is a contentious one, but in simple terms it refers to the idea that economic relations and activities operate on an increasingly transnational scale. Economic globalisation describes the processes through which distant and diverse spaces are integrated through economic exchanges, production systems, communication flows and commodity chains. Approaches to globalisation, however, often take this term to describe not simply these various empirical processes but also a larger historical state of affairs. Globalisation in this sense can indicate both a *process* and a *condition* – a tendency within the economy and other spheres, or the state of living in a globalised world. To get at this double meaning, Beck (2000a) makes a distinction between 'globalization', which refers to a set of (economic, political, cultural) processes that cut across or undermine national borders, and what he calls 'globality', as the condition of living in a 'world society'. Although there is debate over how far back the roots of globalisation (in both senses) stretch, a very prevalent use of the term is to refer to the period from the early 1970s. The question of periodisation is considered more closely in Chapter 2, but this common usage points to the way that current markets in goods, information, labour, money and images tend to operate on an expanding international scale, such that the contemporary economy integrates much, although certainly not all, of the globe.

Drivers of globalisation

How then might we characterise economic globalisation? There are firstly some key factors that lie behind processes of globalisation. These include:

1 Technological innovation in:

- information and communications technology
- transport technologies
- production technologies.

These represent the key *technical* drivers of globalisation. Rapid innovation in information and communication technologies often features in accounts of globalisation, but it is equally important to stress the role of new and improved transport and production technology. If ICTs have been crucial to the globalisation of finance, media, communications and services, changes in transport capacities and production techniques have enabled the globalisation of the 'real' or material economy in goods and resources. Modes of production, transmission and transportation are all critical to processes of globalisation – allowing for the movement and exchange of immaterial as well as material goods.

2 The growing reach of transnational corporations (TNCs)

Transnational corporations can be seen as the *institutional* driver of globalisation. By locating different parts of their activities across different sites, these firms uncouple management, production processes, labour and consumer markets from any one national economy. They represent the key corporate players in world trade, such that a large proportion of global economic activity can be traced around exchanges between and within TNCs (see Dicken 2002). Johnston *et al.* (2002: 21) assert that by the end of the 1990s transnational corporations accounted for up to one-quarter of global output. While TNCs represent only a small number of all exporting firms, they monopolise global trade. Leslie Sklair (2002: 90) notes, for example, that just 15 per cent of US exporters in the 1990s operated from multiple sites, but that these firms accounted for around 80 per cent of all exports – indeed, almost half of US manufacturing exports came from just fifty firms. He sums it up thus:

The global economy is dominated by a few gigantic transnational corporations marketing their products, many of them global brands, all over the world, some medium-sized companies producing in a few locations and selling in multiple markets, while many many more small firms sell from one location to one or a few other locations.

Features of globalisation

These technical and institutional drivers promote processes of economic globalisation in a number of spheres. We might outline the characteristic features of globalisation along the following lines:

1 Trade

Markets in goods and material resources are the most basic and long-standing feature of an international economy. The international trade in commodities has a very long history, but this trade has accelerated greatly in recent decades, eased by transport and production technologies and led by transnational corporations.

2 Capital investment

The stock of foreign direct investment (FDI) in the world economy trebled in the 25 years after 1980. Again, while individual and corporate investors had put capital into foreign schemes for centuries, the growing rate and range of foreign investment is a key feature of economic globalisation.

3 Finance markets

Highly mobile money is central to the contemporary global economy. The globalisation of money markets has been facilitated both by technical innovations – the rapid development of information and communications technologies referred to earlier – and by the political deregulation of key finance markets during the 1970s and 1980s.

4 Organisation of production

Technical innovations and the transnational operations of firms both promote the dispersal of production across space. The component parts for a single product can be sourced widely and moved fairly rapidly, while firms are able to use subcontracting networks and dispersed integration to locate their research, design, manufacture, assembly and distribution functions in different regional and national sites.

5 Organisation of services

The globalisation of services is a distinctive feature of current processes of globalisation. Services now take a growing share of foreign investment and export trade (see Johnston *et al.* 2002: 22). The outsourced IT industry that emerged in India in the first decade of the twenty-first century, for instance, is exemplary of the increase in foreign investment in services and the growth in export of services from developing countries. Such a trend suggests that the transnational organisation of services is rapidly following the model of manufacturing production.

6 The international division of labour

The spatial dispersal of economic processes has shaped a new international division of labour, as manufacturing (and latterly services) shifts to developing economies. While capital remains highly concentrated in the advanced capitalist core, labour increasingly is located in peripheral regions in the global economy. Along with this division of labour across international space, globalisation is also marked by the increased spatial mobility of labour. By 2004, around 200 million people worked outside their own country, at very high and (mainly) very low levels in the international economy.

Patterns of globalisation

These basic features of a globalising economy are structured in quite distinct ways. Indeed, a free-form language of 'globalisation' can obscure the systematic geography that shapes the international economy. It is important, therefore, to underline the structural features of globalisation, as well as certain structural trends:

1 The power of the 'Triad'

The 'global' economy in fact remains dominated by the United States, the European Union and Japan. At the start of the twenty-first century, the US and the EU each accounted for up to one-third of global economic output, with Japan representing around 12 per cent.

2 Changing balance of economic relations

This established balance of power, however, is subject to increasing global integration and penetration. The US is the key case in point here. The US historically has been a highly protectionist economy which until the latter half of the twentieth century traded largely with itself. (It retains, of course, some deeply protectionist instincts which only seem to work in tandem with its will for other economies to liberalise.) In 1960 US exports were just 5 per cent of its GDP; by the turn of the century they accounted for over 10 per cent. The level of US *imports*, more markedly, has greatly increased. The US has, in the course of a few decades, gone from being the largest net creditor in the world to being its largest net debtor. This turnaround initially was based on the US's spiralling trade deficit with Japan, but its trade debt to the EU has also escalated, and in early 2005 China's trade surplus with the US was running at around 16 billion dollars per month.

3 The shift to Asia

In the twenty-first century economic weight is moving towards Asia. China and India are growing rapidly as economic forces, with their huge markets in labour and in potential consumers. At least one projection suggests that, if recent trends continue, China will by 2041 have overtaken the US as the world's largest economy, with India in third place (see Gyngell 2004: 3). This represents a correction to what may then appear as a twentieth-century 'blip' – both countries were significant economic actors into the nineteenth century, accounting for around one-half of world output, whose power diminished during the following century (see also A. G. Frank 1998). At its low point in the mid-twentieth century, the Asian region as a whole represented less than a 20 per cent share of the world economy, but this reversal of fortunes looks likely to be temporary (see Maddison 2001).

The generic concept of globalisation, then, takes in a diverse range of economic processes, characterised by Cox (1997: 1) in terms of:

> the growth of multinational and transnational corporations, the expansion of trade and foreign investment, the New International Division of Labor, the enhanced mobility of money capital across international boundaries, intensified international competition with the rise of the Newly Industrializing Countries (NICs), and the globalization of markets for consumer goods.

Doubtless one might add to this list. There are, moreover, some critical questions that arise in this context. How adequate is the concept of globalisation in accounting for this complex of economic factors? To what extent does globalisation represent a *new* set of economic processes and relations? How do these processes reconfigure economic and social power? Can these processes be controlled or opposed? The discussion in this chapter, and in the two chapters that follow, is concerned with questions such as these. In this chapter, I am particularly concerned with globalisation as a mode of capitalist accumulation across time and space. I begin with the historical view offered by world systems theory, before examining the spatial perspective of Harvey's (2003: 1) 'historical-geographical materialism'.

The capitalist world economy

The most sustained historical view of the trend towards capitalist globalisation is to be found in world systems theory (Chase-Dunn 1998, 1999; Hall 2000; Hopkins and Wallerstein 1996; Wallerstein 1974, 1979, 1987, 2003). This body of work offers an historical analysis of the long-term structural development of a capitalist world economy, reaching back to the early modern period in Europe. Originating in the early 1970s, world systems theory pre-dates wider debates over globalisation, although a number of world systems theorists more recently have taken up the terms of this debate (see, for example, Chase-Dunn 1998, 1999). Thinking about globalisation in such a way places current trends against the long-run historical expansion of a capitalist world economy. This sort of long view therefore runs counter to any notion of globalisation as a new and distinctive stage of economic and spatial organisation.

World systems theory is most closely associated with the work of the sociologist Immanuel Wallerstein. In very broad terms, Wallerstein's thesis can be outlined as follows: the capitalist mode of production has shaped a world economy since the sixteenth century. It is economically integrated by a single division of labour, but includes different cultural and political systems. Capitalism originated in northern Europe, but the search for profit and for expanded production opportunities means that its boundaries have gradually extended to take in much of the world. The capitalist world economy historically has been structured around three major economic zones, and around two world classes. Within these broad spatial and social contours, it has also been marked by ethno-national conflicts and internal inequalities, repressions and revolts within nations.

In these terms world systems theory can be seen as an extremely grand narrative in historical social science. Large-scale theory of this kind has fallen out of favour since the 1970s, but it is important to stress that the very scale of world systems theory represents a critical response to the intellectual context in which it developed. Wallerstein insists that the study of world systems is not about a total theory of the world; rather, it is a rejection of the way the social sciences typically have taken the nation state or national society as their frame of enquiry (Wallerstein 1987: 309; see also Braudel 1984). World systems theory emerged in the 1970s as a challenge to conventional analyses which understood economic development largely as a domestic story. The issue of development (and, indeed, that of economic 'backwardness') was seen as a local question, determined by national political and institutional arrangements, and by the ability or readiness of given economies to make the most of their comparative advantage in international trade. Models of economic development more generally assumed a central standard or developmental path along which individual nations would travel, or otherwise lag behind. Theorists such as Wallerstein and Frank (1966), in contrast, argued that national economic development – and 'underdevelopment' – should be placed in the context of an international capitalist economy which systematically advantaged certain regions and nations and systematically exploited others (see also Sklair 1994). This capitalist system emerged in Europe, but over the modern period it came to incorporate more and more regions across the globe, especially through projects of imperialism and colonialism. Such patterns of incorporation, then, were not simply a matter of bloodless market processes extending their reach through trade: the expansion of the capitalist world economy over time was the work of material interests and actors, 'utilizing military, political, and economic pressures of multiple kinds, and of course involving the overcoming of political resistance in the zones into which the geographic expansion was taking place' (Wallerstein 1990: 36). While world systems theory is primarily an account of economic integration and interpenetration, it underlines the ways in which economic expansion has been and still is tied to forms of military, political and cultural domination.

Accounts of globalisation often see this as a distinctly late-modern phenomenon, but Wallerstein dismisses the idea that capitalism only became a world system in the twentieth century. Rather, he traces the origins of a capitalist world economy to the early modern period. This is not, what is more, merely an historical description of how economic processes happen to have unfolded over time: it involves a more basic analysis of the logic of capital itself. Echoing Marx, Wallerstein argues that capital has never respected national borders. Its logic is always to expand and extend – capitalist accumulation is in this sense an intrinsically mobile process. If by the end of the twentieth century the capitalist world economy had become almost fully globalised, the antecedents of this global system are to be found much earlier, and its impetus lies in the underlying logic of capital.

What, then, is meant by the term 'world system'? The notion of a 'system' is central to this body of work, and has a particular definition within it. World systems theory takes the 'system' (rather than 'society' or 'nation') as its basic unit of analysis. A social system is defined by a single division of labour that draws its members into economic interdependence. It does not require either a shared political structure or a common culture to hold it together. Wallerstein distinguishes between two types of system: mini systems and world systems. Mini systems, firstly, are based on a single division of labour and also have a unified culture. On Wallerstein's (1974, 2003) account, such bounded mini systems have only been evident in 'simple' agricultural or hunter-gatherer societies that do not interact economically with cultural outsiders, although other systems theorists define them more broadly (see Hall 2000). World systems, in contrast, are characterised by a single division of labour across different cultures. They involve economic networks that extend beyond and between societies and states. World systems take two forms. A *world empire* (as represented by the cases of ancient China, Egypt or Rome) operates under a common political structure, usually imposed by a dominant power through conquest. A *world economy*, however, does not have a common political structure. It follows that the empires of the nineteenth century, notably Britain and France, 'were not world-empires at all, but nation-states with colonial appendages operating within the framework of a global economy' (Wallerstein 2003: 63). Wallerstein's specific interest is in the modern world economy. Although complex economic networks existed in pre-modern times, as the seminal work of Fernand Braudel showed in the case of the ancient empires, the modern period has come to be dominated by a single capitalist world economy, driven primarily by economic rather than political interests. This capitalist world economy is notable in that it has become a global economic system without being politically unified as a world empire (see Hall 2000: 4).

The capitalist world economy has developed in a cyclical manner, through 'long waves' or Kondatrieff cycles of economic expansion and contraction, as well as through dynamics of war and peace, and phases of colonisation and decolonisation (see Wallerstein 1982). It also is subject to more 'secular' or persistent trends: the gradual proletarianisation of the world workforce; the growing commodification of labour, land and resources; the concentration of capital in increasingly large firms; internationalisation of trade and investment; and the internationalisation of political institutions (Chase-Dunn 1999). It is this set of changes that characterises a global capitalist economy today. Indeed, the last of these trends – towards international political institutions – increasingly puts into question Wallerstein's older distinction between a capitalist world economy and a world empire, as common political structures come to assert themselves on the global scene.

World systems theory takes both a long historical view and a very heightened overview, but this perspective makes it possible to analyse the world economy as single social space – segmented and uneven, but nevertheless observable as a system. The story goes like this: a modern world economy began to take shape from the sixteenth century in tandem with the emergence of market capitalism. The origins of this world economy lay in northern and western Europe, as regional agriculture became more specialised and diversified (and therefore more amenable to trade), and was augmented by such emerging industries as textiles and metals. Economic growth led merchants and nascent capitalists to demand more specialised kinds of labour, raw materials and new markets. Such demands were met both by extended trading networks and later by colonisation. The logic of expansion, however, was principally economic rather than political. It follows that the capitalist world system was organised by economic networks rather than by political structures. From the early modern period, capitalism developed around an international division of labour and growing economic interdependence, but not around a unified political structure or a common culture. The modern world system remained 'multi-centric' because it was based on networks of trade in capitalist commodities (Chase-Dunn 1999). Capitalism was, as Wallerstein tells it (2003: 66) 'from the beginning an affair of the world-economy and not of nation-states'. Indeed, 'capital has never allowed its aspirations to be determined by national boundaries in a capitalist world-economy'. The logic of capital has always been international; lately, it has gone global.

The map of the modern world economy, then, is not based on nation states. Rather, the modern history of capitalist development divided the world into three broad economic zones, establishing distinct structural positions for different regions. Wallerstein (1974, 1979) claims that this general structure was in place by the middle of the seventeenth century (in fact by around 1640), although its geographical detail has shifted over time as different regions were integrated into the world economy. The resulting model is one of the best-known and most contested features of world systems theory. It marks out three structural zones in the world economy: the core, periphery, and semi-periphery.

Core

The 'core' is the dominant region in the capitalist world economy. It originally was located in northwestern Europe, based on specialised agriculture, emerging property relations and the spread of wage labour. With the rise of industrial capitalism, the core came to be characterised by manufacturing production, strong states, a powerful bourgeoisie and a large working class (Hall 2000). By the end of the twentieth century, the capitalist core was focused on advanced productive and communication technologies, information and financial capital, producer services and other high-level service sectors. While northern and western Europe has never been dislodged from its starting position in the capitalist core (now consolidated through the bloc power of the European Union), other regions and nations have joined it – most notably, of course, North America and Japan.

Periphery

The capitalist 'periphery' is a source of raw material and commodities exports to the core, historically typified by weak states and large peasant populations. In the early capitalist period it included eastern parts of Europe and the Western hemisphere (that is, the Americas and the Caribbean). These early capitalist relations between core and periphery were based on slavery, indentured labour or cash-crop production by peasant workers. Later colonial expansion brought regions in Africa and southern Asia into the world capitalist economy. The basic division of labour between core and periphery divides the world economy between those regions that produce high-grade products using more advanced technologies, and those peripheral economies that supply cheap labour, resources and agricultural products. These entrenched relations of inequality and dependency structure terms of trade within which peripheral economies are compelled to sell cheap and buy dear. The language of core and periphery has become very contested, and the division of labour Wallerstein posits between different regions in the world economy is destabilised in a global context in which manufacturing functions increasingly have shifted to developing economies, and agricultural producers in poorer regions find themselves unable to sell as cheaply to world markets as can heavily subsidised producers in the capitalist core. Even so, it can be argued that the model of structured inequality the core-periphery model implies continues to provide a template for changing economic relations between the global North and the global South.

Semi-periphery

The 'semi-periphery' is positioned between core and periphery. It is based on intermediary or transitional economies, with either quite specialised or uncertain economic and political roles. Mediterranean Europe, Wallerstein (1979) argues, occupied the semi-periphery within early capitalist relations: certain specialised products were traded, but share-cropping in agriculture insulated the region from wider trade in resources. Later, semi-peripheral economies were characterised by moderately strong states and less 'advanced' economies. In the twentieth century the semi-periphery was taken to include communist states which – although not excluded from international trade – were based on distinctive economic and political systems (see Chase-Dunn 1980). It also included oil-producing states with their heavy reliance on a single commodity. Newly industrialising economies in Southeast Asia assumed semi-peripheral status in the latter part of the twentieth century, while China, Brazil and parts of India could be seen to sit between core and periphery in the contemporary global economy. The debate as to whether China would join the World Trade Organization as a 'developed' or a 'developing' country gives some sense of this in-between status (see Lai 2001). Wallerstein (1974) suggests that the semi-periphery, whatever different political structures it might contain, is critical in maintaining the overall stability of the world economy. Its intermediate status ensures that the world system is never simply polarised between the exploited majority in the periphery and the privileged minority in the core. Chase-Dunn (1980, 1999) makes a stronger case for the role played by the semi-periphery in the world economy. To take one example: he argues that US post-war policy towards Japan and Korea only makes sense in terms of the threat posed by Chinese communism. Both nations were reconstructed by heavily state-driven industrialisation, rather than being exploited as peripheral economies in relations of dependency with the US. Such international Keynesianism worked in the general interest of stabilising a liberal and capitalist world system, although not necessarily in the immediate and particular interests of US capitalists. In this way, it contrasts quite strikingly, Chase-Dunn notes, with US policy in Latin America during the same period, which systematically reproduced conditions of 'underdevelopment' and dependency in the absence of any regional counterweight.

The model of core, periphery and semi-periphery is subject to serious question for its broad-brush and frankly Eurocentric approach. However, there are two important points to be made for it. First, Wallerstein's work in the 1970s and early 1980s was a critical attempt to analyse conventional models of first, second and third worlds in terms of their integral 'roles in the rise to dominance of capitalism and industrialization' (Hall 2000: 4). There are not different 'worlds', understood in terms of different models or stages of development, but a single world economy structured around unequal exchange and uneven power relations. Second, it sought to show that capitalist exploitation inhered not only in the relation between owner and worker, or between national economic classes, but between regions of the globe. These patterns of unequal exchange amounted to the 'appropriation of surplus of the whole world-economy by core areas' (Wallerstein 2003: 65). The world economy could be understood as a single economic system integrated via an international division of labour, and characterised by exploitation and structured inequality.

Such an account of the origins of the capitalist world economy has been criticised on the basis of its (quite explicit) Eurocentrism (see Dussel 1998). It begins with Europe, and it traces the spread of capitalism as a world system dominated by this core region. Janet Abu-Lughod (1989) argues, in contrast, that the lineaments of a world system are visible some three hundred years prior to Wallerstein's sixteenth-century starting point: the 'rise of the West' in fact is predicated on the eclipse of the East. Wallerstein's work focuses on a capitalist core which he locates in Europe and later in North America, but A. G. Frank (1998) contends that China was at the centre of a more extended Afro-Eurasian world system for a far longer period, one that did not simply disappear with the ancient Chinese 'world empire'. China was more advanced than most of Europe in the eighteenth century, and remained an important economic power into the nineteenth century. The shift to Asia in the late twentieth century – and the much-anticipated 'rise' of China in the twenty-first – does not therefore indicate the emergence of a new economic core, but the revival of an older power after a relatively brief period of decline (see also Castells 2000a: 7–8; Hall 2000: 10–11; Maddison 2001).

These are important criticisms of Wallerstein's orientation, but his own analysis also helps put into question certain Eurocentric assumptions about the course of economic development. His account of how exploitation operates between core and peripheral regions in a world economy builds upon his own work in the 1960s and early 1970s on post-colonial Africa. In this connection it extends earlier arguments concerning the systematic 'development of underdevelopment' (Frank 1966; see also Chase-Dunn 1989, 1998; Hall 2000; So 1990). As Frank argues in his classic article on the topic, 'underdevelopment' does not describe a state prior to economic modernisation. Underdevelopment is a capitalist process, not a pre-existing condition. He rejects the linear version of economic progress that is central to conventional models of modernisation and development. Underdevelopment is a consequence of being incorporated as a dependent or peripheral region in the world economy, providing raw materials, labour and captive markets to the core. It is in this sense a *function* of capitalism and not a precapitalist state. As Wallerstein (1974, 2003) points out, the status of 'developed' economies in turn is premised on expropriative economic relations – it is not primarily a state project, much less the effect of having a more 'advanced' culture.

To follow the analysis offered by world systems theory is indeed to take a long view. Its value in this regard, however, is in setting contemporary globalisation in its historical context. The model of core, periphery and semi-periphery may be a rather blunt instrument for analysing lines of economic power and inequality, but it retains some real critical currency. For one thing, the world systems thesis puts capitalist accumulation at the centre of globalisation processes. Against sanitised versions of globalisation which see economic exchange in terms of global 'cooperation' (see Sen 2002) or the neutral play of competitive advantage, this account depicts a capitalist world economy fundamentally organised by an uneven geography of power. The international division of labour draws distant parts of the world into a system of economic interdependence, as more recent notions of globalisation suggest, and at the same time entrenches relations of exploitation between them.

World systems theory occupies an interesting place within current debates over globalisation. On one hand, it is clearly tied to some of the positions that have been subject to serious criticism in the social sciences in the last twenty years or more: grand narratives in general and Marxism in particular; theses concerning the 'rise of the West', and so on. It also falls foul of certain neoliberal orthodoxies concerning the progress and benefits of globalisation. Yet the historical and geographical scope of world systems theory fits it well to telling a big story like globalisation. Moreover, this body of work takes a consistently critical stance in relation to global patterns of integration and expropriation. In this way it has proved relevant to the theoretical demands of recent anti-globalisation movements in their efforts to 'think global'. This kind of global thinking, however, also requires a finer understanding of how global capitalism carves up space. Relations of inequality exist not only *between* regions within the global economy (as the core-periphery model might suggest), but within regions, nations and even cities (see Sassen 1998, 2001). Sweated labour happens in the metropolitan centres of the advanced economies (see Cohen and Rogers 2001; Ross 1997). The outward movement of capital, colonisers and ideologies from the core has been paralleled by patterns of migration from periphery to core – propelled in large part by the poverty, debt and conflict that have been such pervasive aspects of the post-colonial experience (see Castles and Davidson 2000). If, following world systems theory, it is possible to think about global economic relations in terms of an integrated social *system*, it is one marked by extreme affluence and severe immiseration in close proximity as well as at a distance.

The 'new imperialism': accumulation by dispossession

World systems theory offers a large-scale account of capitalist expansion over time, but it also looks to the way this economic system integrates and segments space. Such a concern with the spatiality of capital is key to the contemporary analysis of globalisation. For the critical geographer David Harvey (1990: 344), 'the widening and deepening of capitalist social relations with time is, surely, one of the most singular and indisputable facts of recent historical geography'. Even so, his writing largely avoids the language of 'globalisation' (see Harvey 1995). The extension of capitalist exchange across international space is, after all, not in itself new: capitalism by definition is 'expansionary and imperialistic'. Harvey's work is alert to the new features of globalising capital while stressing its continuities with earlier forms. It is certainly the case, for instance, that advances in information, communications and transport technologies have re-made many people's experience of time and space. Harvey's notion of 'time-space compression' points to the way that objects, images, ideas and people can move ever more rapidly over ever greater distances. This is not simply a technical fact but a subjective effect: one's sense of location in time and space is framed by the potential for real-time exchanges with people on another continent; it is possible to fly from one side of the globe to the other – from the depths of winter to the height of summer – in less than a day. The speed and stretch of transport, travel and communication is a distinctive feature of the current global condition, but it is also a persistent tendency in capitalist development. 'The reduction in the cost and time of movement', as Harvey (2003: 98) puts it, is a 'compelling necessity of a capitalist mode of production', making as it does various kinds of capital move faster. In particular, recent technological innovations have given even greater scope to the protean nature of finance capital. Harvey's work has always stressed the importance of finance in the international economy, and he argues that mercurial finance capital represents the 'cutting edge' of current capitalist accumulation (Harvey 2003: 147). At the same time, we might note that Lenin also remarked – in 1916 – on the growing importance of finance capital over commodity exports in the nineteenth-century imperialist economy (Lenin 1988). Indeed, this is an important point of reference for Harvey's own work, on two grounds. First, his work involves a crucial argument for the continuing relevance of Marxist critique to the analysis of contemporary capital. Second, Harvey's approach to globalisation stresses capital's *imperialistic* urge towards non-capitalist (or less capitalist) spaces. The discussion that follows begins by looking at Harvey's spatial treatment of capitalist expansion, and then considers his argument that globalising processes might be understood as a new form of economic imperialism.

While the contemporary economy has distinctive features, for a thinker such as Harvey it remains vulnerable to certain established lines of analysis. Globalisation can be seen as an advanced version of what he calls the 'spatial fix' for problems of capitalist accumulation (Harvey 1982, 1990, 2001, 2003). Versions of a spatial fix are also evident in systems of imperialism, colonialism and neo-colonialism. Capitalism, to put it simply, has certain crisis tendencies – particularly the tendency for over-accumulation and under-consumption. The basic orientation to constant growth and competitive markets demands continual innovation, whether in technologies of production and distribution, changes in productive organisation, or in products themselves. As Harvey (1990: 180) puts it, capitalist enterprises are driven to 'leap-frogging innovations in their search for profit'. As production and distribution systems advance via technological changes and efficiency gains, more goods and services can be produced and circulated, typically requiring fewer workers in those parts of the production process. The capacity to supply outstrips existing markets' demand for goods, while corporate growth leaves in its wake redundant or under-employed workers. Problems of over-accumulation appear both as excess capacity in the economy (surpluses of capital, commodities, plant or labour power that can find no profitable or productive use) and as under-consumption (a lack of effective demand in labour, consumer and other markets). Periods of sustained capitalist crisis, such as the 'stagflation' of the early 1970s which stubbornly combined high inflation with high unemployment, are marked by surpluses of productive or finance capital alongside surpluses of labour power (see Harvey 1982). The point of crisis, here, is in the system's inability to bring together these surpluses in any profitable way. The expanded reproduction of the system is stymied.

Harvey outlines two strategies for dealing with these problems of accumulation, one based on time and the other on space. 'Temporal displacements' occur when surpluses of capital or labour are directed to investment in capital projects (for example, in transport and other infrastructure, housing or commercial property) or in social spending (for example, in education, health or scientific research) which will foster economic accumulation in the longer term – via more skilled workers, technical innovations, or enhanced productive infrastructure. Such initiatives, that is, 'defer the re-entry of capital values into circulation into the future' (Harvey 2003: 109). 'Spatial displacements', on the other hand, involve the search for new locations for investment and market opportunities – whether in new resource, commodity, consumer or labour markets. Dealing with excess economic capacity often involves a bit of both strategies, displacing investment and accumulation across both time and space: what Harvey calls the 'spatio-temporal fix'.

One – as it turned out, temporary – fix for capitalism's accumulation problems was found in the post-war politics of corporatism and welfarism. This sought, amongst other things, to regulate relations between capital and labour, to provide public investment in infrastructure and social projects, and to stabilise demand by shoring up workers' conditions as well as ensuring a social wage for the unemployed. It offers a key instance of Harvey's notion of a 'temporal' response to accumulation crises, whereby investment in long-term capital projects or social spending is geared to the expanded reproduction of the economy. Such a system of regulation, however, was grounded in national economies and is widely seen as simply untenable or quaintly quixotic in an increasingly international economy. That, at least, is what the rhetoric of neoliberalism would tell us. In practice, various neo-Keynesian strategies remain crucial to the management of contemporary economies, however 'post-national' or 'post-welfare' they might appear. The strategy of temporal displacement is evident in the British government's economic golden rule of the early twenty-first century – that the government may only borrow to fund long-term investment – while deficit spending by the Bush administration to finance infrastructure projects (and of course defence contracts) and to underwrite ailing industries (notably the airlines) was central to its response to the US's economic troubles after 11 September 2001. Even without economic shocks of this kind, accumulation problems seem particularly acute in the contemporary economy – Brenner (1998, 2002) argues that over-accumulation has dogged capitalist economies since the 1970s. Capitalism's tendency to over-accumulate has been redoubled in this period by intense innovation (automation, robotisation, computerisation, containerisation), which has greatly augmented the technical capacity of production and distribution systems. If economic globalisation has undercut (if not actually negated) the viability of welfarist responses to problems of capitalist accumulation, globalisation in itself offers an alternative solution. Harvey (2003) suggests that the key contemporary 'fix' for capitalism's crisis tendencies is through the spatial expansion of economic networks and the colonisation of new markets.

Various spatial fixes – whether via systems of imperialism, colonialism and neo-colonialism, or in current processes of globalisation – involve the geographical search for new investment and profit. Harvey's analysis of the current progress of international capital suggests that, as with earlier forms of capitalist imperialism, it is 'typically about exploiting the uneven geographical conditions under which capital accumulation occurs', as well as the social and economic asymmetries which 'inevitably arise out of spatial exchange relations' (Harvey 2003: 31). His work on the international economy as a kind of new imperialism has precedents in both liberal and Marxist approaches to imperialist systems. Imperialism, in each of these earlier conceptions, is analysed as a response to domestic economic crises or constraints via the hunt for new markets and investment opportunities (see Hilferding 1981; Hobson 1988; Lenin 1982; Luxemburg 1968). In her 1913 work on *The Accumulation of Capital*, for instance, Rosa Luxemburg argued that the capitalist crisis predicted by Marx had not come about because capital was able to shore up profits by exploiting 'pre-capitalist' social formations as cheap sources of raw materials and labour. Expanded accumulation in this way was premised on the colonisation of new economic territories.

In his treatment of *The New Imperialism* (2003), Harvey draws on Luxemburg's arguments to consider contemporary modes of what he terms 'accumulation by dispossession'. His account, moreover, offers a compelling reworking of Marx's notion of 'primitive accumulation'. Marx used this concept in volume one of *Capital* to refer to the preconditions for capitalist production that marked the transition from feudalism. Those original acts of predation or usurpation by which the rising bourgeoisie broke the power of guilds over artisan production, and the power of feudal lords over both land and the labour of serfs, laid the ground for a capitalist system based on the buying and selling of 'free' labour. Harvey elaborates the acts of primitive accumulation which underpin modern capitalism: these include the enclosure of land, involving the eviction of peasant populations and the creation thereby of a landless class of workers, but also the 'suppression of rights to the commons; commodification of labour power and suppression of alternative modes of production and consumption; colonial, neo-colonial and imperial appropriation of natural assets . . . monetization of exchange and taxation; slave trade; usury, national debt and the credit system' (Harvey 2003: 145; see also Marx and Engels 1848: 222–5). As might be guessed from such a list, Harvey's argument is that this offers more than an analysis of capitalism's sixteenth-century origins, or its development from feudal preconditions in Europe: similar acts of 'primitive' accumulation remain crucial to its contemporary reproduction and expansion across the world. He prefers, however, to call current processes 'accumulation by dispossession' – a term that both avoids the idea that these practices are somehow archaic or rudimentary, and also underlines the often stark relations of power and expropriation they involve.

How then might we think about current strategies of accumulation by dispossession within an international economic system? Such processes can be seen at work in a number of ways, including the following.

Access to new markets

One obvious way of responding to over-supply or stagnant growth in existing markets is to seek alternative markets elsewhere. This was the basic premise of both liberal and Marxist analyses of nineteenth- and early twentieth-century imperialism. It is no less evident as a feature of contemporary capitalist expansion. The 'opening up' of Eastern Europe to capitalist consumer markets in the 1990s is a key example of such a strategy, while the ongoing move to market forms in China reproduces this logic on an even larger scale. This is not only a matter of 'opening up' new markets, however: it can also depend on usurping existing market arrangements. Such an effect is at work in practices of export dumping where producers in advanced economies market goods abroad, especially in developing countries, at prices lower than their costs of production. These practices have been most apparent in heavily subsidised industries such as agriculture and textiles, where state subsidies allow producers in the United States, Europe or Japan not only to saturate domestic markets but to offload surpluses onto foreign markets. The most significant example is the billions spent annually by rich nations (the United States and the European Union, chiefly) on agricultural subsidies which promote domestic over-production and lead to export dumping in world markets at artificial prices against which producers in poorer nations are simply unable to compete. Out-competing local market actors in contexts where the terms of competition are so stacked offers a very clear example of how more powerful interests can exploit the 'asymmetries' that characterise exchange relations across space (Harvey 2003: 31).

Access to cheaper inputs

Another response to accumulation problems is to increase profit margins by lowering the costs of production. Apart from seeking new markets else-where, producers can also shore up profits in existing markets by seeking to reduce their costs. As Harvey (2003: 139) puts it, it is 'possible to accumulate in the face of stagnant effective demand if the costs of input (land, raw materials, intermediate inputs, labour power) decline significantly. Access to cheaper inputs is, therefore, just as important as access to widening markets.' The search for cheaper inputs – which under the 'old' imperialism largely involved the exploitation of overseas territories for raw materials and resources – is exemplified today by practices of foreign outsourcing and subcontracting. Under these arrangements, production for domestic as well as foreign markets is partly or wholly undertaken in offshore locations, typically in developing economies and often in special export processing zones (EPZs) which offer not only cheaper land and labour but other locational incentives such as tax breaks, low-cost water and energy supplies, tariff reductions and relaxed environmental, labour, and health and safety standards.

Expanded capital accumulation in this way is linked to the spatial restructuring of production, which in turn underpins a new international division of labour (NIDL). Whereas under the older imperialist model manufacturing was concentrated in the core while raw resources were extracted from the colonised periphery, within the contemporary system production increasingly has shifted to developing regions, either through offshoring or through extended chains of production and assembly that stretch across international space. The extent to which the growth of manufacturing in developing economies accounts for its decline in advanced capitalist economies is subject to debate; however, it is easy enough to point to the growth of the *maquila* system of production on the Mexico/US border, or to instance the shift in production of General Motors cars from Michigan to Mexico, of Levi's jeans from Texas to Costa Rica, or the fact that Nike now subcontracts all of its production to Southeast Asia (Sklair 2002: 132–4; Wright 2002: 72; see also Frankel 2001; Goldman and Papson 1998).

The search for lower-cost inputs does not only affect the organisation of production, but is also evident in the 'offshoring' of business activities and services in search of cheaper labour. Innovations in communications and information technology have promoted a trend among US and European companies to transfer business services abroad, including office backroom functions, call centres, finance and accountancy services. These offshore offices in turn require a range of administrative jobs in personnel management, recruitment, procurement, technical support, and so on. It has been estimated that around 60 billion dollars were contracted for offshore IT services and business processing in 2004, with US organisations accounting for more than 40 per cent of that total, and the United Kingdom around 20 per cent. European economies, taken together, sent the greatest proportion of business activities abroad, while companies in the Asia Pacific region accounted for less than 7 per cent of offshore business contracts (Seager 2005). US and UK firms are most likely to send service functions offshore, given the global dominance of the English language – a key example here is the rising number of British firms (particularly in banking, insurance and telecommunications, but including the national customer enquiry line for rail service and timetable information) that subcontract IT and call centre work to skilled, English-speaking, but relatively low-paid workers in India. Clearly the offshoring of business services so far represents a small proportion (less than 10 per cent) of total foreign direct investment, but faster and cheaper communications make it increasingly viable, and it forms part of a larger picture in which services in general, and intra-firm transactions in particular, are taking a growing share of foreign investment and trade (see Dicken 2002: 46–7; 2003). Indeed, Johnston, Taylor and Watts point to the way that surges in the level of foreign direct investment since the 1980s have also been marked by a shift in its content: whereas investment was once largely geared to primary manufacturing and resources, services now account for 'close to 50 percent of all FDI' (Johnston *et al.* 2002: 22).

Privatisation and marketisation

The geographical search for new consumer, supply and labour markets is a tactic of what Harvey calls 'spatial displacement', as capital seeks out opportunities for investment and profit-making elsewhere. In a global context, these spatial displacements are especially pronounced between advanced capitalist regions and transitional or developing (what Luxemburg referred to as 'pre-capitalist') economies. Another way of displacing capital into new uses is through the colonisation of non-capitalist economic sectors. What we might term 'sectoral displacement' is at work when capital looks for investment in goods and services which formerly stood outside the commodity nexus. New opportunities for accumulation are to be found in the privatisation of state assets and services (housing, education, health) or of public utilities (electricity, water, telecommunications). Continued accumulation in this sense is premised on forays both across geographical space – by accessing foreign markets – and across sectors: particularly the division between private enterprise and public functions. This second mode of accumulation by dispossession has been a keynote of neoliberal reforms in North and South America, Europe, Australia and New Zealand since the 1980s, as well as of various structural adjustment programmes and post-communist transitions. It is evident in the free market being established in public goods and services – in health, municipal contracts, water, sewage, power and so on – by IMF/World Bank loan conditions and via the WTO. An agenda of 'progressive liberalisation', as built into the General Agreement on Trade in Services (GATS), has been strenuously supported by leading economies, and particularly by the European Union. The latter has pushed for deregulation of public and other services through multilateral agreements, especially in respect of health services and water supply (see UNDP 2003: 111–12; see also Shiva 2002). It is worth noting, against this backdrop, that two European multinationals control 50 per cent of the world's private water market, an ownership share that is likely to increase with greater liberalisation. Privatisation as a mode of accumulation by dispossession was especially acute in the 'shock therapy' buy-up of Russia's national industries (notably oil) by political oligarchs and their business cronies after the break-up of the Soviet Union. Indeed, Marx's blunter language of 'primitive accumulation' seems more to the point of this fairly raw process of plunder than does the anodyne language of 'privatisation'.

Further opportunities for investment and profit arise in wider strategies of commodification and marketisation. In the endless creativity and innovation of the capitalist logic, new commodities can be invented, for example, via the patenting of novel kinds of intellectual property or of genetic materials (see Shiva 1997, 2001). Commodification is a key feature of the expansion of capitalist markets into new spatial or sectoral contexts. Others, as indicated by Marx's treatment of original accumulation, include monetarisation and the introduction of credit systems. The extension of money and credit instruments makes it possible to integrate a diversity of interactions, goods and services into market transactions. Local, customary and non-market systems of exchange in this way are brought inside a market logic; conventional forms of barter, reciprocity, swapping and so on are rationalised as buying, selling and lending (see Davis 1992; Slater and Tonkiss 2001). The expanded use of money and credit runs from petty capitalist models of economic development funded through micro-finance arrangements, to the spiralling personal debt of Western consumers, to the circulation of complex new instruments (such as derivatives or futures) in international finance markets.

Conversion of alternative property rights into private property

This tactic follows from the previous point: new opportunities for profit arise as various forms of property – collective, public, common, traditional – are converted to private property. Transfers of the public estate or commons into private ownership range from sell-offs of council housing, school playing-fields and cemeteries in the United Kingdom, to the logging of rain-forests in Australia and mineral exploration and extraction in wilderness areas in the United States. The dominance of private property is a familiar feature of advanced capitalist economies, but the conversion of alternative property holdings is also a condition of transnational economic processes. Private property rights have been promoted by structural adjustment programmes, free trade agreements and broader neoliberal strategies for international competitiveness. A prime instance is offered by neoliberal land 'reforms' leading to the enclosure of collective lands in rural economies, as in the privatisation of indigenous lands in Mexico after 1991 (see Nash 2001). The 1917 Constitution which followed the Mexican Revolution had protected the legal rights of indigenous peoples under the *ejido* system of collective land use and possession; in 1991 the reforming Salinas government amended the law to allow for the privatisation (and therefore the sale) of *ejido* land (see also Harvey 2003: 160).

The shift to wage labour

The 'proletarianisation' of the world workforce is one of the clear long-term trends of the capitalist world economy (see Chase-Dunn 1999). The creation of a proletariat – a class of workers who possessed no land or productive capital and were impelled to sell their labour power as a commodity – was of course crucial to Marx's account of the development of capitalism. Such an account offers more than an historical narrative: it also works as an analysis of labour in a globalising system. As capital seeks new and cheaper resources of labour, it also creates capitalist labour markets in places where previously these had not existed. The import of raw materials by foreign capital, as well as the outsourcing of production and assembly processes, is instrumental in producing an agricultural and industrial working class in developing economies. The transition from alternative systems of peasant labour, sharecropping or family labour occurs as the exchange between owner and worker comes to be regulated by the wage relation. It sits alongside the privatisation of property rights and the marketisation of exchange detailed above.

In broad terms, the new international division of labour is based on the transfer of manufacturing and other forms of waged work from 'core' to 'periphery' (Wright 2002: 72; see also Munck 2002), but this division of labour also takes a particular social form. The exploitation of women's and children's labour has been crucial to the emergence of the NIDL. As Wright (2002: 73) points out, 'the NIDL is especially augmented by gendered labor markets and the underpayment and devaluation of female wage labor' (2002: 73; see also Mies 1998). Use of child labour is also prevalent. The International Labour Organisation reported in 2002 that globally almost a quarter of a billion children aged between 5 and 17 years worked, about three-quarters of these in dangerous jobs, ranging from mining to prostitution. The Asia-Pacific region had the highest number of children at work, while Africa – with over 40 per cent – had the highest proportion of children in work. The transfer of work from core to periphery in this way is also a transfer of labour to women and children. The chains that bind underpaid or sweated labour to global consumer items and prestige brands have been increasingly well documented, such that it is difficult for a consumer of certain goods to be ignorant of the fact that at the end of the supply chain that provides their trainers, chinos or burger stands a child labourer, an exploited worker or a dispossessed smallholder (see Goldman and Papson 1998; Klein 2000).

The exploitation of child and female labour in the international division of labour tends to blur the distinction between labour commodification and slavery, each of which Marx saw as elements of primitive accumulation and both of which fit with Harvey's contemporary account of capital accumulation by dispossession. Indeed, substantial amounts of work worldwide remain outside the wage relation, as enslavement not only endures but takes certain distinctive contemporary forms (see Bale 2000). In 2005, ILO figures put the number of workers in forced labour globally at 12.3 million: three-quarters of these were forced into labouring for individuals or private companies, with a quarter subjected to forced labour by states. The majority of these workers were in Asia (as many as 9.5 million), with 1.3 million in Latin America and the Caribbean, and an estimated 660,000 in sub-Saharan Africa (ILO 2005). A significant proportion of forced labour was channelled through an international slave trade: the ILO calculated that 2.4 million people globally were victims of human trafficking. Some 360,000 people in 2005 were in forced labour in industrialised countries, where human trafficking – particularly of women and girls into forced domestic labour and sex work – is a profitable but largely hidden part of cross-border economic flows.

Globalisation as the new imperialism?

Harvey's analysis is a critical one, but this list does not read solely as a charge-sheet against vampiric capital. Access to credit and money exchange are important means of economic development and self-sufficiency, as is evident in numerous micro-credit initiatives involving women in particular (see Lemire *et al.* 2002). The wage relation is in principle certainly no worse – and in practice usually much preferable – to various forms of tied labour. Expanded capital accumulation in the 'core' can also promote economic growth in the 'periphery' (see Harvey 2003: 178–9). What Harvey's treatment of accumulation by dispossession does do, however, is emphasise the respects in which new markets and expanded profits are based on existing social, economic and spatial arrangements. Growth in the international economy frequently involves practices of expropriation, usurpation and theft. In these terms, there is a dual logic at work in capitalist development: 'expanded reproduction on the one hand and the often violent processes of dispossession on the other have shaped the historical geography of capitalism' (Harvey 2003: 142). You can't, after all, make an omelette without breaking eggs. Market opportunities do not simply present themselves as blank slates for development, but are founded on alternative and pre-established uses, spaces, property forms and social relations. Neither are such market openings always the invention of innovative market actors. It is important to note the extent to which these accumulation strategies on the part of capitalist interests are underpinned and prosecuted by states. This is especially clear in programmes of privatisation and property reform, but state actors are also crucial in brokering conventions of trade and regulating (or, more accurately, deregulating) investment conditions, whether in respect of tax, tariffs or labour standards. The 1994 NAFTA agreement between the governments of Canada, Mexico and the United States, for example, opened the door to the low-cost US imports – the spatial displacement of capital – which battered local agricultural producers in rural Mexico (see Nash 2001).

In what sense, though, can this be analysed as a kind of 'new imperialism'? While recognising the links between histories of imperialism and contemporary globalisation, for instance, a theorist such as Sen (2002) rejects the notion that globalisation is simply a continuation of imperialist projects by other means. Harvey's argument is a provocative and in many ways polemical one, but there are also well-founded connections between earlier theories of imperialism and his own more specific treatment of accumulation by dispossession. The economic parallels are particularly clear in tracing an expansionary and predatory logic of capital across geographical space. Recent processes of globalisation can be read as one spatial fix for problems of extended capitalist reproduction, alongside (although not identical to) older forms of imperialism. There are, of course, very significant differences, not least in the contemporary restructuring of an international division of labour. The shift of a considerable proportion of global manufacture from core to periphery inverts the characteristic pattern of nineteenth- and early twentieth-century imperialism, where dependent regions provided raw materials and consumer markets for the industrial powerhouses of the core. This is an especially notable contrast between imperialist economic arrangements and the current state of play, given that the United States – as the dominant power in the international economy – is a massive importer of commodities from elsewhere, whereas the major nineteenth-century powers (particularly Britain) were net exporters of capital and commodities (Dicken 2002: 45; 2003). Indeed, Harvey (2003: 72) wryly comments that, were any other economy to display the levels of foreign indebtedness that the US has sustained in recent years, it would be 'subjected to ruthless austerity and structural adjustment procedures by the IMF' as a macroeconomic basket-case. 'But the IMF', he reminds us, 'is the United States.'

Harvey's account of a new imperialism, however, involves an argument about political as well as economic arrangements. The analytical parallels here are less clear. Harvey's new imperialism is not politically organised, as were nineteenth-century empires, around a competitive system of nation states which possess and control foreign territories. 'Contemporary imperialist practice', in contrast, assumes a different political form and a different kind of state project. As Harvey (2003: 181) puts it, 'an internationalist politics of neo-liberalism and privatization' – the leading edge of accumulation by dispossession – is at the core of the new imperialism. It is a politics that is formalised in the institutions of global governance and dominated by the advanced capitalist states, most notably the US (see the discussions in Chapters 2 and 3). The question of whether the US might, in the early years of the twenty-first century, be seen as an imperial power is highly contentious (see *inter alia* Aronowitz and Gautney 2003; Barkawi and Laffey 2002; Bishai 2004; Boot 2003; Cox 2003; Cumings 2003; Foster and McChesney 2004; Klare 2003; Mann 2003; Nye 2002; Smith 2005; Wood 2005; cf. Hardt and Negri 2000). The ideologies of nationalism and militarism that typified imperial power are certainly consistent with such a diagnosis, as is the commitment to a civilising mission, the network of dependent and client states, and the formal and informal domination exercised variously through occupation, patronage, language and culture. It is the nature, rather than the fact, of America's overseas 'possessions' that marks the key difference, together with what appears at times as a rather fine distinction between direct and indirect rule. Harvey's work, though, is less concerned with an imperialist project on the part of any single nation state than with the role of the United States as the primary power within an international neoliberal settlement.

This brings us back in interesting ways to Wallerstein's historical treatment of the capitalist world economy, particularly his assertion that this should be seen as an economic rather than a political system. The modern world system, that is to say, was integrated through economic relations and did not rely on a common form of political rule or on a common culture. Capitalism therefore formed the basis of a world system but not a world empire. While capitalist accumulation certainly was extended by imperial political arrangements, it did not necessarily require them. On Wallerstein's account, to repeat, the empires of the nineteenth century 'were not world-empires at all, but nation-states with colonial appendages operating within the framework of a global economy' (Wallerstein 2003: 63). This glancing reference to 'colonial appendages' understates the contribution that world systems theory more generally has offered to the analysis of imperialism and colonialism. It also underplays the centrality of these arrangements to the shaping of the international economy. Theorists such as King (1990a, 1990b, 1990c, 1991) and Chase-Dunn (1998) argue that the late modern global economy is deeply embedded in colonial patterns of settlement, trade and dependency. Certain societies 'in particular parts of the world can be understood better when conceptualized as "post-colonial" or "post-imperial" than as "peripheral" or "core"' (King 1990c: 410). Given the immediacy and the extent of global communications, people may now have a sharper sense of being part of an international system, but King contends that it has never really been possible to understand the development of London, say, without understanding its relations to Kingston or Bombay (see King 1990a, 1990b). It follows that structures of power in the global economy are derived in large part from the inequities of colonial modes of exploitation (see Amin 1977). Such relations of exchange and domination are not simply local details in a broader story of capitalist development – one modality in which capitalist economic relations have been played out below the world scale – but are quite basic building-blocks of the global system.

Wallerstein's original analysis of the development of modern capitalism has been critically updated in the context of more recent debates over globalisation. While the language of 'globalisation' may be relatively new, these arguments suggest that the patterns of integration it describes are very long-standing. Chase-Dunn (1999), for instance, examines processes of globalisation from a world-systems perspective. Broadly speaking, he sees economic globalisation as developing over a period of six hundred years (in line with the standard world-systems model), political globalisation stretching back two hundred years to the emergence of the modern state system, and cultural globalisation as gaining ground in the twentieth century and after. Wallerstein's own later work takes up these questions of politics and culture (see Hopkins and Wallerstein 1996; Wallerstein 1990, 1991). The extension of capitalist relations across space did not unfold, after all, according to the imperatives of an abstract economic logic, but frequently relied on military and political pressure, 'involving the overcoming of political resistance in the zones into which the geographic expansion was taking place' (Wallerstein 1990: 36). The use of these forms of coercion in support of the penetration of capitalist social relations has been very marked in the twentieth and early twenty-first centuries. It is also possible to trace the development, over this same late period, of an increasingly coherent cultural and ideological project: Wallerstein (1990: 35) remarks upon 'the degree to which this historical system became conscious of itself and began to develop intellectual and/or ideological frameworks which both justified it, and impelled its forward movement, and thereby sustained its reproduction'. Such an argument speaks quite clearly to Harvey's 'internationalist politics of neo-liberalism and privatization', or what Ulrich Beck (2000a) refers to as a prevalent ideology of 'globalism' (see the discussion in Chapter 3).

Conclusion

This chapter has been concerned with accounts – advanced within historical sociology by Wallerstein and his colleagues, and in critical geography by Harvey – which set global economic arrangements within the long-term expansion of capitalism. Globalisation means that a growing number of the world's population is incorporated into a capitalist economic system, as capitalist relations extend on a transnational scale. Drawing on political economy frameworks, each of these accounts suggests that advanced economic forms remain susceptible to a neo-Marxist critique of capital. Other critical and neo-Marxist theorists, it is worth noting, argue that although contemporary globalisation is dominated by capitalist relations and processes, globalisation in itself is not necessarily or inevitably capitalistic (see Castells 1999, 2000a; Sklair 2002). The arguments we have looked at here offer, therefore, critical takes on 'actually existing' globalisation. Both Wallerstein and Harvey also look to the potential for systemic change opened up by the very contradictions that dog global capitalism (see Amir *et al.* 1982, 1990; Arrighi *et al.* 1989; Harvey 2000; Wallerstein 2002; see also the discussion in Chapter 3).

If this discussion has concentrated on the economic analysis of globalisation, these critical approaches continually give onto other questions – of politics, ideology, culture and space. Economic arrangements, even under conditions of globalisation, remain difficult to disembed from social, political and cultural contexts. The analyses offered by world systems theory and by Harvey's critical geography make valuable contributions to a sociological understanding of economic globalisation, in large part through their fidelity to Marx's insistence that economic phenomena must be seen as social relations. In stressing the continuities between current globalisation and older patterns of capitalist organisation, moreover, they give us critical versions of the history of the economic present.

2 A new global economy?

The previous chapter focused on approaches to the international economy that draw on established lines of critical analysis. It suggested that globalisation, while it may involve certain distinctive features and novel processes, can be understood in terms of the long-range historical and spatial development of capital. Globalisation appears as an extension or intensification of capitalist economic relations. This chapter, in contrast, is concerned with arguments over the *new* or inventive elements of economic globalisation. It begins with a sceptical view, looking to critical approaches – exemplified by the work of Paul Hirst and Grahame Thompson – which put both the extent and the novelty of economic globalisation into question. Other accounts take globalisation more seriously as a distinct shift in economic organisation, arguing that it involves original elements and particular effects that require alternative modes of critical analysis. Notable here are accounts that see contemporary economies as shaped by 'flows' or 'networks' of exchange. The discussion takes up Scott Lash and John Urry's treatment of the 'speeding-up and stretching-out' of social relations and economic processes through dynamic flows in time and space. It goes on to consider Arjun Appadurai's treatment of the complex spatial organisation of a global cultural economy. Finally, it turns to Manuel Castells' work on the emergence of a 'network society' which goes beyond older structures of capitalist accumulation. None of these thinkers are entirely cut adrift from earlier frameworks of analysis. In each case, for instance, Marx remains an indispensable (if not always accurate) critic of what we now call 'globalisation'. However, these accounts all suggest that globalisation is not simply reducible to capitalist business as usual. It may, to be sure, still largely be about doing capitalist business, but the terms on which such business operates are – if not without precedent – at least without parallel in earlier phases of capitalist development. The concept of globalisation in this sense gets at something new and different in social and economic life. Before considering these arguments, however, it is worth examining the counter view.

The globalisation 'myth'

While notions of globalisation have become common currency in both critical and popular discourse in recent years, there are serious grounds for
questioning the extent to which contemporary economies can properly be
described as 'globalised'. Hirst and Thompson (1999) are perhaps the best
known among the critics who put this question, arguing against the terms of
a globalisation 'myth' which they claim both misrepresents current economic arrangements and closes off possible political responses (see also
Bourdieu 1998a; Gordon 1988; Hirst 1997; Hirst and Thompson 1992;
Piven 1995; Rosenberg 2000; Scott 1997). If we follow a strong thesis of
globalisation to its logical conclusions, they suggest, national strategies of
economic management simply become redundant. Capital chases opportunities for profit across a 'borderless world' in which nation states no longer
constitute meaningful economic boundaries (see Ohmae 1989, 1995). A
totalising logic of globalisation appears inexorable, and the international
economy ungovernable. This version of globalisation, moreover, is not
merely a self-serving myth put about by extreme economic liberals; it has
had significant and negative impact on recent programmes of social democratic government. Hirst and Thompson argue that state actors have become
prey to a kind of paralysis in the face of internationalising tendencies, where
they have not been busy creating the conditions that might appeal to
'footloose' global capital. However, political strategies in pursuit of social as
well as economic goals remain viable in an internationalising world – and,
it could be added, more and more necessary. The thrust of Hirst and
Thompson's account reduces to two simple but important assertions: the
international economy is not new, and it's not ungovernable.

Hirst and Thompson characterise the current state of the world economy
as 'inter-national' rather than global, on a number of grounds. Nation
states, firstly, remain the basic economic unit, both in respect of regulating
their domestic economies and in brokering the terms of international
exchange. A highly internationalised economy, secondly, is not in itself
novel: the modern industrial system has been more or less international since
the mid to late nineteenth century. Indeed, the period between 1870 and the
outbreak of World War I in 1914 may have been more highly internationalised (based on measurements of monetary integration via the gold standard,
or of export trade as a proportion of national outputs) than is the current
phase of 'globalisation' (see also Bairoch 1996; Gilpin 2001). Hirst and
Thompson charge that theories of globalisation typically fail to demonstrate
how contemporary economic arrangements differ in substance from earlier
phases of international integration; they lack historical substance, both neg-
lecting the past and missing any real sense that present conditions might not
endure indefinitely into the future.

It should be said that it is not always clear exactly who this argument is
directed against. Hirst and Thompson's 'strong thesis' of globalisation is

based on a highly stylised ideal-type, dominated by stateless capital in the form of wholly transnational corporations, and effectively ungovernable by nation states. It can be hard to pin this version of a globalised economy on any particular theorist, and on the whole Hirst and Thompson don't try to – although Ohmae looks most likely. The authors sketch this ideal-type not so much because it corresponds to a strongly held view on the part of specific critics, but because it provides a pretext for them to develop a more detailed analysis of the current state of international economic arrangements. They begin by sketching the context for recent debates over globalisation. A number of factors point to the liberalisation and internationalisation of economic affairs over the last few decades of the twentieth century.

These factors operated in a number of inter-linked spheres:

Monetary policy

The first is the breakdown of the Bretton Woods system of monetary control, named after the New Hampshire town at which the UN Monetary and Financial Conference met in July 1944. The 45 countries that met at Bretton Woods had signed up to monetary cooperation and exchange stability, overseen by a newly formed International Monetary Fund and underwritten by the US dollar as the world's major reserve currency. The key shock to this system was the oil crisis of 1973 (and another in 1979), which greatly increased oil prices and sparked an inflationary spiral across oil-consuming Western economies. At the same time, high prices created massive liquidity in oil-producing states, with large volumes of 'petro-dollars' washing around financial markets, principally on Wall Street.

Credit and foreign investment

The inflationary problems in Western economies led financial institutions and manufacturing interests to look for alternative credit and investment markets, resulting in large-scale lending and capital investment in developing economies – and followed in turn by various recessions and debt crises in these contexts.

Currency and financial markets

Policy interventions sealed the collapse of the post-war monetary system with a series of measures to liberalise international markets, principally through the abolition of foreign exchange controls and financial market deregulations. Such moves were led in the 1970s and 1980s by the United States, as the petro-dollar splurge reinforced US financial dominance. The United States was effectively enabled to stand outside IMF requirements for financial governance, even while it remained central to the IMF system. This marks the key point in the transformation of the IMF, from a Keynesian device geared to monetary cooperation and financial stability, to a neoliberal instrument of deregulation (see Gowan 1999; see also the discussion in Chapter 3).

Industrial production

Alongside these shifts in currency and finance markets, the bases of industrial production were increasingly unstable, with deindustrialisation and deepening unemployment in advanced economies twinned with the threat of rising foreign competition, especially from Japan.

Trade

The established terms of international trade under the auspices of US economic dominance were disrupted by the entrance of these new trade competitors, including the emergence of newly industrialising countries in East Asia.

Corporate organisation

Finally, deindustrialisation in the core and the emergence of new producers in the former 'periphery' saw a shift in the organisation of production away from large national corporations serving mass domestic markets towards more flexible corporate networks and multinational firms operating across international markets.

This paints a picture of an international economic order undergoing a period of intense instability and rapid change. To what extent, though, does it equate to a thoroughgoing process of globalisation? Hirst and Thompson present two very critical counter-arguments to a strong thesis of globalisation, one based on the role of transnational corporations (TNCs) and one on levels of foreign direct investment. First, they contend, TNCs are only 'weakly developed' (1999: 16). There remain relatively few truly stateless corporations that locate and relocate their operations across different sites in response to local market conditions. Multinational corporations (MNCs) continue to predominate in the international economy, with major operations (including management, research and development, core production and sales) based in the company's primary location and the strategic location of branch assembly or distribution plants elsewhere. These corporate players are best understood as 'national companies with an international scope of operations' (ibid.: 12; see also Allen 1995; Gilpin 2001; Mair 1997). While export sales are highly important for multinational corporations, and foreign market conditions very influential, this is nothing new in itself – it was also typical of how major companies operated during the long post-war boom. The distinction Hirst and Thompson draw between transnational and multinational corporations may seem a rather fine one, but their argument is valuable in emphasising the way that the assets and activities of major corporations tend to remain centred in national economies, and to this extent are subject (at least in principle) to national systems of regulation.

Other globalisation theorists, in contrast, ascribe greater significance to transnational corporations. There are various measures of how many TNCs are active in the world economy, and of their share of global investment and trade. Dicken (2002: 47) describes TNCs as the 'primary shapers of the global economy'. They dominate world trade; indeed, Dicken estimates that up to one-third of global trade consists in transnational trade *within* these firms themselves – that is, 'transactions between different parts of the same firm . . . within their own internal markets'. UN figures indicate that by 2001 there were around 65,000 companies with headquarters in three countries or more, with 850,000 foreign subsidiaries, and generating more than two-thirds of world trade activity (UNCTAD 2002). Johnston, Taylor and Watts (2002) suggest that by the end of the 1990s transnational corporations accounted for more than 20 per cent of global output. However, their analysis does support the Hirst and Thompson view that such corporations remain firmly based in certain national and regional locations: '90 percent of TNCs are headquartered in the advanced capitalist states', with half of them based in five countries alone (Johnston *et al.* 2002: 21).

A second key argument on Hirst and Thompson's part concerns the role of foreign direct investment in the international economy. On their definition, 'FDI is key to the proposition that capital mobility is restructuring the world economy' (Hirst and Thompson 1999: 16). Foreign direct investment in the world economy may have trebled since 1980, but their analysis suggests that flows of foreign capital remain concentrated in exchanges between the advanced economies. Relatively little is directed towards developing countries, with the exception of some rapidly industrialising economies. More generally, international economic flows (including trade as well as investment) are largely between the Triad or G3 economic blocs of North America, Europe, and the Asia-Pacific, rather than being noticeably or inclusively 'global'. While trade between these big three takes a large share of total international trade, it accounts for a relatively small share of their own domestic product – in the case of the United States, export trade accounts for a little more than 10 per cent of GDP. This proportion, it must be noted, has doubled since 1960, but most US trade continues to take place within the boundaries of the national economy.

Again, other theorists who are happier with the language of 'globalisation' would also concur with Hirst and Thompson on this point. Johnston *et al.* (2002: 21) note that 'the triad of Japan, North America, and Western Europe produced 72 percent of global foreign investment flows' in 1997. Underlying this figure, moreover, is not simply the regional domination of FDI flows but its corporate concentration, as the authors assert that around 1 per cent of transnational corporations control half of all FDI stock. In the late 1990s, 48 developing countries attracted around $3 billion in foreign direct investment annually, just 0.4 per cent of the global total (ibid.: 23). Such patterns of investment are mirrored by patterns of world trade, which follow lines of regional advantage and TNC organisation. These uneven geographies mean that 'the vast majority of world trade is focused on the three major regions while substantial parts of the world, notably Africa, parts of South Asia and of Latin America, remain largely peripheralized' (Dicken 2002: 48). Against such a picture, however, must be set the emergence of China as a major trading partner in world markets and a site for intensifying foreign investment, as well as the expansion of foreign investment into economies such as India, Brazil or Mexico (see Sklair 1999).

The primacy of the Triad blocs within the international system both undermines the notion that the contemporary economy is genuinely global, and opens up substantial scope for coordinated international economic regulation. What is more, this regional Triad tends to stand for the interests and activities of its major national players: the United States; the larger European economies such as Germany, Britain and France; and Japan. These dominant nation states have the economic clout to exert a significant degree of control over financial and other markets – the governance of international economic flows therefore remains not only possible but actual. In this context, Hirst and Thompson (1999: 13–14) make an important point. 'The world trading system', they contend,

> has never been just an 'economy', a distinct system governed by its own laws. In this sense, the term 'international economy' has always been a shorthand for what is actually the product of the complex interaction of economic relations and politics, shaped and reshaped by the struggle of the great powers.

Indeed, their account suggests that greater economic integration has historically been promoted by a certain kind of political project. The modern economy has appeared most highly internationalised when it is underwritten by a hegemonic power which sees an open international trading system as coincident with its own national interests. This was the case during the period both of British economic dominance up to 1914, and that of US dominance after 1945. Hirst and Thompson argue that US hegemony in the world system was shaken by the monetary, inflationary and recessionary crises of the early 1970s, but the United States remains the world's largest national economy and its strongest advocate of international free trade – in spite of a lingering attachment to protectionism at home (see also Cox 2003; Cumings 2003). In sum, the integration of the international economy is best understood in terms of an international state project, usually under the stewardship of a hegemon, rather than simply as an effect of the activities of 'stateless' capital.

Hirst and Thompson's argument against the globalisation 'myth' is not to deny that there are certain definite 'trends towards internationalization' (1999: 4). Export trade in both goods and services greatly increased as a proportion of world GDP over the latter part of the twentieth century; foreign direct investment increased three-fold in the two decades after 1980. The substance of their argument, however, is that these flows remain highly geared to exchanges between the leading industrial economies. The contemporary system in this sense is an 'inter-national' rather than a 'global' one. Capital continues to be domesticated in important ways. It can be argued, against Hirst and Thompson, that finance capital (rather than productive or investment capital) represents the really novel, the radically mobile and the distinctly global factor in contemporary economic arrangements (see, for example, S. Amin 1997; Castells 2000a; Harvey 1989, 2003). Gilpin, although otherwise something of a sceptic, argues that international finance 'is the one area to which the term "globalization" is more appropriately applied' (2001: 7). While the US acted as the world's banker during the post-World War II period, the volatile and speculative nature of financial flows evades even its grasp today – Castells (2004: 306) notes that 'global financial markets are largely out of the control of any individual government, including the United States'. There may remain some degree of control, however, for states working in concert. Hirst and Thompson recognise that current short-term financial flows are unprecedented in scale, but at the same time they insist that there is scope, where there is the will, for international controls on financial markets and flows. The liberalisation of finance markets and the abolition of currency controls during the 1970s and 1980s, for instance, have been at least partly corrected by re-regulation through international agreements and institutional fixes in the 1990s and after. This underlines a larger point about the changing nature of international economic arrangements. The world economy has gone through various phases since the late nineteenth century – at times in the direction of greater openness and integration (1870–1914, or 1945–73), at other times towards protectionism and competitive autarky (for example, during the 1920s and 1930s). A shift to a fully globalised economy is neither a simple fact nor an inevitable tendency; Hirst and Thompson suggest that current conditions represent a particular conjuncture in the history of the modern international economy, rather than a decisive break with the past or the outline of a distinctively new economic future (see Chase-Dunn, Kawano and Brewer 2000 for an even longer view).

This cyclical model of phases of integration and isolation, liberalisation and regulation, contrasts with accounts that see the global economy as advancing through gradual stages of incorporation (Dicken 2003; Palloix 1977; Robinson and Harris 2000). The international economy, in this view, has developed around the successive integration of different circuits of capital. It proceeded firstly through circuits of commodity capital – the long-standing international trade in goods. This was followed by the internationalisation of circuits of money capital via foreign investments. Most recently productive capital has internationalised through the rapid spread of transnational production processes (see Dicken 2003: 201). Robinson and Harris (2000) argue that the world economy up to 1914 – for Hirst and Thompson, a high point of international integration – operated primarily through the arm's-length trade in goods. This form of 'shallow integration' is qualitatively different from the 'deep integration' across international space represented by transnational production (see also Dicken 2003). The globalisation of production in this way marks a qualitative change in the organisation of the international economy, even if productive capital has not (yet) become wholly footloose or stateless. While Hirst and Thompson may be right to argue that the international economy was, by certain measures, as integrated at the beginning of the twentieth century as it was by the end, they understate the differences between then and now. Their cyclical model of waves of integration and disintegration, what is more, presents a quite different picture from a stage model of increasing internationalisation in the production and exchange of goods and services over the course of the twentieth century and thereafter. Robertson (1990: 19), to draw out this contrast, sees the period from 1880 to 1925 not as one high point in successive cycles of international activity, but as the 'crucial take-off period of globalization' as it began its inexorable, if uneven, ascent.

This is to make a distinction between Hirst and Thompson's cyclical model of international economic integration, and a long-term tendency towards globalisation which was, by the end of the twentieth century, unrelenting (see also Sklair 1999). One also can go along with Hirst and Thompson's version but nevertheless argue that the current state of the international economy is markedly different in kind from earlier phases. The question of globalisation is in this sense not simply quantitative (a measure of levels of FDI, international trade as a proportion of GDP, number of TNCs, and so on), but a qualitative issue to do with the *content* of transnational economic exchanges (see A. Amin 1997). Dollar and Kraay (2002), for instance, agree that there was a pattern of downturn and upswing in the international economy over the twentieth century, such that levels of foreign ownership only returned to their 1914 peak in 1980. While the sustained rise in FDI since then is important, what is also notable is the real shift in the content of these foreign assets. Whereas at the beginning of the twentieth century, foreign investment was largely directed to natural resources and infrastructure projects (such as canals and railroads), at the beginning of the twenty-first century foreign investment flows were geared to manufacturing production and increasingly to services. Foreign capital, of course, still builds dams and owns mines or oil in overseas economies, but the balance between these different kinds of investment has altered in fundamental ways.

A similar shift is evident in world trade. Dollar and Kraay note that the trend towards rising levels of trade up to 1914 was reversed in the period from the Great Depression through World War II, and in 1950 international trade as a proportion of global income was lower than it had been in 1914. Under the post-war GATT regime, however, greater cooperation and grad-ual trade liberalisation promoted an upsurge in trade between the major industrialised economies, with some of the new industrialisers – notably Taiwan and South Korea – later getting in on the act. From the 1980s, foreign trade began to expand more widely to other developing economies. Dicken (2003), too, would agree with Hirst and Thompson on the regional-ised nature of current global trade and the uneven patterns of world eco-nomic growth, yet still sees a substantive shift taking place in economic organisation. He argues that the late nineteenth-century economy was indeed highly internationalised, but functioned chiefly as a 'core-periphery system', with the core states producing nearly all manufactured goods and the periphery providing raw resources and consumer markets (see also Dicken 2002: 45; and see the discussion in Chapter 1). The restructuring of production across geographical space, the new international division of labour, the globalisation of services, the rapid movement of money: this complex of factors produces a quite new map of the international economy. According to the measures Hirst and Thompson set up (levels of FDI, activ-ity of TNCs, regional patterns of trade), the contemporary economy may not appear significantly more 'globalised' than it was one hundred years ago, but the work of analysts such as Dicken suggests that the basis of international integration has been remade in substantive ways. We are not simply witnessing 'one of a number of distinct conjunctures or states of the international economy that have existed since ... the 1860s' (Hirst and Thompson 1999: 2), but are seeing a more fundamental global shift to a 'new geo-economy' (Dicken 2003: 7).

In many ways, however, the weight of such arguments lies not in disputes about the rate or degree of economic change, but in their social and political consequences. For Hirst and Thompson, the language of 'globalisation' is not simply lazy, overdone or historically shallow, it has political con-sequences. In their view, discourses of globalisation are not merely a popular economic myth but a convenient alibi for neoliberal government (see also Boudieu 1998a, 1998c). Arguments about the need for global 'competitive-ness', particularly against imports from newly industrialising economies, provide a rationale for the drive to more flexible labour markets in advanced economies, as well as offering an external explanation for local processes of deindustrialisation and associated job losses. The notion that national econ-omies are more exposed to international pressures and external shocks has also underpinned arguments that extensive welfare systems have become unviable and unaffordable. The highly mobile nature of footloose capital, finally, is seen to preclude any serious moves to tax corporate wealth, regu-late corporate capital, or control financial markets. In these ways, the spectre of unfettered globalisation is as much a political fiction as it is an economic fallacy. The assumption that global economic processes are ungovernable on an international scale and unanswerable on a national level stems from a lack of political will, rather than from any recognition of hard economic fact. The expedient 'myth' and the unexamined rhetoric of global-isation work to obscure the fact that an international economy is not the same as an uncontrollable one.

Modes of global integration

The discussion in Chapter 3 takes up these questions concerning the politics of globalisation. At this point, it may be instructive to return, by way of conclusion, to two of Hirst and Thompson's basic propositions. The first of these is the distinction between an economy that is 'inter-national' (as they put it), and one that is fully *global*. The second is their assertion that con-temporary arrangements represent a particular phase in a modern economic system which has been more or less international since the mid-nineteenth century. Hirst and Thompson's argument, in both connections, is based on the empirical analysis of specific economic factors. It makes for a very com-pelling argument – and their work has been crucial in challenging theorists of globalisation to qualify and historicise their claims. Other theorists, how-ever, offer a more conceptual approach to understanding the degrees of difference between international and global relations, between cycles of integration and step changes in economic organisation. Held *et al.* (1999: 2), for instance, develop an account of globalisation that goes beyond the eco-nomic: for them, globalisation is 'the widening, deepening and speeding up of worldwide interconnectedness in all aspects of contemporary life, from the cultural to the criminal, the financial to the spiritual'. The typology they outline for assessing different modes of global integration, however, is also relevant to the more limited study of economic globalisation with which we are concerned here.

Whereas Hirst and Thompson base their account on specific economic indicators, Held and his colleagues put forward a general analytic frame-work for adjudging the extent of globalisation in different domains. Global integration, they suggest, can be analysed along four lines:

1   *extensity* refers to the spatial extent or reach of international networks and connections;
2   *intensity* concerns the density of international networks or connections;
3   *velocity* measures the speed of international interactions and flows;
4   *impact* describes the wider effects of international linkages on the organisation of political power, on social and cultural relations, and on everyday experience.

According to these four criteria, the current phase of international integra-tion is one of 'thick' globalisation. International connections are extensive and densely networked, exchanges are rapid and in many cases instant-aneous across international space, and these global relations can shape local conditions quite profoundly. 'Thin' globalisation, in contrast, would refer to the old trade routes that brought silks and other luxury goods from Asia to Europe in the early modern period. Although these routes were very extended in space they did not score highly on the other measures – being quite thinly drawn, extremely slow, and having relatively little impact on the majority of people's lives at different points along the route. A more inter-mediate form, such as 'expansive globalisation', might be seen in the period of European imperialism. Imperialist connections were extensive across space and had major impact on the lives of colonised peoples in particular, but the density of interconnections and the velocity of flows were compara-tively low and slow. 'Diffused globalisation', finally, measures highly in terms of extensity, intensity and velocity, but relatively low in terms of wider impact on the local organisation of people's lives. Held *et al.* ascribe this last version of globalisation to those who continue to argue for the sovereignty of nation states in an international system of trade. Hirst and Thompson, if unwillingly, would be in this camp.

The Held approach sidesteps the question of when, if at all, a modern international system became globalised by analysing early modern trade and imperialism as themselves more limited versions of globalisation (see also Keohane and Nye 2000). There is a clear danger of anachronism here, but the model is interesting in that – while committed to an idea that the recent period has been marked by real 'global transformations' – it does not treat contemporary globalisation as an unprecedented or incomparable moment in economic and social organisation. It admits of an historical view (indeed a rather long one) which assumes that degrees of international interdepend-ence vary over time. It becomes possible therefore to speak of 'a partially globalized world or processes of deglobalization' (Held and McGrew 2003: 7). It also recognises the basic unevenness of different regions' and social groups' access to global networks. This typology suggests that the current phase of global integration is distinguished by the extension and intensity of transnational networks, and by the weight of their impact on social and political life. If contemporary globalisation is not entirely without prece-dent, it nevertheless represents something new and distinctive. How then might we tease out the distinct features of this 'thick' mode of globalisation?

The economy of signs, flows and networks

The discussion so far has focused on accounts of globalisation that stress its continuities with earlier phases of economic organisation. In the critical approaches discussed in the previous chapter, globalisation appears as a further stage and a logical extension of capitalist accumulation, one that remains subject to its in-built crisis tendencies and susceptible to a critique of capital. In Hirst and Thompson's view, discourses of globalisation obscure the way that recent arrangements fit into a longer history of the international economy, and tend to overstate both the novelty and the extent of contemporary patterns of international integration. Alongside such arguments, however, might be set alternative accounts that emphasise the distinctive features of current economic processes. While they may continue to see globalisation in terms of a logic of capitalist development, these perspectives maintain that it also involves new economic features which in turn demand new modes of analysis. Of particular relevance here are approaches that view the global economy in terms of a geography of 'flows' or 'networks' (see Appadurai 1990, 1997; Castells 1999, 2000a, 2000b; Lash and Urry 1994).

Such approaches place special emphasis on the reconfiguration of time and space. Lash and Urry (1994) refer to this in terms of the 'speeding-up and stretching-out' of social relations and economic processes. Innovations in communications and transport technologies make it possible for things – whether goods, information, money, images or bodies – to travel further, faster. In simple terms, it is cheaper and easier to move things around. This plain technical fact, though, is tied to a more fundamental shift in social structures and subjectivities. In line with David Harvey's (1990) treatment of 'time-space compression', Lash and Urry suggest that economic and social life involves a new experience of time and space (see also Thrift 2002a). It is marked by the temporal intensification ('speeding-up') and spatial extension ('stretching-out') of processes of exchange – from the sale of goods across borders to social interactions over the Internet. Such an account treats the contemporary economy as distinctive on two levels: firstly that of form, and secondly that of content. In formal terms, the advanced capitalist economy is organised around dynamic *flows* of commodities, people, information and images. The notion of the flow captures both the spatial complexity and the temporal velocity of economic exchange. In relation to content, secondly, the economy is distinguished by the kinds of products that are circulated. An increasing share of global economic flows is taken by the exchange of non-material goods – knowledge, expertise and information, financial products, signs, images and media texts (see the extended discussion in Chapter 5).

Although Lash and Urry are dealing with a novel set of economic conditions, they find a pedigree for their treatment of the economy of flows in the work of Marx. In particular, they look to the argument Marx sketched in the second volume of *Capital* on 'the process of circulation of capital' (Lash and Urry 1994: 1). We have encountered this argument already: capital circulates in three forms – as money or finance capital, as commodity capital, and as productive capital. Lash and Urry note that this third category, productive capital, is subdivided between the technical means of production (constant or fixed capital) and labour power. There are therefore four types of capital that circulate across time and space, comprised of money, commodities, means of production, and labour power. Here is the basic conception that underlies a contemporary economy of flows. Different forms of capital 'move through space and they work to different and changing temporalities' (ibid.). In Marx's unfinished work, however, this model of the circulation of capital remains a technical one. Lash and Urry take Marx's abstract conception and seek to locate it in historical time and social space. They suggest that during the twentieth century circuits of capital were largely coordinated around the space of nation states. By the end of that century, they stretched across international space. The expanded reach and speed of capitalist circulation is aided by the fact that various forms of capital are increasingly 'immaterial': money-capital exchanges as symbols on screens; commodities circulate as images, information or sounds; means of production (historically the most 'fixed' form of capital) are found in digital software and electronic networks; labour power takes the form of knowledge. Bodies and things, it must be emphasised, also circulate in greater volumes, over greater distances and at greater speeds than they ever have before, but the distinctive tendency of current economic flows is towards the production and circulation of *signs*.

Global 'scapes'

This notion that economic flows are increasingly concerned with the circulation of signs is elaborated in Arjun Appadurai's treatment of the global cultural economy (Appadurai 1990). While he has a particular focus on exchanges of cultural goods, Appadurai's approach has broader relevance to the mapping of global economic processes in which 'money, commodities and persons are involved in ceaselessly chasing each other around the world'. He breaks with older models which divide social and economic space into core and periphery, or explain international migration in terms of push–pull factors between set points of origin and destination. Rather, Appadurai sees the global cultural economy as a complex and overlapping space characterised by patterns of disjuncture and difference. This system is oriented around various flows of goods, images, ideas and people. Global cultural flows – if they do not correspond to the geography of nation states or to maps of core and periphery – are not shapeless or placeless. They produce particular spatialities, which Appadurai terms 'scapes'. The idea of the 'scape' is meant to suggest that these are not fixed or objective geographies, but compose themselves in relation to the perspective and position of specific actors, whether corporations, states, social groups and movements, diasporic communities or individuals. Appadurai develops this argument in terms of a number of 'scapes' which coordinate different modes of exchange and circulation.

Ethnoscapes

These map the mobilities of social actors – of tourists, immigrants, refugees, exiles, migrant and guest workers; these cross-cutting routes are shaped by flows of capital as well as constrained by the strictures of nation states.

Ethnoscapes track material patterns of movement and interaction, as well as forming imagined communities which stretch across international space (cf. Anderson 1983).

Technoscapes

These describe the spaces mapped by mechanical and information technology, both of which are becoming more mobile. These technical infrastructures can no longer simply be plotted around conventional economies of scale, but involve complex networks of communication, finance, expertise, political regulation and so on. Production processes may be dispersed across geographical space, but reintegrated through electronic networks and computer-controlled production technologies. Technoscapes in this way facilitate the operations of multinationals in cross-border production, assembly and distribution, as well as rapid exchanges of information in management, research and trade.

Finanscapes

These mark flows of global capital – which Appadurai describe as being 'now a more mysterious, rapid and difficult landscape to follow than ever before'. These capital flows operate through the information technoscapes outlined above, which allow for the rapid movement of 'mega-monies', extremely fine and fast margins of calculation, and the creation and circulation of diverse immaterial financial commodities.

Mediascapes

These are the geographies inscribed by media technologies and media content. They are subject in various ways to the regulatory actions of nation states, but also are more and more open to transnational flows and patterns of ownership and production. Mediascapes are highly variable in terms of technology, genre, ownership, audience, but their chief importance is in circulating a set of common images and narratives across international space, in which 'the world of commodities and the world of "news" and politics are profoundly mixed'.

Ideoscapes

These are also based on information and media technologies, and are composed of political discourses and images oriented both to states and to movements of opposition and resistance. They circulate dominant ideologies of sovereignty, democracy and freedom, as well as counter-discourses of self-determination or anti-imperialism, militant particularism or racism. Ideoscapes can be understood in terms of a global 'public sphere' of debate governing forms of international cooperation and conflict, trade and economic regulation. Ideoscapes can also be conceived in terms of international movements of solidarity with such groups as the Zapatistas in Mexico or the Ogoni in Nigeria, or with the international electronic forums established by far right groups or radical fundamentalist movements.

Appadurai's conception of scapes gives a shape to what otherwise appears as a mutable logic of flows. While he suggests that scapes alter in relation to the position of specific actors (as a landscape composes itself differently depending on where one is standing), his argument also takes in key elements of structure, stability and power. The notion of disjuncture disrupts any idea that circulation within an economy of flows is smooth, free or unimpeded. Appadurai looks to the way that different scapes overlap, intersect and come into conflict with each other. The rapid and fairly free flows of ideas, images and goods via techno-, finan- and mediascapes, for instance, contrast with the political restrictions and material constraints that limit movements of people within ethnoscapes. While states may work to facilitate flows across finanscapes through deregulation and liberalisation, they frequently seek to set controls on flows of media content as well as on movements of people, whether citizens or 'aliens'. People are not so mobile as other objects within the global economy, or are only problematically so. There is a deep contradiction between global capital's demands for labour mobility – requiring 'continuous migrations across national borders' (Hardt and Negri 2000: 400) – and political efforts to limit these movements. The role of Mexican and other Latino workers in US agriculture, or of migrant workers from Palestine or Pakistan in the Arab oil industries, underlines the extent to which contemporary capitalism relies on the mobility of labour (ibid.: 397). Leading economic nations and regions (the EU, US and Japan, but also such economies as Saudi Arabia or Singapore) are 'utterly dependent on the influx of workers from the subordinate regions of the world' (ibid.: 400), even as political and mediascapes work to criminalise or demonise economic migrants. These kinds of disjuncture represent contradictions in a global economy of flows, producing points of conflict, patterns of inequality, and knots of inefficiency. In this way, flows or networks might be said to 'fail' in a manner analogous to market failure, distributing information unevenly, externalising social costs, requiring and subverting regulation.

The network economy: Castells

Perhaps the most influential treatment of a new global economy of flows is to be found in Manuel Castells' work on the rise of the network society (Castells 2000a, 2000b). Like Appadurai, Lash and Urry, Castells sees technological advances in recent decades as having profoundly altered the organisation of social and economic life in many parts of the globe. In what he terms the 'information age', more and more dimensions of economic and social interaction are based on flows of capital, information and symbols through networks, especially electronic networks. 'Networks', as he puts it, 'constitute the new social morphology of our society' (Castells 2000a: 500). This network model – extensive, complex, integrated, rapid – is quite different from older analytic models which understood economic and social arrangements in terms of *structures*. More structural approaches emphasise the relative entrenchment and stability of social and economic arrangements, and tend to depict social relations in terms of hierarchy, segmentation and stratification. Structural analysis has been central to social science, and underpins the models of economy and society offered by such thinkers as Marx or Durkheim, Parsons or Merton. The image of the network society, in contrast, stresses fluidity over fixity, horizontal over vertical relations, process over causality. This shift in analytic language marks a profound shift in social forms. 'Flows', Castells (ibid.: 442) argues, 'are not just one element of the social organization: they are the expression of processes *dominating* over economic, political, and symbolic life'. Any material analysis of social organisation must therefore look to the means by which these flows are enabled, integrated and reproduced – to what Lash and Urry refer to, a little ironically, as the 'structure of flows'. For Castells (2002a: 442), it is the network that gives shape to a contemporary economy and society which is 'structured around flows'.

Castells asserts that a new economy emerged in the 1970s. It is 'informational, global, and networked' (ibid.: 77). On the protracted debates over whether the contemporary economy is really global, or indeed how new any of this is, Castells (ibid.: 101) is simply unequivocal: 'The informational economy is global. A global economy is an historically new reality, distinct from a world economy.' With a nod to Braudel and Wallerstein, Castells moves on. The new economy is distinguished by its form (the network), its content (information), and its spread (global). In this way, Castells' model is marked off from the structural analysis of an economy based on material goods and organised around nation states: in place of structure or system, the network; in place of goods, information; and in place of the national, the global. Clearly economies still produce things, and nation states have not disappeared, but the dominant logic of contemporary economic life is that of the information network. Castells accepts many of the sceptical arguments that may be put forward against the globalisation thesis. It is true that most production, most work and most firms remain local or regional, rather than global. It is true, too, that foreign trade and investment remain less significant to GDP than domestic trade and investment. 'Yet', he insists (ibid.: 101), 'we can assert that there is a global economy because economies around the world depend on the performance of their globalized core.' It is around these core sectors – in finance, trade, production, technology and expertise – that a global economy is integrated. The key to Castells' argument here is his assertion that the global economy has the capacity to function as a single unit in time. This was not the case for the international economy of the late nineteenth century – with its high levels of trade and foreign investment, its dense linkages, its free flows of money and people, but its steam and telegraph technology. It is only with what Castells calls the 'information technology revolution' of the 1970s that it has become possible to annihilate economic space by electronic time.

The extension and intensification of electronic networks is therefore central to processes of globalisation. Castells argues that two features fundamentally distinguish contemporary capitalism from preceding periods. First, it is global: on Castells' account, 'for the first time in history, the capitalist mode of production shapes social relationships over the entire planet' (ibid.: 502). Second, it is organised around networks of financial flows. While earlier phases of capitalist accumulation were propelled by finance capital (money), commodity capital (trade) and industrial capital (production) in varying balances, the current phase is dominated by finance (see also Harvey 1990, 2003). Circuits of commodity and productive capital are secondary to, and tend to be slower than, the electronic circuits of finance. The value of financial commodities which exchange daily on global currency and stock markets massively outstrips the value of global trade in material commodities – as Robinson and Harris (2000) have it, in the contemporary global economy the value of 'real' trade equates to around only 1 per cent of the volume of 'fictitious' trade (see also Gilpin 2001: 6). Financial capital simply is more mobile, more densely networked, and more easily transferable – it is more truly 'footloose' – than other forms of capital.

Global financial flows therefore represent the master or 'meta-network': indeed, the 'network of networks' (Castells 2000a: 505). This is the clearinghouse for the global economy, where different forms of capital are converted, valorised, depreciated – or more simply, gambled. Castells (ibid.: 503) states that:

> whatever is extracted as profit (from producers, consumers, technology, nature, and institutions) is reverted to the meta-network of financial flows, where all capital is equalized in the commodified democracy of profit-making. In this electronically operated global casino specific capitals boom or bust, settling the fate of corporations, household savings, national currencies, and regional economies.

National debts, pension funds, company assets, individual endowments – all of these are washed out and frequently washed up in the flows of finance capital that give the network society its central logic. Conversions between different circuits of capital are a basic feature of capitalist economies, and finance capital is the crucial medium for this process. In the contemporary context, however, finance capital assumes the form of 'an integrated, global capital network, whose movements and variable logic ultimately determine economies and influence societies' (ibid.: 505).

The network society therefore remains a capitalist society. Indeed, the network offers itself as the ideal organisational model for a 'capitalist economy based on innovation, globalization, and decentralised concentration' (ibid.: 502). Even so, there is nothing intrinsically or inevitably capitalist about network society. In order to make this claim, Castells draws a distinction between the 'mode of production' which determines economic relations and distributes the social product (as in a feudal, capitalist or communist mode of production), and the 'mode of development' – the technical means which underlie different kinds of economic organisation (as in agrarian, industrial or informational modes of development). The relation between these economic and technical modes is not fixed. As it stands, the capitalist mode of production is articulated with an informational mode of development as capital is brokered through electronic networks. The result is what Castells calls 'informational capitalism' (ibid.: 18). At an earlier stage, the capitalist mode of production was highly compatible with an industrial mode of development; this did not mean, as Marx and others maintained, that industrialism was *necessarily* capitalistic. Castells points to the strong contemporary links between the capitalist mode of production and the informational mode of development, but is not prepared to assert that capitalism determines the technological form of the network. This argument in turn does two things. First, by stressing the capitalist nature of contemporary network society, it disputes any notion that post-industrial society is somehow 'post-capitalist'. While production and accumulation have altered in substantive ways, while patterns of capitalist ownership have become more dispersed and complex, while capitalist class structures may have fragmented, the network society remains deeply subject to the logic of capital. Second, and by way of contrast, Castells' argument opens up the possibility that network society does not *have* to develop along capitalist lines. In this way he offers both a critical account of contemporary network arrangements, and a space for conceiving these arrangements differently. Network society is currently, but not inevitably, driven by capitalist interests and imperatives.

In working around this paradox, Castells seeks to avoid both economic and technological determinism. Although economic and technical logics – the mode of production and the mode of development – are tightly integrated, it is very difficult to discern what comes first. 'Of course', he insists (ibid.: 5), 'technology does not determine society', but only because 'technology *is* society'. Society cannot be thought of separately from its technological forms. Ultimately, however, Castells does see the network format as shaping the social and economic exchanges which take place within it. The logic of the network takes precedence over the social interests operating through the network: 'the power of flows', as he puts it, 'takes precedence over the flows of power' (ibid.: 500). This is a nice line, but it is also a big claim. It points to one of the thornier problems in recent approaches to a network economy: the way in which a language of 'flows' can appear to level off structural disparities between different points in the network, to render invisible or anonymous the places and people around whom power is concentrated. At the same time, the flow or network, rather than being the expression of the social relations that produce it, appears to take on a life of its own. This is a fetishism of the network, as it assumes a kind of power not reducible to the social interests that underlie it.

This problem is not confined to Castells. Indeed, it is a basic problem for sociological analysis. Institutions, social forms and structures are products of social action. People make and re-make the conditions of social life, but these nevertheless appear as stubborn realities, as simply given, as immoveable objects or immutable facts. Social phenomena have a durability and density that outlast and exceed any given individual or group; they have effects that are not matters of human design or intention. The power of the network is, in this sociological sense, analogous to the power of the law or the state or the family or religion, or anything else that social actors have invented and which in turn directs and constrains them. But Castells' argument goes further, compounding the sociological sense of the sheer weight of institutions with economic assumptions about the autonomy of markets as mechanisms, and a Frankenstein version of technology. Networks are not seen primarily as institutional forms (like the state or the legal system), but as technological artefacts, with an internal effectivity that operates independently of social agency or intervention.

In this account social and economic power does not disappear, but power relations are reshaped by the logic of flows. Real power is power in and of the network, especially at those points where different (political, cultural, economic) nodes intersect. 'Switches connecting the networks (for example, financial flows taking control of media empires that influence political processes) are the privileged instruments of power', Castells (ibid.: 502) writes. 'Thus, the switchers are the power holders.' The argument here is both very persuasive and more than a little frustrating. There is a real tension in Castells' work between the totalising logic of the network, and his efforts to map out the systematic ways in which social interests and inequalities structure and reproduce the network form. Let us look first at the image of the total network.

Castells stresses that the network society remains, at least so far, a capitalist society. It can even be seen as the exemplary form of capitalism, 'in its pure expression of the endless search for money by money through the production of commodities by commodities' (ibid.: 505). Networks, that is, give expression to capital in its most disembodied, dematerialised form. Electronic flows of information and finance, such as dominate the current network economy, are increasingly detached from the production of things and the control of social actors. Real 'human-flesh' capitalists still exist but are subsumed by a 'faceless collective capitalist, made up of financial flows operated by electronic networks' (ibid.: 505). The logic of the network is non-human, as information is generated and exchanged, value produced and destroyed, within an electronic calculus that is virtually instantaneous and radically complex. These processes exceed the control and even the grasp of any given social actors. Castells (ibid.: 504) refers to the way that high-level managers may oversee firms and regulate certain economic sectors, but they 'do not control, and do not even know about, the actual, systemic movements of capital in the networks of financial flows, of knowledge in the information networks, of strategies in the multifaceted set of network enterprises'. In spite of the shock of the new that runs through Castells' account, there is a clear precedent for this model of economic organisation. Castells' network can be seen as a reworking of liberal versions of the market, as a complex system of information, interaction and allocation which operates according to its own logic and which goes beyond the design of social actors. It has never been the case – contra ideal models of perfect knowledge – that economic actors can know, let alone control, what goes on across an extended market system. Castells maintains, however, that networks do not simply follow an abstract logic of the market because they do not work according to laws of supply and demand (ibid.: 505). Network processes are subject to turbulence, unpredictability and irrationalities, to social and psychological noise. The movement of values in shares or currencies on trading screens, for instance, tend to produce demand as much as respond to it. But this is also true of supply and demand in most 'real' markets. Just so (and in spite of his disavowal), it can be argued that Castells' network is a souped-up version of the market, with all of its usual imperfections.

At an extreme, these networks appear to operate almost independently of human actors. It is difficult to identify key agents of command and control, or to pin down the purposive interests which direct interactions within the network. There no longer seem to be any commanding heights from which to regulate a network economy. This is a further marker of a new economic condition. 'For the first time in history', Castells (ibid.: 214) writes, 'the basic unit of economic organization is not a subject', whether individual or collective: *'the unit is the network'*. It is not clear what this means for economic analysis, with its focus on individuals, households, firms, national economies. More broadly, such an argument has critical implications for the understanding of power and class. Class relations are distributed across the network, as workers may labour 'alongside' others in different countries, capitalist owners are dispersed in electronic space, corporate managers oversee the production process on factory floors where they have never set foot. The capitalist class, in particular, becomes more difficult to define, as capital circulates in the virtual space of information networks. Castells (ibid.: 505) puts it this way:

> While capitalism still rules, capitalists are randomly incarnated, and the capitalist classes are restricted to specific areas of the world where they prosper as appendixes to a mighty whirlwind which manifests its will by

spread points and futures ratings in the global flashes of computer screens.

Appendixes to a whirlwind? It would seem that the logic of the network exceeds even Castells' ability to make sense of it, here. Yet there is a common-sense reality to Castells' account: electronic networks process information and convert values in volumes and at speeds that simply defy real-time human reckoning. The electronic displays that tick across the fascias of Bloomberg offices or run across the foot of CNN screens, the frenzy of the trading floor, are only slow-mo suggestions of just how quickly informational values move. Gold or the greenback never really close up or down, because they never really close. It is hard to think coherently about capitalist class power – with the exception of some old-style corporate magnates and some new-style millionaire cadre – when ownership is so dispersed and control so attenuated.

Where, though, is the critical bite of this sort of account? Peter Marcuse (2002) has written persuasively on the 'depoliticising' effects of a network approach to globalisation. The logic of the network, in Castells' depiction, appears inexorable. It is not quite the case, as it is implied by neoliberal approaches to economic globalisation, that there is no alternative, but the alternative is exclusion from the network, electronic isolation and economic immiseration. At the same time, the morphology of the network and the smooth language of flow can make it difficult to think in terms of hierarchies of power and status, structural inequalities or barriers to inclusion, the systematic fixing of social and economic divisions. This gets at the other side of the tension in Castells' work. His account of a disembedded network of financial and informational flows is broken up by his efforts to map more closely the relations of power and inequality which shape the network society.

Critics such as Hirst and Thompson question the concept of globalisation because it falsely suggests an inclusive process, whereas economic integration in fact is limited to particular regions, cities and sectors. Castells, although he holds to the assertion that contemporary capitalism is both new and global in form, would agree. Global capitalism is based on a geography of segments and networks, rather than incorporating a 'planetary' economy (Castells 2000a: 132). This network economy has a global reach and it has global impacts, but extensive spaces of social and economic life are marginalised or peripheralised by it. In spite of the free-form language of 'flow', the new economy of informational capitalism has a definite geography. Its core, firstly, is in the United States (ibid.: 147–8). In addition to its status as the leading world economic power, the US (California in particular) was at the centre of the information technology revolution and underwent capitalist restructuring – including deregulation and liberalisation – earlier than other advanced economies. It leads in Castells' two key sectors: information technology and finance. While the US is at the core of this new economy, however, it is networks rather than nation states that are the key trading units. The older regionalism of the international economy in this way is undercut by multilateral networks of firms interacting across geographical space (ibid.: 115).

This network economy is organised – structured even – in definite ways. Castells argues that the 'space of flows' produced by global networks is not exactly 'placeless', but it does not accord with a geography based on linear or proximate relations between different sites. Instead it can be traced around the technical infrastructure, physical places and social actors that are integrated into global networks. It is a specific rather than an inclusive geography. In mapping such a discontinuous spatial system, Castells points to three layers of 'material supports' which underpin the space of flows (ibid.: 442). The first of these is the electronic network, the technical and institutional infrastructure that mediates flows of information, images and finance. This is a physical as much as a virtual network, with real gaps where fibre-optic cable does not extend, where there is no reception for telephone or television, where there is – more simply – no electricity. The second layer of support is provided by the geographical 'nodes' or 'hubs' which compose the network. Electronic flows are coordinated around specific centres or 'communication hubs', key points of exchange which concentrate information and technical functions, and facilitate exchanges within the network. Various silicon valleys and satellite installations perform these functions as 'exchangers'. Other local sites act as nodes in the network by performing 'strategically important functions' (ibid.: 443) – whether as information sources, sites of surveillance, tax havens, centres of expertise or regulatory powers. Such nodes extend from leading stock exchanges or councils of ministers in the economic and political field; to television studios and mobile news units in the media sphere; to 'poppy fields, clandestine laboratories, secret landing strips, street gangs, and money-laundering financial institutions' in drug trafficking networks (ibid.: 501). Any network is, in this sense, 'a set of interconnected nodes'. Networks are in principle open and expansive forms, but Castells also points to blockages, black-outs and points of exclusion. The spatial economy of network flows is pocked by 'black holes' and dogged by uneven development. The system of nodes is organised hierarchically around concentrations of social, economic and political interests. At certain times, Castells (ibid.: 443) suggests, 'some places may be switched off the network, their disconnection resulting in instant decline, and thus in economic, social and physical deterioration'. The switching off of a node has effects for the wider locality in which it is situated, as when certain national currencies or stocks are dumped by financial networks, when media companies switch production to alternative sites, or when back office functions of major banks are moved to offshore call centres. This mode of spatial exclusion in the information age is akin to the older fate of towns when the railway stopped passing through. Abandoned nodes become something like electronic or informational ghost towns. Meanwhile, other sites never get onto the network in the first place.

The third material support that organises the space of flows is the spatial formation of a managerial and expert élite. Networks, after all, are not simply technical forms, but are enacted and reproduced by social actors. It follows that the technocratic and managerial élite that dominates network society organises its interests and activities in particular spatial ways. This élite spatial formation is based on privileged and protected sites of work, residence and consumption: in corporate headquarters and high-rent enclaves; in the global core of global cities; in cultural centres, five-star resorts and designer stores; in meetings of the World Economic Forum at Davos or in first-class departure lounges. Castells notes the curious uniformity of élite sites within this cosmopolitan space of flows – the familiar hotel lobby aesthetic of a postmodern international style is symbolic of 'an international culture whose identity is not linked to any specific society but to membership of the managerial circles of the informational economy across a global cultural spectrum' (ibid.: 447). This is a significant point: while theorists such as Hirst and Thompson stress the importance of national location for the activities of multinational corporations, this exists in tension with a strong global outlook on the part of the élites who work inside them. Labour markets for high-level work in such corporations are international – although hardly, it should be said, global – and Sklair's interviews with senior executives and middle managers in a sample of Fortune Global 500 corporations found consistent evidence of a strategic and cultural orientation to the global rather than to the national scene (see Sklair 2001).

There is, then, a logic of polarisation at work in the organisation of the global network economy. Globalisation, like other forms of capitalist accumulation, is uneven and inequitable. As Anthony King (1990a: 45) puts it: the current phase of 'internationalisation . . . is internationalisation under the particular conditions, and with the particular outcomes, determined by the interests of international capital and the particular countries where these interests are particularly based'. The sentence is unwieldy, but its repetitions are meant to stress the way that 'global' interests and power in fact are condensed in quite specific sites. Lash and Urry trace these concentrations of power around a reworked core-periphery model, mapped not at the macro-level of regions but in terms of the core cities that integrate global networks. In their account 'the core comprises the heavily networked more or less global cities, as a "wired village of non-contiguous communities". And the periphery consists of isolated areas in the same countries, in the former Eastern Europe or in the Third World' (Lash and Urry 1994: 28). The new core of global cities includes the head offices of major transnational corporations; the communication centres that service them; advanced business services (big law, big accountancy, etc.); major cultural industries (in media and entertainment); and significant tourist and leisure industries. This dispersed geography of economic and cultural power is integrated by networks of airlines, satellite technology and fibre-optic cable (see also Sassen 1999).

The (not so) new periphery comprises of redundant industrial sites and isolated rural areas in the same countries, and the greater part of the developing world. On first glance, this may not look so different from the 'old' core-periphery model traced by world systems theorists, but the point to note here is that the new geography of economic power does not correspond to a hierarchy of regions, but to a hierarchy of spaces based on their position within a global economy. It involves deep divisions, as ever, between the advanced core and the excluded periphery, but it also produces marked inequalities within nations and inside cities (see also Sassen 1994). Degrees of integration into global networks draw a dividing line between different cities within an urban system. When London's economy is the same size as that of Saudi Arabia, or Sydney's the size of Singapore's, the gaps between these global centres and other cities (even large cities like Manchester or Melbourne) become more pronounced. Such gaps can be measured in terms of inter-urban disparities in wealth, job creation, cost of living, in-migration and population growth, but also in the extreme urban inequalities that tend to exist *inside* global cities.

Conclusion

Chapter 1 was concerned with how a contemporary global economy could be understood within the long-term development of capitalism. It suggested, therefore, that globalisation formed part of a much older economic story. This chapter, in contrast, has asked what might be seen as 'new' about current conditions. In addressing such a question, the discussion divided into two broad approaches. The first involved a sceptical view that questioned not only the novelty of recent economic arrangements, but also the extent to which contemporary economies can properly be seen as 'global'. Exemplified by the work of Hirst and Thompson, such an account contends that recent patterns of economic integration represent a particular conjuncture in an international economy which has waxed and waned since the mid-nineteenth century. While there are significant trends that characterise the period since the 1970s – particularly in respect of finance capital, trans-national production chains, and information and communication exchanges – the contemporary economy is nothing like wholly 'globalised': if by this we are to understand either an economy dominated by stateless capital, or an inclusive economic playing-field for a wide range of nations and regions.

The second approach focused on a set of arguments that sees contemporary economies not only as global in their orientation, but as characterised by features that mark off the current period from earlier phases of capitalist development. Socioeconomic analysis therefore requires fresh categories to describe these new conditions. The principal element at work here is the restructuring of relations in time and space – the speeding-up and stretching-out of social and economic exchanges which advanced communications and transport technologies have made possible, and which continue to intensify. This reconfiguration of spatial and temporal relations means that an expanding field of economic activities is based on a geography of flows or networks. It alters the extension and the intensity of economic movements of capital, images, goods and people. It also redistributes power across economic space. This issue of power leads us into the discussion in Chapter 3. Hirst and Thompson argue that the 'myth' of globalisation has serious consequences in relation to questions of power and control. If we follow the logic of a strong thesis of globalisation, then footloose capital and disembedded corporations become virtually ungovernable. And indeed, Castells suggests that the leading sectors of the global economy (notably finance capital) increasingly escape the cognitive grasp, let alone the regulatory reach, of individual or collective actors. Still, strategies and institutions of global economic governance do exist, and oppositional movements seek to set limits on, to defeat or to reform global capital. It is to this politics of economic globalisation – formal and informal, for and against – that the discussion now turns.

3 The politics of economic globalisation: governance and resistance

It is a basic precept of economic sociology that economic arrangements are instituted and regulated by various means. Market exchanges, network relations, commodities, contracts and currencies are all organised by specific institutional forms, rules of conduct and conventional norms. An economy, as Polanyi (1992) put it, is an 'instituted process', held together by a variable mix of formal and informal relations, explicit and tacit rules, legal devices, social custom and policy measures. This article of faith for economic sociologists sits in an interesting relation to contemporary processes of globalisation that at times are seen as unbound and ungovernable.

This chapter offers a critical analysis of structures of governance and strategies of resistance in the global economy. On one level, it looks at high-level measures to regulate and steer global economic and political processes, considering the role of nation states and international institutions in such a project. On another level, the discussion considers the range of non-state actors – from private firms to business associations, trade unions, non-governmental organisations and social movements – that are engaged in coordinating and shaping economic relations in a transnational context. These operate both 'for' and 'against' existing global arrangements, seeking either to extend transnational markets and opportunities for profit, or to reform the terms of global exchange to promote a more redistributive or equitable political economy. The chapter begins with a brief account of key terms, before considering accounts of a contemporary 'crisis' of the nation state as an economic and political agent. The next section outlines the major multilateral institutions at work in the field of economic governance – focusing on the International Monetary Fund, the World Bank and the World Trade Organization – looking at their origins and current status, as well as critiques of the 'Washington Consensus' that came to dominate the governance of international economic affairs from the 1980s. We then turn to the role of civil society actors in economic governance, beginning with corporations and business coalitions and going on to address more oppositional non-governmental organisations active in the economic field, from labour unions to campaigning bodies. The chapter concludes with an account of a broad 'anti-globalisation movement' which seeks to link struggles and protests across geographical space. The central concern throughout this discussion is the politics of globalisation in relation to *economic* governance, rather than with wider questions of political democracy, national self-determination, military security or cultural autonomy. Its interest in multilateral institutions of governance, for instance, is largely focused on finance and trade bodies rather than on the broader political structures or human rights agencies of the United Nations and other bodies. The analysis of economic governance, however, inevitably overlaps with extended problems of political globalisation, and therefore with issues of sovereignty, democracy, representation and justice. The politics of economic globalisation both operates through specific institutions and networks, and opens onto more general political problems of global integration and membership.

Globalisation and the question of governance

The terms 'governance' and 'resistance' both require some clarification in the context of economic globalisation. A concept of governance is used to refer to practices of regulation that go beyond the structures of the state. It takes in the range of public, semi-public, private, and civil actors that are engaged in the steering of economic processes and the shaping of economic relations. Governments, in this sense, represent one element in a variable 'governance mix' involved in the coordination of economic life (see Williamson 1985). On an international level, nation states remain major players in networks of economic governance, but they interact with (or are circumvented by) numerous different agents, from multilateral bodies to private firms to lobbying organisations. Economic governance, furthermore, should not be understood only in terms of positive modes of intervention, planning and regulation. Strategies of deregulation are also practices of governance. This point is particularly important given the way that global economic governance, particularly via multilateral institutions, has been pursued through programmes of deregulation and market liberalisation. If it is now well accepted – among all economic sociologists and at least some economists – that markets do not simply work of their own accord, then this argument is redoubled in a global context. Market operations are conditioned by local, national and international organisations, legal frameworks and social networks: it follows that global markets are shaped by a complex architecture of political, organisational and contractual forms – at times in the direction of deregulation, at others in pursuit of tighter rules of conduct and compliance (see Fligstein 2001).

The notion of resistance is also a slippery one in this context. Opposing current global arrangements is not exactly the same as being 'anti-globalisation'. A range of initiatives to make the terms of global trade more fair, to alleviate international debt, to improve labour conditions in export-processing zones, on farms and in sweatshops, all seek to bring about economic reform within the framework of globalisation. For Sen (2002), these questions of economic justice are not questions about globalisation as such. Rather, they concern the distribution of its benefits and the management of its costs. Globalisation, he contends, is neither 'fair' nor 'unfair' by definition: issues of equity are institutional and political problems. Market outcomes, both economic and social, depend on different political, legal and social arrangements. This argument suggests that an abstract logic of globalising capital cannot be assumed to have any interest (for good or bad) in social or environmental outcomes; arguments over equity or injustice are therefore not, in themselves, arguments *for* or *against* globalisation. Attention instead should be directed to those institutions (governments, in the main) that may be expected or impelled to have a stake in such outcomes. However, this is not merely a matter of how the costs and benefits of market processes are to be managed. From the standpoint of economic sociology, market outcomes are harder to separate from the structuring of market relations and the conduct of economic interactions. Relations of inequity may be built into the basic terms of economic exchange, not just the distribution of economic goods. This kind of argument is reflected, for example, in campaigns to redress the unequal terms of world trade between producers in richer and poorer countries, as fixed market relations which exist prior to questions of distribution. A politics of 'resistance' to globalisation in this way includes not only anti-global positions, but struggles over how economic globalisation is to be managed through political and economic institutions and less loaded rules of exchange.

The 'crisis' of the nation state

Economic globalisation raises acute problems of political regulation, producing what has been seen as a 'crisis' of sovereignty on the part of nation states. Effective government appears less viable at a domestic level, given the difficulties of controlling flows of goods, information, money, people and risks across national boundaries. This is not simply a question of regulating economic flows: economic globalisation brings with it a range of new or more severe challenges in numerous other domains, as networks of organised crime, people trafficking, money laundering, drug routes, health and environmental problems mirror the transnational routes carved out by finance and commodity capital. Nation states in this context appear as what David Held (1991) has called 'fractured domains of political authority', as both external and internal pressures are brought to bear on their functions, jurisdictions and capacities.

Held considers the erosion of the state's political authority on two levels: those of autonomy and sovereignty (Held 1991, 1995; see also Holton 1998; Mann 1997; Strange 1996). State autonomy, firstly, refers to a nation state's capacity to act independently in making and enacting domestic and foreign policies. Such a capacity is weakened in a number of spheres, as the local conditions for policy-making are buffeted by international economic

trends and competitive threats; by cross-border flows of cultural, information and media content; by transnational environmental problems and social
currents. State sovereignty, secondly, concerns the legitimacy of the nation
state's authority over a given territory and its citizens. This is undermined by
the growing influence of international institutions and the sway of multilateral agreements and initiatives, not only in relation to trade but also and
more importantly in respect of law and human rights, humanitarian interventions and other military strategies. Taken together, these challenges to
autonomy and sovereignty mean that individual nation states find it harder
both to act unilaterally in making policy, and to enforce their legal or
coercive powers over their own population and territory. The environment
in which states operate is increasingly transnational, as external conditions
press on internal problems, and different political functions are transferred
upwards and outwards to international bodies – whether the United
Nations, the European Union, the International Criminal Court, the World
Trade Organization, or the 'coalition of the willing' in US-led military
ventures.

These challenges to the nation state arise across diverse political and legal,
military, economic, social, cultural and environmental spheres. They are
especially sharp in relation to economic governance, where the effects of
globalisation can be seen to make nation states simply redundant. One of the
clearest statements of such a position is offered by Kenichi Ohmae's thesis
on the 'end of the nation-state' (see also Guehenno 1995). Ohmae argues
that transnational flows are creating a new map of economic activity which
does not follow the contours of a political geography based on nation states.
Indeed, nation states have become mere bit-part players in a global economy
dominated by regional networks and corporate interests that operate
beyond the domestic state's regulatory reach (Ohmae 1995: 11). There are
four key planks to Ohmae's argument here:

1   Nation states have little to offer in the way of strategies for economic
    growth, and considerably less autonomous scope to do so. Moves in
    local interest rates, for instance, will have as much to do with fluctu-
    ations in world oil prices as with domestic policy designs – where gov-
    ernments have not already ceded controls over this economic instrument
    to independent banks or to the requirements of the IMF. While the
    nation state was once an important engine of economic growth, more
    recently it has been left behind by the rise of multinationals and the
    cross-border extension of major economic networks. Indeed, the nation
    state is now more likely to impede wealth creation by attempts to inter-
    vene in market processes or to redistribute wealth within a national
    society. Nation states may still give in to their 'reflexive twinges of sov-
    ereignty', but global markets tend to punish this reflex by moving cap-
    ital, investment and information out of the reach of states that seek to
    tax or regulate them too heavily. Ohmae notes the irony of a situation in

which the efforts of national governments to promote economic growth and social welfare using conventional tools of economic policy in fact can rebound in the forms of capital flight and lowered productivity. Nation states have limited powers to intervene in transnational economic processes, and their attempts at intervention within their own borders tend to produce negative economic effects.

2   The idea of the nation state has become a 'nostalgic fiction'. It may carry with it various patriotic, romantic or tragic associations, but the nation state does not work as a meaningful economic entity. Ohmae points out that countries such as Russia or China (or even Italy), with their diverse and variably performing regions, cannot be sensibly understood as integrated or coherent economic units. Neither can they be effectively governed as such. The force of the argument here is perhaps most evident in the project of the European Union, where member states' concession of certain economic powers to the regional bloc have been accompanied by anxieties over the effects of economic integration on such matters as culture and language. In Britain, for example, the Euro-sceptic view has traded on the idea that the very national character depends on maintaining a separate, sovereign currency – grounding an economic argument in part on a patriotic sentiment. Ohmae's account suggests that the two issues might safely be separated. Nation states no longer function very well as independent economic units: this is not to say that they no longer have a place as the contexts for sports teams or various national myths.

3   It is increasingly difficult to think about production in national terms, or to locate firms in national economies. Ohmae asks how far US performance in technology can be gauged by the success of IBM's foreign operations, or by its overseas research activities in Europe or Japan. Similarly, Robert Reich (1991) poses the question of whether an ordinary American worker (or even a federal Labor Secretary) should be heartened on seeing General Motors' share price go up, as more motor cars roll off its factory floors in Mexico and greater returns are made to investors in overseas funds. If one accepts that 'transnational corporations are the primary movers and shapers of the global economy' (Dicken 2003: 509; see also Dicken 1994; Sklair 2002), then by definition nation states are secondary at best. Some sense of the relative weight of TNCs to states is given by the measure that, in 2001, 245 corporations in the Fortune Global 500 list of the world's largest companies enjoyed revenues in excess of 20 billion US dollars, while only 60 countries generated GDP of this volume (Sklair 2002: 36–7). It might be argued in reply that there is necessarily, therefore, a clear concentration of the richest corporations in the richest states (see the discussion in Chapter 2). Nonetheless, these corporations do not tend to nest neatly inside given national boundaries.

4   Economic nationalism is more a question of emotion or jingoism than a strategy for economic success. Indeed, economic chauvinism can be seen

largely as the recourse of the most beleaguered or pariah states, cut off from global flows by incapacity, sanctions or ideology. Burma or North Korea – and, in a more limited but still significant sense, Cuba – are amongst the most 'nationalist' economies of the present day, although all have links with economic partners. Even in less extreme cases, pangs of protectionism tend to go with conservative or insular politics – for example, the opposition to the accession of a liberalising government in Ukraine's 'Orange Revolution' of 2004 came largely from the country's east, with its heavily protected coal industry. The argument over nationalism in economic policy is, however, more complicated than Ohmae's account might suggest. The strongest economies are still subject to nationalism and protectionism in the economic sphere, in ways Ohmae would contend are at odds with good economic sense. However, it is not clear that gestures of economic nationalism are such ineffective strategies on the part of more powerful players. The vexed question of agri-subsidies by leading economies, for instance, may involve significant tax transfers to a fairly small proportion of the national population in the United States or France, but it does give their big agricultural producers a competitive edge in global trade (as well as allowing their smaller producers to just about stay afloat). In this way nationalist strategies – which, as Ohmae argues, may have more to do with domestic politics than with economic rationality – can reinforce the advantage that large economies have in international exchange. So the United States has been able to use its economic weight to broker bilateral deals with weaker trading partners such as Mexico or Australia in ways that serve particular economic and political interests at home, whether agricultural or media producers or the political lobbies that represent them. On the other hand, it can be argued that the role of interventionist states in industrial and banking policies was a factor in the 'crisis' of East Asian economies in the late 1990s, particularly in the Korean case (cf. Stiglitz and Yusuf 2001). Economic nationalism, then, may play rather differently depending on the contexts in which it takes place.

Ohmae's argument makes the radical case for the redundancy of the modern nation state as an economic actor. Trans- and sub-national *regions*, he contends, are the core units of a borderless economy in which economic flows do not respect national boundaries and competitive advantage is worked out on complex spatial scales which operate both above and below the national level (see also Ohmae 1989). The most feasible task that remains for nation states is to devolve autonomy to the leading-edge 'region states' that sit wholly or partly inside their national territories; to promote the globalising strategies or potential of such economic regions; and to enable the access of different forms of global capital to relevant industries and enterprises. The role of the nation state, in short, is to do itself out of economic business. There are elements of this strategy in the formation of regional trading blocs, again as exemplified by the European Union. It should be noted, however, that the protectionist and interventionist features of EU bloc formation is sharply at odds with Ohmae's commitment to borderless economic flows and a merely 'enabling' state. Such a model is visible in a rawer sense in the creation of export processing zones in developing economies, in the Special Economic Zones for foreign investment in southeast China (see Sklair 2002: 244–9), and of local tax and regulatory havens for finance and investment capital.

Ohmae's argument is especially valuable in setting out the case for the crisis of the state in such stark terms. There are, equally, a number of basic critical points to be made in response to it. The first of these is that the geographies of economic accumulation and those of political regulation have never exactly matched up under capitalism. While it is difficult to speak any longer of distinct 'national capitalisms', there has always been a tension between the expansionary logic of capital and the domesticating logic of the nation state. It is fair to argue that this tension has intensified in the context of globalisation, but the lack of fit between economic and political space is not in itself an effect of globalisation. The notion that the nation state has become redundant as an economic authority, secondly, tends to overplay its previous autonomy. In liberal capitalist contexts especially, strategies of economic governance have always gone beyond the domestic state apparatus to incorporate a range of public and private actors and institutions (see Hirst and Thompson 1999; Miller and Rose 1991; Slater and Tonkiss 2001). These include not only firms but central, investment and commercial banks, stock exchanges, securities commissions, regulatory bodies, trade cartels, labour unions, chambers of commerce and employers' confederations – all operating at various local, national and transnational scales, and all with a range of strategic relations to the national state.

The capacities of individual nation states, thirdly, are highly variable. There is no single version of the nation state, which once ruled the economic scene and now is thrown into crisis. Dicken (2003) argues that specific states play a number of roles in the global economy: at times as regulators of foreign trade, investment and production; sometimes as competitors with each other for inward investment and export sales; at other times as collaborators within regional economic blocs or bilateral deals. Nation states employ different strategies in response to globalising conditions, variously adopting 'developmental' or 'deregulatory' tactics in their efforts to manage the relation between domestic and international capitals (Dicken 2003: 510). The paths taken by particular states will depend not only on the external challenges or opportunities they face, but also on the strength of the state itself. In this sense the ability to intervene in a larger deregulatory climate – the degree to which a state retains a 'strategic selectivity' in the use of economic policy (Jessop 1990a, 2002) – is an indicator of relative power. Moreover, deregulation or low taxation are not the sole incentives that governments can offer in the bid to attract inward investment and keep existing enterprise. Legal frameworks relating to contracts, property rights, anti-trust and other forms of corporate conduct; transport, resource and communications infrastructure; education and skills support; effective law enforcement and policing – all of these may provide positive incentives for the location of firms. Cheap labour markets are not the sole lure for roving capital (see Hirst and Thompson 1999). In this sense, governments have a broader role to play in securing the legal and physical environment for enterprise and investment.

These counter-arguments suggest that state capacities are reworked under global conditions, not simply eroded. The internationalisation of the nation state is not the same as its decline (Jessop 2002). Indeed, as the UN Secretary-General Kofi Annan (2003: 241) has contended: 'Globalization makes well-organized states if anything more necessary, not less.' There is a critical distinction to be drawn between the relative loss of sovereignty or autonomy on the part of certain strong states, and the very real 'crisis' of weak or failed states that are scarred by corruption or conflict, unable to secure economic welfare or social stability, incapable of protecting domestic economies from rapacious capital or of brokering access to global networks (see Weiss 1998). Debates over the crisis of the nation state tend to take a stable, liberal democratic state as the starting point, in a wider context in which relatively few states have accorded with such a model (see Mann 1997). If the effects of economic globalisation on political authority signal a challenge to the nation state as an economic actor, such a status is already highly variable across different national economic contexts.

International economic governance

The key way in which the capacities of nation states are being remade is through their involvement in international economic and political arrangements. If national governments now find it hard to steer their domestic economies in an autonomous manner, the high-level tasks of economic steering are increasingly vested in a global 'command structure' (Blustein 2001) which oversees different aspects of national and international economic activity. At its apex sits the World Trade Organization (WTO), set up in 1995 as the successor organisation to GATT, with responsibility for setting and regulating the terms of international trade. The WTO is therefore concerned with managing circuits of commodity capital. It is charged with brokering trade negotiations, administering trade agreements, adjudicating trade disputes, monitoring trade policies, and providing technical support and training to developing economies. It was established following completion of the Uruguay Round of trade negotiations under GATT, which ran from 1986 to 1994. GATT originally had been designed to regulate and reduce tariffs, and to mediate trade disputes between its signatories; the WTO has a broader role in promoting and managing global trade relations. Just as the shift from GATT towards the formation of a WTO greatly increased the number of states that were party to international trade agreements (from 23 countries at the inception of GATT in 1947 to 148 WTO members in 2005), the Uruguay Round greatly expanded the range of trade activities that came under this remit. This includes the highly contentious sectors of agriculture, textiles, services and intellectual property, as well as trade-related investment measures – all sectors inherited by, and critical to, negotiations within the WTO (see Dicken 2002: 52–3). The gradual inclusion and complex framing of different trade and trade-related sectors under the GATT and WTO belies any notion that international trade represents the limit case of unfettered market exchange. Rather, the conditions of international trade are brokered via protracted negotiations and regulated by institutional means.

Circuits of finance and investment capital, meanwhile, come under the auspices of the International Monetary Fund and the World Bank, as the principal forums for negotiation of international financial arrangements. Both organisations originate in the Bretton Woods Agreement of 1944, with the aim of ensuring stability in the world economic order as a key part of the post-war settlement. The principal concern of the IMF, inaugurated with 45 members in 1945, was to promote monetary and financial coordination between nation states, and thereby avoid the volatility of the post-World War I period. It also sought to foster economic growth and employment, and could act as an international lender of last resort for economies facing balance of payments crises. The World Bank was designed to underwrite post-war reconstruction and development, principally by providing investment loans for infrastructure projects. Over ensuing decades, however, the remit of these bodies has been adapted to changing economic conditions. There has been a shift from the demands of post-war rebuilding towards the purposive shaping of a global market economy. The IMF has the key regulatory role, overseeing not only states' monetary, finance and banking policies, but patterns of government borrowing and spending (whether on public services or military hardware), as well as tax and regulatory policy (including corporate regulation and labour standards). The World Bank retains a more developmental function in respect of national economies. While its initial brief had been the reconstruction of post-war economies, its focus later shifted to wider development contexts, and in the 1970s it came to place increasing emphasis on poverty alleviation. In the 1980s, there was a move away from investment in infrastructure towards policy reform. Such a move may be viewed in different ways. On the one hand, major infrastructure projects have been subject to serious criticism on the grounds of their environmental and social effects, as well as their economic costs. On the other, critics have argued that economic development in poorer countries was stunted not by a lack of investment finance but by bad policy-making. It is in this context that World Bank funding became increasingly tied to domestic policy reforms – known as conditional lending or 'structural adjustment' (see Dollar and Svensson 2000). The developmental aims of the

World Bank therefore exist in tension with its structured role in the architecture of global governance. Most notably, its part in enforcing IMF structural adjustment programmes as a condition of funding, particularly during the 1980s and 1990s, saw World Bank support closely bound to neoliberal forms of deregulation. Indeed, at this international level it becomes clear how far the deregulatory effects of neoliberalism rely on interventionist measures, prosecuted in this case by institutions of international governance (see George and Sabelli 1994; Taylor 1997; Tickell and Pick 2003).

If these represent the peak bodies of international economic governance, the political architecture of globalisation operates on a number of levels:

1   At a macro-level, economic governance is coordinated by international bodies (such as the WTO, IMF, World Bank, OECD or OPEC) and formalised in international agreements. The latter include not only those brokered through GATT or WTO negotiations, but the various accords established by summits of the G7 (now G8) group of leading industrialised economies – especially insofar as these set the agenda for IMF policy. The United Nations, too, involves key economic programmes, in particular its development programme (UNDP), Food and Agriculture Organization (FAO), and standing conference on trade and development (UNCTAD).

2   Trade areas have emerged as important players in international economic governance. Economic regions are basic features of a globalising economy, but the formal organisation of such blocs gives them an institutional presence and specific regulatory capacities in respect of cross-border economic flows. These regional actors are more or less formalised, from the highly integrated European Union to trade confederations such as NAFTA in North America, MERCOSUR in Latin America, or APEC in the Asia Pacific.

3   Nation states have not disappeared, and retain significant – although very uneven – powers in relation to international economic governance. The leading economies, firstly, maintain a decisive influence over international governance, notably via the G7 network. Individual states, secondly, are able to determine certain terms of international trade through bilateral trade agreements. More generally nation states, finding it harder to act unilaterally, are given to work in concert through international institutions and agreements at different scales. They constitute the formal membership of the WTO, IMF and World Bank, and also enter into networks based on strategic or regional interests to pursue particular agendas within these institutions.

4   Non-governmental networks and organisations are both dense and diverse in the economic field, with bodies representing the interests of international capital as well as those of international labour, lobbying and private interest groups, and more oppositional pressure groups (see Koenig-Archibugi 2002). International non-governmental

organisations (INGOs) tend to be seen as the good conscience of global politics, but they also have strategic roles to play in relation to economic governance. The International Labour Organisation, founded alongside the League of Nations in 1919 and now a UN agency, considerably pre-dates much else of the architecture of international governance, and is based on a corporatist model of interaction between labour, governments and business. Labour interests have been represented, if rather shakily, by the International Confederation of Free Trade Unions (ICFTU), and by international trade unions in specific industrial sectors (see Sklair 2002: 100–1; see also Herod 2002; Munck and Waterman 1999; Munck 2002). Anti-sweatshop and anti-slavery networks, meanwhile, have gained prominence within a wider anti-globalisation movement in campaigning for the rights of less organised labour. Business interests are represented by the International Chamber of Commerce (ICC) and other peak business bodies, but also tend to coalesce around more informal networks, as in the *Fortune* magazine annual Global conferences or the Caux Round Table meetings of leading business figures (Sklair 2002: 99). A range of regulatory standards governing legal and financial transactions, furthermore, have been designed or instituted by such agencies as the International Standards Organisation, the International Organization of Securities Commissions, the International Accounting Standards Committee, and the International Bar Federation. The most striking contemporary instance of an international network active in the economic sphere, however, is the World Economic Forum (WEF), which convenes annually at Davos. The WEF has superseded the Trilateral Commission formed in the 1970s to bring together business and political elites from North America, Europe and Japan in claiming a 'world' remit, however dominated it remains in fact by the interests of the Triad. It includes as its core members the CEOs of the largest TNCs; together with 'World Media Leaders' drawn from major media groups; 'World Economic Leaders', represented by policymakers from national governments and international institutions; and various academics and experts as 'Forum Fellows' (see Robinson and Harris 2000). This high-level shindig brings together global financiers with international business and political leaders. For the few days of the meeting, this Swiss town can be seen as the 'nerve center of the global body politic' (Hardt and Negri 2004: 167), as it captures in place an extended, and not always so visible, network of economic and political interests.

These layers of international governance suggest that a globalising economy is less the result of capital unbound, than the outcome of complex networks, laborious negotiations, and institutional fixes. Both the terms of international trade and the deregulation of national economies are pursued by organisational and policy means. The tortuous trade rounds conducted over several years by the GATT or WTO give a sharp sense of the way that economic exchange, even in a global context, is secured by formal as well as informal strategies, and underwritten by quite explicit terms of agreement. These institutional structures not only regulate but in a substantive sense *institute* the global economy as a system of (more or less free) market exchange, rules of engagement, and conventions of conduct. If the structures of governance are complicated, however, the balance of power that under-pins them is perhaps more straightforward. Harvey (1990: 170) sees the shift towards international economic governance in terms of 'a struggle to win back for the collectivity of capitalist states some of the power they have individually lost' in recent decades. This concerted effort to steer economic processes in line with state interests, however, is not founded on simple equality between states.

On a formal level, the stakes are organised in particular ways within intergovernmental bodies. The World Trade Organization, for instance, fol-lows the model established by the UN in giving voting rights to individual nation states on a straight membership basis. The balance of power in the IMF and in the World Bank, in contrast, is weighted – as in a share-holding company – to individual members' investment stakes. These are two differ-ent modes of representation, equally plausible and both fairly 'transparent', which involve different claims to legitimacy. Criticisms of these multilateral institutions, however, focus not only on their formal structures but on their capacity for the mobilisation of bias by leading economies, and the latter's influence over both the agenda and non-agenda of international governance. It is at least clear that the US Treasury, as the single largest funder of the IMF, will have a significant say; and US interests have been paramount in driving IMF policies on deregulation and structural adjustment, as well con-ditions of membership which now require open capital and finance markets (see Gowan 1999; Harvey 2003). In 2005, the G7 states together controlled over 45 per cent of the votes at the 184-member IMF, with the United States alone taking a more than 17 per cent share. The economic distribution of power at the World Bank is similar to that of the IMF, and the leadership of each institution is understood as being in the gift respectively of the United States and the European Union. The formally more democratic structure of the WTO, meanwhile, is quite compatible with back-room dealing and stand-over tactics on the inside, and special interest lobbying from without.

The IMF and the World Bank began as broadly Keynesian institutions, with the founding aims of avoiding the kind of post-war depression and discord seen in the 1920s and 1930s, and of aiding domestic programmes for reconstruction and economic development. The International Monetary Fund sought to ensure that national governments kept their balance of pay-ments in check, fostered domestic savings and investment, promoted eco-nomic growth and employment, maintained overall demand and avoided high levels of public debt. As Joseph Stiglitz, former chief economist of the World Bank, has pointed out, these institutions were founded on the assumption that markets were given to *fail* in various ways – to produce unemployment and instability, to create economic bubbles and lapse into slumps (see Stiglitz 2002). Moreover, local difficulties, as the 1920s to 1940s had shown, tended to have more general consequences – not only in severe problems of economic depression, social crisis and political turmoil, but ultimately in military conflict. International economic stability, it followed, depended on coordination at an international level. How is it, then, that the IMF in particular has come to stand for neoliberalism on an international stage? In large part, this has to do with the role of the United States within such international institutions. The neoliberal turn taken by the IMF can be seen to follow the deregulatory impulses of the US Treasury, especially pronounced since the oil crisis of the early 1970s. Previous chapters have remarked on the US's ironic position as the chief power behind the IMF while at the same time being very selective in submitting itself to IMF rules, whether on levels of government indebtedness, financial controls or balance of payments. The move to deregulate financial and currency markets at home and abroad was led from the front by the United States, and served – especially in the later 1970s and the 1980s – to consolidate Wall Street's financial power (see Harvey 2003: 128–9).

The Washington Consensus

It is this kind of alignment between IMF policies and US interests that has led a number of critics to charge that international institutions are dominated by the terms of a 'Washington Consensus'. This is an accord on economic governance which draws together the US Treasury, the IMF and World Bank, networks of bankers and foreign finance ministers who are signed up to the creed – together with their various camp-followers amongst academics, media pundits and think-tankers (see Sklair 2003: 84–5). Stiglitz argues that the Washington Consensus is characterised by a kind of market 'fundamentalism'. It is based on a commitment to privatisation, market liberalisation, and decreases in tax and public spending. When prosecuted by the IMF in tandem with the World Bank, these elements represent the familiar ingredients of structural adjustment and austerity programmes, offering a one-size-fits-all programme for developing and transitional economies. While such neoliberal strategies are most closely associated with a politics that developed during the 1970s and was instituted in government during the 1980s in the United States and Britain (as well as in other states that acted as neoliberal laboratories, such as Chile and New Zealand), they have since become a policy orthodoxy across advanced and emerging market economies (Tonkiss 2002). Such an orthodoxy was progressively institutionalised at the level of international governance, as open financial markets and the abolition of exchange controls became a condition of IMF membership, trade policies under the WTO operated via a system of competitive deregulation, and IMF bail-outs and World Bank loans were tied to liberalisation and austerity measures, typically in the form of privatisations and cut-backs in public spending (see Dunkley 2000; Gill 1995).

There are exceptions to these neoliberal rules. The United States, of course, is the primary case of a member nation bucking the IMF austerity and balance of payments system, as it runs ever deeper public deficits and accrues a spiralling trade debt to Japan, the EU and now China. Stiglitz (2002) argues, moreover, that the East Asian economies which prospered on the basis of early 'globalisation' (actually, massive increases in export trade), tended to do so in locally managed ways. This involved a variable mix of foreign direct investment, local enterprise development, and growth in manufacturing and services: what was common was the absence of any single model which held that globalising expansion should rely on minimum state intervention twinned with robust programmes of privatisation and liberalisation. These strategies meant that economic growth was combined with relative social stability from the 1960s to the 1980s. The Asian crisis of the late 1990s can in turn be linked, he suggests, to the radical liberalisation of capital and finance markets at the behest of the US treasury and the IMF (see also Stiglitz and Yusuf 2001; Wade and Veneroso 1998). Other critics agree that the 'Asian miracle' of the 1960s to 1990s does not conform to any single model of growth, but argue that the 1997 crisis was commonly due, at least in part, to the long-term unsustainability of excessive government intervention, state subsidies and managed exchange rates (see *The Economist* 1999; see also Krugman 1994).

Both cases are arguable. The events of 1997 can be seen in terms of a fall-out between parochial banking systems and hot foreign money. Stiglitz's larger point, though, may hold. The rapid economic development in East Asia from the 1960s was not marked by the kind of inequalities that charac-terised economies later subject to 'one-size-fits-all' IMF structural adjust-ment programmes, where cuts in public subsidies and spending tended to impact most heavily on the poor, while deregulation and liberalisation trans-ferred assets to those who already had them – including, often, foreign owners. Dollar and Svensson's (2000) evaluation of 220 structural adjust-ment programmes, which suggests that failures tended to be due to unpromising local environments rather than to the programme design itself, nonetheless may underline the problem of lack of fit between a fairly stand-ard SAP model and specific social and economic conditions. Adjustment lending was most effective, they conclude, where local governments and other institutions were already willing to make SAP-style reforms. There was therefore a case for limiting policy-based lending to countries which were 'promising reformers' – volunteers, rather than conscripts, for struc-tural adjustment. Stiglitz's contention, however, is that the benefits of global-isation have been socially most widespread where nations have controlled the terms of their economic engagement in global exchange, notably in East Asia. The greatest inequities, on the other hand, have occurred in countries whose 'engagement' with the global economy has largely been dictated by the IMF. It is the form globalisation takes, then, rather than globalisation itself, which he sees as the problem. The market fundamentalism that dominated international institutions in the 1980s and 1990s was premised on spurious models of, and zealous beliefs about, the market which were untenable even for advanced market economies and proved disastrous for many developing economies.

The terms of the Washington Consensus have, since the problems of the late 1990s, become subject to serious doubt. The liberalisation of finance and capital markets left economies exposed to severe financial risk, vulnerable to seduction and abandonment by speculative 'hot money' (see Blustein 2001). The supposed 'disciplines' of liberal capital markets are rather variable: foreign direct investment can provide critical inputs to economies which lack sufficient savings to support productive investments. More footloose capital, however, especially rapid movements in finance, chase the quickest and easiest profits on a sharp-in, sharp-out basis, and can be seen as a key factor in financial crisis. Blustein (2001) argues that this kind of hot money played a major part in the meltdown of Asian financial markets in 1997–98. What is more, the global command structure proved at first unable to deal with the flight of capital and currency freefalls that began in Thailand, spread through East Asia and shook Brazil and Russia. In the absence of effective international strategies, individual states simply opted out of the IMF rules, as Malaysia imposed currency controls in 1998 and Russia – more dramatically – declared bankruptcy in the same year.

It remains unclear how far this 'chastening' of the international governance system might lead in terms of its reform (Blustein 2001; see also Fine *et al.* 2001). One problem is that the IMF, in spite of its Keynesian origins, is not well placed to take into account the ways in which economics does or should fit into a wider social system. All its powers are vested in its Board of Governors, made up of national finance ministers and the governors of central banks. Stiglitz and other critics argue that IMF measures have undermined political, economic and civic democracy in its client states, and are themselves the product of an undemocratic institution. The World Trade Organization, meanwhile, gives the representative role to national trade ministers. In both cases, the national representatives are closely tied to particular domestic interests – speaking for the financial and commercial communities, respectively. For Stiglitz, this represents a technocratic model of international governance in the absence of legitimate government. The formal institutions may be there, but democracy, transparency and accountability in various degrees are not.

The notion of 'governance without government' was coined by James Rosenau to describe an international regime which involves practical effectiveness but lacks normative legitimacy (see Rosenau and Czempiel 1991). This question of the 'democratic' nature of international economic governance is a vexed one. Stiglitz (2002) rightly points out that organisations such as the IMF are *public* organisations, funded by tax-payers, but not directly accountable to them. In this way it shifts the problem of the relation between taxation and representation – hardly resolved at national levels – to a further remove. These are important arguments, but there are a number of points to be raised in response to such depictions of opaque and undemocratic institutions of global economic governance. The first is to say that the legitimacy of the WTO or IMF rests on the nation states that constitute them. The lines of representation may be highly attenuated, but they are not simply absent. Not all trade or finance ministers are answerable to their domestic populations, but many – at least in principle – are. Given the profile of international trade and finance negotiations in recent years, and the amount of lobbying these attract from various private interest and citizens' groups, it is not clear that national governments are *less* answerable for the positions they take in these bodies than they are, say, for domestic security policy, where decisions may be far more hidden. To argue that the agenda of the WTO is neoliberal or pro-capitalist is not the same as saying that it is undemocratic. Members of such bodies may be (and clearly are) nobbled, co-opted or coerced by more powerful interests, but similar strong-arm or seduction techniques are also commonplace within national parliaments. If international institutions can be seen as undemocratic on the grounds that voting members of the IMF or WTO are not directly elected by citizens, it is also the case that they are not directly elected as finance or trade ministers within European parliaments, and are generally not elected at all in the case of US trade or finance secretaries. The design of international bodies in this way reproduces some of the problems of democratic design at the level of nation states. The more salient argument concerning governance without government has less to do with questions of formal legitimacy or democracy than with the distance between the sites where decisions regarding economic governance are made, and the local spaces where their effects are felt.

Nation states, furthermore, hold key powers in respect of international institutions. Negotiations within these bodies are largely dominated by national or regional interests, rather than representing any putative 'global' interest. It may be somewhat contradictory, but there is nothing very sinister about the fact that the US pursues its national interest via these organisations in the form of liberalisation abroad and protectionism at home. Nation states, particularly strong states, protect key elements of sovereignty and reserve strategic powers of opt-out and veto. While it would be difficult to dispute the extent to which international organisations are subject to capture by the most powerful nation states and regional blocs, it may also be argued that these structures offer poorer and smaller states an enhanced bargaining position within international negotiations – usually preferable to the terms on which bilateral deals might be struck with richer partners. Coalition-building (such as regional partnerships in southern Africa, South Asia or Latin America) and alliances around specific issues (for example, the grouping of 22 less-protected agricultural producers that blocked the WTO trade negotiations at Cancun in 2003) can give states a strategic weight they do not have when acting by themselves. The direct interests of the dominant states do not simply hold sway in institutions that are oriented to negotiated procedures and multilateral decision-making (see Held and McGrew 2003: 27). International bodies in this way appear as quite complex domains of economic governance: limited in definite ways by the prerogatives of nation states, but also remaking the terms on which states operate and interact. Indeed, the United States' shift in the early 2000s away from multilateral trade negotiations to bilateral deals illustrates both sides of this picture: pointing to how international governance structures can get in the way of even the most powerful interests, but also to how such players may simply then opt out of the game – taking their weaker partners with them.

Is it the case, finally, that the gap between government and governance should always be seen in negative terms? Both Rosenau and Stiglitz are concerned with the lack of fit between formal legitimacy and practical effectiveness. Such a split reproduces the tension between government and bureaucracy which is evident in many national contexts, such that expert and technical personnel are oriented to professional and institutional object- ives, rather than simply to political objectives. The gap between governance and government in the international sphere – if this can be understood as a gap between negotiated processes and national interests – may therefore create a margin for positive action. It is arguable that an efficient and 'neu- tral' bureaucracy pursuing negotiated goals is more viable than (and pos- sibly even preferable to) an untenable ideal of global democracy (see McGrew 2003: 508). States are not always the guarantors of their peoples' interests or well-being. International institutions at times carry greater nor- mative legitimacy than national government. The question here remains, however, whether the objectives of such institutions can be reformed in the direction of more general economic and social welfare as distinct from unfettered trade and capital flows. Hardt and Negri (2004: 174) point out, for instance, that many officials working within the World Bank have a genuine commitment to eradicating poverty and reducing global inequality. The pursuit of these objectives too often is hampered, however, by the neces- sity of working through corrupt or incompetent state structures, such that government actors and their cronies siphon off or fail to distribute the bene- fits of World Bank investment. One solution to this problem, as we have seen, was the placing of conditions for policy reform on World Bank fund- ing. The effects of such policy-based lending, however, have been compli- cated by the way that reforms aimed at reducing government corruption and graft were bundled in with other conditions concerning market liberalisa- tion and privatisation. The loss to local oligarchs went with the gain to private capital.

Civil society and economic governance

This gap between government and governance suggests that the architecture of the state never quite gets at the complex of institutions and agents which are involved in systems of economic governance. One critical response to the idea that globalisation has put the nation state into 'crisis' is that the state has never been the sole agent of economic governance, particularly in market societies. A similar argument may be made at an international level, where states represent one – even if the major – strand in a complex system of economic governance. Nation states, international institutions, regional bodies and non-governmental actors interact in various ways to make economic decisions, regulate economic exchanges, steer economic processes and mediate economic relations. Debates over global civil society have a key focus on broadly political issues: such as cosmopolitan democracy, social movements and human rights (see Anheier *et al.* 2004; della Porta *et al.* 2000; Held 2004; Kaldor 1999). Civil society organisations and movements, however, also have significant roles to play in respect of transnational economic governance.

The most obvious of these economic actors in civil society are businesses. Theories of civil society remain somewhat ambivalent about the place of such private actors in a wider civic realm, often defining civil society in contrast to both state and market. There are however clear precedents for including them: classical accounts – particularly in the English and Scottish traditions of thinkers such as Locke, Ferguson and Smith – placed commercial activities and exchanges at the centre of civil society. Moreover, it seems crucial to consider corporations in any account of the role of civil organisations in international economic governance. The first point to make here is that private corporations are not simply subjects but are *agents* of economic governance. In contrast to a version of the firm as beset by legal rules, government red-tape and cross-border regulations, a more critical approach to economic governance takes in the way that businesses and business networks intervene in and steer economic processes (see Hall and Biersteker 2002). On one level, this operates through corporatist structures and private interest networks which seek to influence the actions of governments and international bodies, as well as through the apparently seamless flows of personnel between the worlds of politics and business. This model of organised business is found in such bodies as the Business and Industry Advisory Committee to the OECD, the International Chamber of Commerce, or the World Economic Forum – while the private activities of government representatives are at least partly disclosed by various registers of members' interests. Vice-President Dick Cheney's interest in Halliburton or former Prime Minister Margaret Thatcher's role with British American Tobacco represents only the tip of these government–business networks on a transnational scale.

Below this more or less overt level of organisation and networking, corporations shape economic processes through their own strategies of accumulation. These include decisions on location and investment, the uses of technology, industrial relations and labour conditions. Such factors impact directly on workers, contractors, suppliers and localities; they also have an impact on government policies. The actual or threatened mobility of firms is a key element in the drive towards competitive deregulation by local and national states. Multinational firms' capacity to relocate different parts of their operations to sites where local conditions are most favourable (for which read, *laissez-faire*) acts as a spur to governments to create such conditions through deregulations of labour, planning and environmental standards, and cuts in business rates and corporate taxation. Different kinds of corporate investment, of course, are harder to move, depending on such factors as the level of sunk investment, technological requirements, and the composition of the workforce: private companies frequently find themselves able to live with outcomes they threatened would send them off-shore, whether changes in government or meagre improvements in the minimum wage. The extreme case of capital mobility is that of finance capital; other capital circuits move at slower speeds. As noted above, what is more, deregulatory measures are not the sole means available to governments for attracting or keeping business investment. A range of public functions, from provision of transport infrastructure to the stable rule of law, to education and training, can act as supply-side strategies for influencing business location. This is a worthy argument, if not always convincing in the face of footloose capital. The ability and propensity of different governments to provide positive incentives rather than blank slates for corporate investment is itself an index of relative strength. The larger point, however, is that deregulatory tactics should be seen, as much as government interventions, as modes of economic governance. Deregulation does not represent an absence of governance, but a definite mode of governance through the market, pursued by governments and pushed by business.

A rather different role for private firms within economic governance has been highlighted by recent moves towards corporate social and environmental responsibility. Here the stress is on self-governance by multinational firms in particular, based on the principle that companies have (or should have) responsibilities not only to their share-holders but also to their workers, subcontractors, suppliers, consumers, and to local populations in the sites where they operate. This idea has become especially relevant given the way that transnational companies are able to side-step regulation in their countries of origin by outsourcing production, assembly and back-office functions to locations with more liberal (or simply non-existent) standards on pay and labour conditions, health and safety, or environmental impact. Shifting operations off-shore in this way becomes an extremely cost-effective way of externalising a firm's social and environmental by-products. A number of high-profile cases of social harm, environmental damage and labour exploitation, however, have put these corporate tactics under public scrutiny

– as the practices of corporations including Nestlé, Exxon, Shell, Nike and Gap have been targeted by anti-corporate campaigners (see Starr 2000). The costs to both governments and businesses of containing or suppressing protests against environmental and social abuses increasingly weigh against the profits corporations derive from them (see Sklair 2002: 284). One counter-response to such protest campaigns has been the shift to a corporate citizenship agenda, largely promoted by the corporate sector itself, as an exercise in self-regulation and in the interests of public relations.

An important feature of the move towards corporate social responsibility concerns labour conditions in off-shore (as well as domestic) production, assembly and distribution sites. Networks of subcontracting relations and licensing arrangements mean that lines of responsibility become very blurred, as numerous major corporations do not directly employ the workers who produce their goods. This may provide cover for severe abuses of worker rights, vicious exploitation, and brutal forms of coercion and violence. Coca-Cola, for instance, has been able to deny any responsibility relating to the paramilitary murder of trade unionists at one of its bottling plants in Colombia, on the grounds that it did not directly own or control the plant (Wright 2005). Increased opposition to these kinds of abuse, however, both by local labour activists and by transnational campaigners, has impelled a more serious engagement by TNCs with issues of social responsibility (see Fung *et al.* 2001; Klein 2000; Starr 2000). The ability of corporations to secure certain labour conditions from local contractors as part of contractual arrangements is substantial: their will to do so, or effectively to monitor standards, is less clear. Still, one can argue that the power, if not always the will to reform and to monitor, remains at the centre. It is important to note that the nature of employment practices in off-shore sites tends to vary across sectors and locations, according to plant size, and based on whether factories are directly owned, subsidiaries, or subcontracted. Indeed, Sklair (2002: 125) points out that a number of major TNCs take issues of corporate identity and responsibility seriously: while they may not offer better wages than local employers, they may provide better conditions and workplace facilities. The operation of foreign subsidiaries, however, is a rather different thing from the activities of subcontractors. Emerging corporate strategies have aimed to address issues of subcontracting and sweat-shopping through practices of monitoring, reporting, and the gradual revision of standards. These generally work outside formal structures of regulation or independent monitoring, and non-disclosure agreements may make full transparency difficult. In a 2005 report on employment conditions in the 700 factories with which it contracted globally to produce its branded products, Nike represents corporate responsibility as good practice both for major buyers such as themselves and for their suppliers (who can demonstrate their 'investment in CR and use it as a part of their proposition to other buyers'). Its own report aims to promote joint corporate efforts at 'factory remediation', to lower the 'price of entry into CR', and support 'the development of a marketplace where responsibility and competitiveness go hand-in-hand' (*nikebiz.com/Responsibility/Workers&Factories*). Such initiatives respond to criticisms of corporate practice through a framework of self-monitoring and self-regulation, with industry regulation assumed to occur largely via demonstration effects.

Issues of corporate responsibility have been especially pronounced in the environmental sphere. Concerted efforts at environmental regulation by states, multilateral agencies and non-governmental organisations – the UN Earth Summit in Rio in 1992 or the Kyoto agreement on climate change drafted in 1997 – are joined by such organisations as the Business Council for Sustainable Development or the Global Climate Coalition, which lobby to ensure that environmental measures remain congruent with business interests. The Business Council for Sustainable Development successfully lobbied for corporate interests at the 1992 Earth Summit (Sklair 2002: 276–7). The Global Climate Coalition, formed in 1989 to represent business in international debates on climate change, 'deactivated' in 2005, declaring that it had served its purpose in shaping US policy on global warming, particularly through its opposition to the Kyoto Protocol. Sklair (2001) sees this kind of mobilisation on the part of business as central to the formation of a 'sustainable development historical bloc' within the transnational capitalist class, not only comprising business networks and globalising politicians but also co-opting élite members of the environmental movement in leading INGOs. Such moves towards the 'greening of the corporation' work in different ways (Sklair 1998: 302). Sklair does not deny, for instance, that there may be genuine concern on the part of certain individuals and institutions for environmental issues (see also 2002: 283). The imperatives of sustainability, however, are likely to impinge only so far on the profit motive: the aim being to make environmental protection at least compatible with – maybe even an opportunity for – capital accumulation (ibid.: 277). A crucial part of this corporate agenda, moreover, is to ensure that environmental and social regulation remains a matter of *self-regulation*. Corporate citizenship in this way is governed largely by voluntary codes of practice, non-binding agreements, and good or less good intentions.

Private corporations, of course, do not exhaust the field of civil actors with a stake in international economic governance. Mathews (1997) argues that nation states are not simply losing autonomy in the face of global economic processes and interests, but that they increasingly are 'sharing' aspects of sovereignty – not only with business, but with INGOs, NGOs and citizen groups. As noted above, there are a range of non-governmental forms active in the economic sphere, from labour organisations to international regulatory bodies and private interest networks. Labour unions are old players in this field, whose internationalist politics have frequently been at odds with their nationalist and protectionist impulses. The expropriation of value in a globalising system, however, remains highly dependent on the exploitation of labour; changing patterns of exploitation in this context offer new challenges to labour movements in making connections across geographical space and industrial sectors (Herod 2002; Munck 2002; Munck and Waterman 1999; Waterman and Wills 2001). The global struggle for workers' rights and even the most rudimentary labour conditions sees unions making common cause with NGOs and activists in the anti-slavery and anti-sweatshop movements, as well as with unemployed workers' organisations (see Moody 1997). The Service Employees International Union (SEIU), for example, has mobilised for the rights of poorly protected, often migrant workers, notably through the Justice for Janitors campaign. This campaign, founded in 1985, has targeted the exploitation of workers in the cleaning industry, employed (usually indirectly) by corporations including Safeways, Target and United Parcel Service. Similar initiatives have developed elsewhere. In Britain, the Transport and General Workers Union (T&G) has focused on organising casualised, outsourced workers in low-grade service jobs: in 2004, for instance, cleaners working for contractors at Canary Wharf in London (many of them at Morgan Stanley bank) gained union recognition for the first time. In 2005, a three-year campaign in the US seeking labour justice for migrant farm-workers was concluded with an agreement between the Coalition of Imokalee Workers and the parent company of the fast food chain Taco Bell. The company stood accused of buying tomatoes from farms operating an effective system of slave labour. Organisation by workers, including the formation of their coalition and hunger strikes outside the company headquarters, were supported and publicised by student campaigns to ban Taco Bell outlets from university campuses. In this way, labour struggles for organisation and representation, for protection of workers' rights and even unionists' lives, can be reinforced by pressure from consumer and campaigning groups using organised tactics of boycott and lobbying.

A wide range of NGOs and citizens' groups – such as the International Labor Rights Fund, Anti-Slavery International or Survival International – are concerned with such economic questions as workers' rights, land reform and ownership rights, privatisation, bio-piracy and seed wars, farmers' and peasants' rights, fair trade and ethical trade (see Goldman 1998; Shiva 1997, 1999, 2000). Moreover, issues of economic governance, justice and regulation often fall within or overlap with the remit of ostensibly 'non-economic' INGOs. Environmental organisations, such as Greenpeace or Friends of the Earth, campaign on issues of sustainability and bio-diversity which inevitably come up against economic interests, whether in respect of carbon emissions, oil exploration or logging. Human rights organisations, such as Amnesty International or Human Rights Watch, frequently challenge the organisation of economic power, as in their campaigns for domestic workers' rights and against people trafficking, or where individual or group rights come up against private interests: evidence the case of the Ogoni people in Nigeria, where human rights violations were directly linked to the exercise of property rights by the multinational Shell corporation.

Development organisations, notably through trade and debt initiatives, have a quite clear concern with issues of economic governance (see, for example, Oxfam 2002). The terms of global trade represent a key site for thinking about economic justice and the effectiveness of multilateral governance (see Said and Desai 2003). It is interesting, in this context, to see the shift that has taken place on the campaign agenda in recent years. A fair trade platform – anti-capitalist to the degree that it contested the 'normal' workings of capitalist markets – has been well established in this domain. However, such arguments for fair trade more recently have translated into a stronger trade justice position. It departs from the earlier concern with setting up less capitalist trade alternatives in development contexts (by supporting collective producers or setting minimum prices, for instance), in order to criticise the *anti-market* activities of powerful nation states and economic blocs. This shift – from fair trade to free trade, as it were – reflects a move from a micro- to macro-level economic analysis, from interventions in local markets and supply chains, specific commodity sectors and consumer behaviour, to address an international trade regime. Such an approach seeks to promote the links between trade and poverty reduction, and is highly critical of the way global markets are rigged by the forms of protectionism and subsidy which richer nations selectively deploy. Processes of reform in this sector are evident but patchy, particularly given US moves after the breakdown of the WTO trade talks at Cancun in 2003 towards a series of bilateral trade agreements. The cautionary model here is that of the 1994 NAFTA agreement, under which the flow of low-cost US imports pummeled local agricultural producers in Mexico. The European Union remains divided over the question of subsidies, while in 2002 the US Congress approved $180 billion in domestic agricultural subsidies over a ten-year period. The problem in this case is not so much one of unbridled capitalism – nor, properly speaking, one of a generalised 'global' capitalism – but an uneven geography of managed economies for some, and a raw version of the market for the rest.

These terms of trade are further skewed by the dependence of many poorer nations – particularly in sub-Saharan Africa, the Andean region of South America, and Central Asia – on the export of a limited number of primary commodities in contexts of low and unstable prices. By the end of the 1990s, UN figures estimated that primary commodity prices were at their lowest for a century and a half (UNDP 1999: 2). To take the example of coffee: in 2002 the international price for coffee beans hit a low at US 4 cents per pound. Given the prices at which coffee retails in Western supermarkets, it is clear that a significant amount of value is being extracted further along the supply chain. And given, too, that four multinational companies control over 50 per cent of world coffee production, agreements to regulate supply and price are not beyond the imagination. However, the attempt to establish a kind of OPEC for coffee-producing countries has advanced only slowly. On a more general scale, the establishment of an international institution to regulate supply and prices in respect of primary commodities remains a Keynesian dream, although we might note that an international political apparatus has proved itself capable of setting up governance structures for rather more complex economic sectors (services being a good example), and oil supply and prices have been more or less effectively regulated for decades, in spite of the instabilities inherent in that sector.

One alternative solution to low commodity prices is diversification. This remains, however, a luxury of the economically better-off, or a local initiative highly dependent on development funding or alternative credit systems operating outside of international financial regimes. Poorer economies' capacity to diversify is highly constrained by, amongst other factors, the effects of the global debt regime. The Debt Relief Initiative for 41 'heavily indebted poorer countries' is an important starting point, although somewhat undercut by the way that any debts written off by creditor nations tend to be outweighed by continuing trade deficits. Outside the HIPCs, there is little protection for indebted countries in a context where international debt trading has been on the increase in global finance markets, such that hedge funds potentially can buy up large chunks of national debt.

In campaigning for controls on commodity prices and for debt relief, NGOs are calling for forms of multilateral intervention to manage the terms of international economic exchange. In other contexts, the argument is for deregulation. Liberalisation of intellectual property regimes, for example, is crucial to the development of affordable technologies in poorer countries and regions. The model of (and protracted struggle over) pharmaceutical products is a clear case where intellectual property has been regulated to the benefit of powerful corporations and rich nations, with serious consequences for health and mortality in poorer countries (see Shiva 1997, 2001). Critics of existing international arrangements therefore find themselves in the position of arguing for and against regulation at different moments and in different contexts. Campaigns such as Oxfam's Make Trade Fair or Jubilee 2000's call for debt relief advocate a mix of regulation and deregulation, liberalisation and intervention. There is in this sense no straightforwardly anti-globalist or anti-market logic at work in efforts to transform the terms of international economic governance and to promote economic justice.

The argument of critics such as Mathews is that these non-governmental bodies alter both the structure and the processes of international governance. Governments, to put it simply, are hierarchies, whereas civil society organisations tend to develop and work through networks. NGOs, citizens' groups and campaigning bodies are often more responsive and more innovative than unwieldy government structures, and able to work closer to the issues they highlight and the groups these affect. While they may lack formal authority, they can carry a high degree of moral force. Such organisations can combine local with international orientations, mobilising both in relation to localised problems (specific dam projects, particular producer or worker groups) and via transnational networks of campaigning and lobbying, especially via the Internet. In this way, they work both above and below the level of the nation state, where interests get locked in and inventive solutions can get stuck. Mathews compares the outlook of such groups to those of international civil servants, working for example in UN or EU agencies or in the World Bank, whose commitment is (or should be) to the organisation and its projects rather than to any national interest.

At the same time, international non-governmental organisations can be seen as a form of special interest group: unrepresentative, unaccountable and undemocratic. Such arguments are made by critics of NGOs from both left and right. Moral force is not the same as majority rules, and in any case non-governmental bodies may be just as likely to advocate for the cause of big tobacco as for the peasant farmer. This is an important criticism, although it points to the way that notions of representativeness and democracy remain tied to the nation state – even in an international context where not all nation states can claim to be democratic, or where any such claims are open to serious question. The transnational orientation of certain non-governmental actors, what is more, can be read in terms of a progressive commitment to cosmopolitan values (see Held 2004), but can also be seen as a kind of élitism. As Mathews (1997: 51) points out, new global élites include 'not only the rich but also citizens' groups with transnational interests and identities that frequently have more in common with counterparts in other countries, whether industrialized or developing, than with countrymen' (see also Sklair 2001, 2002: 315–16). The capture or co-optation of non-governmental organisations is a common criticism of the sector, particularly given the way that lobbying networks interact with state agencies, private foundations and businesses. Non-governmental organisations and networks are important players in the politics of economic globalisation, but do not fit neatly into any simple opposition between 'for' and 'against', governance and resistance.

Anti-globalisation movements

The politics of resistance is more clearly associated with the development of a broad 'anti-globalisation' movement. Of course, acts and movements of resistance have sought to counter capitalist expansion throughout its history. As Wallerstein (1974: 233) puts it in his early work on the capitalist world system:

> The mark of the modern world is the imagination of its profiteers and the counter-assertiveness of the oppressed. Exploitation and the refusal to accept exploitation as either inevitable or just constitute the continuing antinomy of the modern era, joined together in a dialectic which has far from reached its climax in the twentieth century.

Wallerstein argues that the expanding reach of capitalist social relations has been tied to deepening forms of capitalist contradiction, producing various forms of resistance over time: whether in the shape of social movements (trade unions and socialist parties), new social movements (environmental, women's or civil rights movements), nationalist movements, local insurgencies, or populist struggles. These different politics – working at transnational, national and local levels – each can be seen as 'antisystemic' in their aim to transform existing systems of economic and social organisation (see Arrighi *et al.* 1998; Wallerstein 1990). In recent work, Wallerstein (2002) analyses the emergence of the anti-globalisation movement as a new antisystemic movement, one that is capable of taking in diverse groupings at different geographical scales: in this sense it can be seen as a 'movement of movements'.

These 'new revolts against the system', however, have earlier antecedents. One of the most important is to be found in anti-imperialist or anti-colonial struggles, not only against direct foreign occupation but also against foreign corporate influence and expropriation. This history of resistance remains a significant element in more recent protests against major institutional players, particularly the IMF and World Bank, as leading agents of a brand of neo-imperialism that undermines local autonomy and opens up developing economies to foreign penetration. World Bank funding of large infrastructure projects, especially dams, became a target of mobilisations in the 1980s. The long-running protest against the damming of the Narmada River in India has highlighted the consequences of such mega-dam projects for local environments, communities and livelihoods, as well as the way profits tend to be directed towards foreign owners (Roy 2000). The late 1970s and 1980s saw waves of 'IMF riots' in response to austerity packages imposed on such developing economies as Brazil, Jamaica and Egypt (see Walton 1987, 1998). In 1994 the Zapatista rebellion in Chiapas mobilised against the effects on indigenous rural populations of land privatisations and NAFTA's free trade rules (see Nash 2001). Over time, a network of local struggles 'began to coalesce around issues such as IMF-imposed structural adjustment, the predatory activities of finance capital, and the loss of rights through privatization' (Harvey 2003: 66). It follows, Harvey suggests, that the 'tone of anti-imperialism began to shift towards antagonism to the main agents of financialization' within multilateral institutions of global governance (see also O'Brien *et al.* 2000; Petras 2003; Petras and Veltmeyer 2001).

This focus of antagonism became clear in the mobilisation against the World Trade Organization at its meeting in Seattle at the end of 1999. The 'Battle of Seattle' is generally taken to symbolise the emergence of a joined-up anti-globalisation movement. The Seattle protests captured a wide slate of grievances against the global command structure in general and the WTO in particular, including neoliberalism and neo-imperialism, global poverty and injustice, labour exploitation, and environmental degradation (see Kaldor 2001). The WTO meeting was abandoned in the face of mass protest, leaving some protestors to take their fight to the signature brands of global consumerism, vandalising Starbucks and McDonalds shopfronts. Such violence against property was met by local police with tear-gas and rubber bullets (see Hardt and Negri 2004: 286–7; Yuen *et al.* 2001). Subsequent protests against the World Bank/IMF in Washington in April 2000 were subject to more conciliatory police tactics, including the memorable sight of a local police chief wielding a flower on television news reports of the violence that wasn't. There followed a series of protests – against a regional meeting of the World Economic Forum in Melbourne in September 2000; a World Bank meeting in Prague the same month; the Davos World Economic Forum in January 2001. Levels of security and policing escalated as the wave of protests continued: in June 2001 a protestor in Gothenburg was shot by police, and in July Carlo Giuliano, a protestor at the G8 summit meeting in Genoa, was killed by a military conscript (see Hardt and Negri 2004: 287; Sklair 2002: 292). Subsequent multilateral meetings have largely been protected by exclusion zones which keep protestors at a clear distance from delegates.

It is very notable, of course, that the symbolic emergence of the anti-globalisation movement took place in the metropolitan core, whereas the range of specific struggles which lie behind it have occurred in such cities as Kingston or São Paulo, or in rural areas in India or Mexico. Even so, the spatial politics of urban protest in Seattle, Washington or Genoa has sought to draw out the links between sites of political and economic power, typically concentrated in the North, with sites of exploitation and dispossession in the South: in sweatshops, forests and river valleys, on plantations and factory floors. This form of politics is premised on making connections across space, but also relies on specific campaigns in local sites and at particular times. The idea of a contemporary 'space of flows', however compelling as a socioeconomic analysis, can belie the ways that power still tends to fix quite reliably in certain places, and around certain institutions and agents. Anti-global protests reject the notion of unbounded flows, targeting economic power in definite sites, as embodied in its political or financial élites or its bureaucratic functionaries. Indeed, one measure of these movements' success in calling out abstract structures of global power is the security zones set up around trade negotiations, summit meetings and finance talks, as well as the co-opting of local police forces and military as the enforcement arm of a global command structure. Such protests can be seen as local moments in a much broader politics of resistance (see Klein 2002; see also Cohen and Rai 2000; Gills 2001; Mittelman 2000; Smith 2001; Smith and Guarnizo 1998; Smith and Johnson 2002).

To what extent, though, might these forms of protest be characterised as a 'movement'? While the list of campaigns, groupings, protests and issues which come under the general banner of 'global justice' continues to expand, it is not clear whether a shared programme or even a shared critique runs through these different forms. Writers such as Amartya Sen (2002) and

Joseph Stiglitz (2002) argue that the very notion of an anti-globalisation movement makes little sense: its mobilisation relies on global networks of communication and information, while anti-global protests are 'among the most globalized events in the contemporary world' (Sen 2002: 5; see also Held and McGrew 2002). Critics on the left agree. David Harvey (2003: 176) refers to 'alternative globalization movements' (see also Sklair 2002: 291–321, on the prospects for 'socialist globalization'). Alex Callinicos (2003) concurs that the so-called 'anti-globalisation' movement is in fact deeply reliant on global networks and transnational bases of support. It is more properly understood as anti-*capitalist*. What this movement mobilises against is not globalisation but global capitalism (see also Sklair 2002: 277–8). The system of global capitalism is composed around multinational corporations, advanced capitalist states, and the international institutions that pursue the interests of both: it is these that provide the focus of anti-capitalist resistance, although marching on the World Bank building is unlikely to be enough. Real opposition to global capitalism, on this reading, ultimately calls for revolutionary social transformation.

The anti-globalisation movement, however, is not straightforwardly anti-capitalist. It also takes in movements for capitalist reform, particularly via NGO networks and trade union activism. A critical instance of this reformist politics is seen in the movement to levy a tax on foreign exchange transactions (see Haq *et al.*1996). Taxation policy, of course, has been understood as a key factor in corporate location in an international context, and the flight from tax can be seen as one of the motors setting footloose capital on the move. Once capital *is* on the move, of course, it becomes harder to tax. The rapid flow of electronic transactions across time and space works to disembed vast sums of income from national taxation systems, and the ability of states to levy taxes at this level has been significantly outstripped by the capacity of firms to evade them. The rapid flow and massive valorisation of finance capital represents the extreme case in this context. Still, taxation at an international level is possible to the degree that capital and currency movements can be monitored, measured and taxed at the points where they occur. This is not so unfeasible as it might appear: the taxing of currency transactions should be facilitated by the same information technology that allows for large-scale currency movements and rapid calculations of value. The possibility of such a tax was suggested as long ago as 1971 by the Nobel economist James Tobin. The international campaign for the taxing of currency transactions in this way takes its name (if not its wider politics) from a committed free market economist. The Tobin Tax campaign has gained wide support amongst NGOs, and briefly had backing in the French parliament. While certain critics may see such a politics as 'anti-capitalist' (Said and Desai 2001), the mobilisation around the French campaign by ATTAC – the Association for Taxation of Financial Transactions to Aid Citizens – can also be seen as an attempt to marry 'state interventionism with participatory politics' at the level of social movements (Ancelovici 2002: 427; see also Ruggiero 2002).

Debates over strategies of anti-globalisation or anti-capitalism underline the extent to which various factions tend to have different, and sometimes conflicting, goals. A central problem here is the way that political mobilisations can reproduce a divide between 'core' and 'periphery' in the global system. Harvey (2003: 176), for instance, points to a tension between social movements concerned with the expanded reproduction of capital in core economies (as in labourist and welfarist politics), and movements against processes of accumulation by dispossession, as seen in struggles for peasant and indigenous rights and in the new anti-globalisation movements. It is not always clear where common cause may be made, although Harvey is persuasive on the organic links between class politics in the core and the politics of dispossession more generally. Chase-Dunn (1999: 206) argues that the politics of neoliberal globalisation are especially acute in the developing world: 'It is there that the capitalist world-system is most oppressive, and thus peripheral workers and peasants, the vast majority of the world proletariat, have the most to win and the least to lose.' At the same time, related processes have been at work in the core, as 'hyper-mobile capital has attacked organised labor, dismantled welfare states and down-sized middle-class work forces' (ibid.: 207). An important framework for making connections between struggles in different places has been the World Social Forum which has met at Porto Alegre in Brazil since 2001, as well as its offshoot regional forums. The WSF brings together networks of activists, trade unionists and NGOs to discuss global problems and highlight local issues, to exchange information, develop skills, build solidarity and coordinate campaigns (see Fisher and Ponniah 2003; World Social Forum 2001). It is counter-opposed to the World Economic Forum, which brings the leading players in the globalising economy together each year at Davos. While that annual gathering of global CEOs, media leaders, financiers and politicians gives an impressive sense of unity of purpose – 'It is', as Kees Van der Pijl (1998: 133) puts it, 'a true International of Capital' – the World Economic Forum is nevertheless marked by the competing interests of different political and economic agents. Still (and among its many other advantages) the WEF works within the frame of actually existing global capitalism. The World Social Forum declares that 'Another World is Possible', but it is not obvious how we might get there from here. Its diverse politics of labour unions, non-governmental organisations, indigenous and popular struggles, student activism and new social movements is cut through by old tensions between how far opponents of existing conditions are prepared or required to work for change through existing political and economic structures.

It would be a mistake, finally, to imagine that 'resistance' to globalisation is always a matter of radical or progressive politics. Some of the most robust and coherent anti-globalisation positions are to be found in reactionary, right-wing and nationalist movements. Anti-immigrant and neo-fascist movements are a primary case in point. Such a politics is concerned not with reforming (let alone revolutionising) the terms on which global exchanges are governed – as in the case of the 'anti-globalisation' movement – but with insulating itself from global conditions, particularly cross-border movements of workers and refugees. A further challenge to globalisation comes from millenarian, extremist, and some fundamentalist movements, which in part can be understood as opposing processes of global modernisation or cultural homogenisation. Again, the paradox of 'anti-globalisation' shows up in these cases. Defensive political networks, as well as terrorist actions, are facilitated by the practical features of globalisation: cheap, light and fast communications; the rapid and often hidden electronic movement of money; international travel and global media.

Conclusion

The logic of economic globalisation is not simply one of liberalisation, the creation and extension of free markets. An uneven global geography of regulation and liberalisation is reproduced by the ability of certain actors to avoid the effects of the free market through subsidies or favoured terms of trade, while others elsewhere are fully exposed. The argument in this chapter has been that practices of regulation, deregulation and 're-regulation' should all be viewed as strategies of governance. In this context, nation states do not always appear as the principal agents of economic governance. At times their role – particularly when acting in concert – is decisive, but there are a range of other actors who take part in processes of economic steering, the organisation of economic relations and the regulation of economic exchange. Practices of economic governance knit multilateral, corporate and social actors into networks of regulation and reform at international, national and very local scales. The political and economic geography of contemporary nation states, what is more, is deeply uneven and inequitable, such that it makes little sense to talk about the 'crisis' or the 'sovereignty' of the nation state without specifying whether the nation state in question is the US, Zimbabwe or Peru.

In looking at the different scales on which processes of economic governance take place, as well as at strategies of opposition or resistance, it is evident that the politics of the international economy does not polarise around arguments 'for' or 'against' globalisation or market liberalisation. It is interesting to note, in this connection, the extent to which contemporary globalisation can be seen as an international version of managed capitalism. Comparative advantage in a global system is in no small part based on the strategic ability of nation states (singly or in federation) not only to capitalise on but to insulate themselves from free markets, and to regulate in their own interests. This is not an unbridled global market. Rather the current system represents degrees of managed capitalism for some, globalisation or exclusion for the rest. An important source of economic injustice in the system as it stands, then, is the way in which strategies of regulation and liberalisation are applied selectively in different contexts, and overwhelmingly to the benefit of richer nations.

The politics of economic governance can be problematic in this context if it is over-simplified in the contest between pro-globalisation and anti-globalisation positions. Within arguments *for* globalisation, economic welfare and economic rights are seen as positive outcomes of globalisation. It is access to global markets that improves living and working conditions for growing numbers of people (see Dollar and Kraay 2002). Economic welfare, then, can be secured inside a global system. On the other side, anti-globalisation arguments often assume that economic justice is simply incompatible with globalisation (see Hines 2000; see also Bello 2002). The only way to secure economic rights and welfare is by resisting the forces of globalisation. Clearly I am simplifying here, but there is a tendency for questions of economic justice or inequity to become moored on either side of arguments for and against globalisation. Problems of economic justice, however, appear rather differently within various economic sectors and struggles, and are difficult to reduce to a coherent pro- or anti-globalisation position. Neither can the anti-globalisation movement simply be represented as anti-capitalist. Anti-capitalist factions have been important elements in the emergence of a broader anti-globalisation movement; however critiques of economic globalisation are not straightforwardly critiques of capitalism. Certain anti-global actors – particularly within the international labour movement and development NGOs – mobilise around arguments for more just forms of managed capital. It is a truism of economics after neoliberalism that 'successful' economies (that is, those that combine growth with relative social stability) generally are based on mixed economies where markets coexist with, and are secured via, extended state intervention, including in respect of welfare measures (see Stiglitz 2002). The capacity that different nation states have to manage their capital in this way might be seen as a key indicator of their relative strength within an inequitable global system. Economies, as Polanyi argued, should be seen as instituted processes, and the global economy is not an exception. The organisation of economic relations, the architecture of economic regulation, the terms of global exchange – as well as strategies of economic resistance – are instituted at various scales via a complex governance mix of states, bureaucracies, corporations, private interest groups, non-governmental organisations and social movements.

Part II
Production

4 Fordism and after

Within the wider debates over globalisation considered in Part I, issues of production play a particular role. Key features of production in a globalising context include the dispersal of industrial processes across international space; the growth and economic clout of multinational corporations; and the increasingly 'immaterial' character of production based on knowledge, information and communications technology. It is with these issues that the next two chapters are concerned, moving from the broader analysis of economic globalisation to focus more closely on the organisation of production and the nature of products within contemporary economic life. This chapter centres on accounts of the shift from Fordism to post-Fordism as systems of economic production and social reproduction. Theories of post-Fordism became prominent in the 1980s and after as attempts to explain processes of restructuring in advanced capitalist economies, particularly in light of the downturn of the early 1970s (see Kilmister 2000). The notion of Fordism, however, has much older antecedents. Taking its name from the US car manufacturer Henry Ford and the innovations he introduced in factory production early in the twentieth century, this mass industrial system received one of its sharpest critical treatments in the *Prison Notebooks* written in the early 1930s by the Italian Communist Antonio Gramsci. It is Gramsci who gives us the precedent for thinking about Fordism not simply as a means of organising production and industrial work, but as an economic basis for the organisation of social life. This is an important move for the sociology of economic life, going beyond the study of production as a technical process to consider its integral place in a larger social formation. It suggests that the forms in which economies produce goods and services is closely tied to the ways in which they reproduce social relations, institutions and norms.

The discussion begins with the anatomy of Fordism, setting this system of mass industrial production within a wider framework of social organisation and political regulation. The work of the French regulation school is central to this early part of the discussion. Regulation theorists such as Aglietta or Lipietz take Fordism as an exemplary case of how capitalist reproduction is secured through the interaction of economic, political and social arrangements. Such an integrated Fordist regime, however, did not turn out to be failsafe. This chapter looks at the crisis of Fordism in advanced capitalist economies that can be dated from the early 1970s. During this period the economic system grounded in mass production became subject to serious internal and external pressures, facing structural problems of over-capacity and new forms of international competition. These pressures were felt not only within production systems, but at the levels of political and economic regulation. Large-scale production fitted into a broader picture which included patterns of mass consumption; a negotiated settlement between government, industry and labour; and an established system of international trade and coordination. The crisis of Fordism in this way signifies more than the exhaustion of mass industrial production.

The chapter goes on to look at debates over what has come 'after' Fordism. While a transition to post-Fordism may be analysed in terms of a shift to more flexible production methods, product diversity, technological innovation and corporate restructuring, a number of theorists have questioned how far these changes in production have reached, as well as the larger coherence of any post-Fordist system of economic and social organisation. The last part of the discussion highlights certain critical problems that emerge from the analysis of post-Fordism, and considers the uneven mix of Fordist and post-Fordist arrangements which remains evident in contemporary economic life.

Fordism

'Fordism' refers to the mode of industrial organisation which came to characterise advanced capitalist economies from the early twentieth century and which reached its height in the post-World War II boom. It also had its counterpart in developed communist economies during this period, at least in terms of the technical organisation of mass industrial production. As a mode of accumulation, however, Fordism can be seen as distinctly capitalist. David Harvey (1990: 125) offers a neat symbolic starting date for the development of Fordism. We might say it begins, he suggests, from that moment in 1914 when Henry Ford introduced the eight-hour, five-dollar day for workers on his new car assembly line in Michigan. This instituted in one move the mechanised production of standard goods, a routinised labour process, and a set working day. Ford's car plants provide a model for what would become a more general form of industrial organisation on a number of levels.

First, the assembly line signalled the replacement of craft production in workshops (which had been typical of early car manufacture) with mechanised production on the factory floor. This is what Piore and Sabel (1984) call 'the first industrial divide' – the shift from manual or craft production to automated production which took hold around the turn of the twentieth century and was fully realised in the leading economies and industrial sectors by the mid-twentieth century. For Piore and Sabel, a mix of craft and mass production techniques had characterised manufacture from the earliest days of the Industrial Revolution, but a clear divide opened between the two during the twentieth century, as large-scale production displaced small-scale, more specialised and decentralised enterprises. This shift was marked, what is more, by the growing concentration of economic power in corporations, as big capital – and they still don't come much bigger than Ford Motor – came to direct industrial production.

Increased mechanisation, secondly, involved changes in the labour process, as production was organised into distinct tasks along the assembly line. The technical division of labour simplified and routinised work, as the production process was broken down into its parts and distributed between a number of workers performing specific functions. This allowed for greater supervision of the labour process, as exemplified by the 'scientific management' of work advocated by Ford's contemporary Frederick W. Taylor (1911). Even as the working day grew shorter (remember the eight-hour, five-dollar day), mechanisation and assembly-line discipline made workers more productive: simply, you got more out of them in less time. Using Marx's categories, Michel Aglietta (1979) analyses this effect as a shift from the production of 'absolute' surplus value – extracted via lower wages and longer working hours – to 'relative' surplus value, achieved by increasing labour productivity.

Mechanisation also allowed, thirdly, for the production of standardised goods on an expanding scale. The assembly-line system of industrial production was in this sense a system of *mass* production. It is also critical to note the nature of these mass goods. Large-scale industrial activity, which formerly had centred on the production of capital goods such as iron or steel, became increasingly geared to the production of consumer goods, such as Ford's cars. The standardisation of these goods was the basis for achieving economies of scale: high-volume production at low unit costs. In such a context, the mechanisation process went together with a broader process of rationalisation. In addition to the use of assembly-line technology, Ford's 'experiment' integrated transport and distribution functions under the direct management of the plant, economising on overall production costs and bringing transport and distributive workers into the employ of the producer (Gramsci 1971: 285). These economies helped bring down the price of finished products, such that a formerly luxury item like a motor car gradually became available for mass consumption.

Such changes in production went with broader changes in social and economic organisation. 'Fordism' in this way refers not simply to what happens inside the factory, but to the larger setting of work, consumption, and the socialisation of both workers and consumers. At the centre of the system, though, was the settlement between worker, management and machine on the factory floor. This mode of industrial production rested on a division of labour not only along the assembly line, but also at a broader level between a mass labour force of semi-skilled workers, and a technical and managerial class that oversaw the productive process. In Ford's particular case, Gramsci writes (1971: 285), 'it was relatively easy to rationalise production and labour by a skilful combination of force (destruction of working-class trade unionism on a territorial basis) and persuasion (high wages, various social benefits, extremely subtle ideological and political propaganda)'. Ford's Michigan plant mainly employed non-unionised immigrant labour, and the relatively high wages offset some of the drudgery of the work. Elsewhere in the United States, and more generally in Europe, organised labour movements and stronger traditions of craft skill proved barriers to the introduction of the disempowering and de-skilling assembly-line techniques associated with Fordist-style production (Harvey 1990: 128).

It was only in the post-war period that this model of mass production became more widely generalised. The Fordist emphasis on efficiency, rationalisation and productivity turned out to be particularly well suited to the growth industries of the reconstruction, many of which had been proved by war-time expansion: ship-building, car-making, steel, construction, petrochemicals, and consumer goods (Harvey 1990: 132). The more stable context of post-war growth also allowed for a brokered settlement between capital and labour. As Fordist-style mass production became embedded in the economies of the capitalist core, the reproduction of this system was founded on the wage relation between organised labour and corporate capital – with the state often acting as steward of such an industrial compact (see Jessop 1994). This, we must note, represents an ideal-typical Fordism: systems of industrial production varied between countries and between industries, with variations in union power and collective bargaining. Neither effective trade unionism nor amenable employers existed everywhere. Fordist systems of production in this sense proved compatible with a range of state and social forms (see Lash and Urry 1987 for an account of different Fordist systems).

The Fordist wage settlement, however, was crucial to the larger stability of the socioeconomic system. Fordism was, after all, a mode of mass production which depended on patterns of mass consumption. The social and economic reproduction of the system was secured by this linkage between production and consumption, as a mass industrial workforce, in relatively secure employment and earning a living wage, also formed part of a mass market for the goods that rolled off these factory floors. The wage settlement on which Fordist production typically rested – decent earnings for semi-skilled industrial workers – equally constituted the basis for Fordist consumer markets. In bringing home a family wage, the worker on the assembly line created the market for the very goods he produced. Michel Aglietta (1979) argues that the mass commodity, such as the family car or the suburban home, formed the material link between Fordist production and consumption. Standardised, suburban housing (with all its consumer items) was the site for the reproduction of the nuclear family as the basic social and economic unit. The motor car mediated a spatial design for living in which the home was separate both from the workplace and from mass consumer spaces. In forging the material link between a system of production and new norms of consumption, Aglietta suggests that these mass commodities shaped a Fordist *commodity aesthetic*, based on functional, uniform design. Such a functional aesthetic was founded in the automated production of standardised goods. The mass production of automobiles is a good example here, as is the growing market in consumer goods after the 1950s – as the wives and children of the Fordist worker (and, even more so, the Fordist manager) provided markets for the washing machines, mix-masters and record players of the new consumerist dream. 'Fordism' in this context is a shorthand term for an economic system where mass production both fuels, and in turn is fuelled by, mass consumption.

Aglietta's study of the United States is a leading contribution to the work of the French regulation school which has been central to the analysis of Fordism and post-Fordism. The regulation school approach originates with French economic and social thinkers, and provides an important point of reference for wider approaches to capitalist restructuring within political economy, economic sociology and critical geography since the 1980s (Aglietta 1979; Boyer and Durand 1997; Lipietz 1986, 1987, 1994; see also Harvey 1990; Jessop 1990b, 1994). The chief concern within the regulation approach is the reproduction of capitalist economies, analysed in terms of different 'regimes of accumulation'. This focus derives from a basic problematic: the endurance of what is an inherently volatile system. How is it that capitalist economies, in spite of their in-built contradictions and crisis tendencies, are able to reproduce themselves in a fairly stable way over extended periods? Capitalism, as well we know, has not collapsed either under the weight of its own structural contradictions, or in the wake of severe periodic shocks such as the Great Depression. In fact it has proved very resilient in riding out its episodic crises, bubbles and meltdowns. In the regulation view, this relative durability comes from the way that a complex of production, distribution, exchange and consumption processes hold together as a 'regime of accumulation'. Fordism is a primary example of such a system. A regime of accumulation includes dominant methods of production, distribution and exchange; standards of organisation in work and management; norms of consumption and patterns of demand. In this way it refers to the 'fit' between economic accumulation and expanded social reproduction. The latter takes in such factors as the socialisation of workers, cultures of consumption, and the management of relations between different economic groups. The 'regime of accumulation' is therefore the principle concept for understanding the economic reproduction of capitalism; not only in terms of how things are produced or how money gets made, but in the wider context of economic life – in ordering practices and relations of work, distribution, and consumption.

The political reproduction of capitalist systems, secondly, operates through the 'mode of regulation'. This term describes the institutional setting of government, law and politics which underpins a given regime of accumulation. It provides the formal regulatory framework within which capitalist processes operate, as well as the political settlement between different social classes. Certain theorists (for example Lipietz 1994) also use a third concept – the 'societal paradigm' – to refer to the underlying social contract, or mode of organisation of social life. This shapes social arrangements and identities beyond the economic field. To simplify these arguments we might say that the three terms – regime of accumulation, mode of regulation, and societal paradigm – point to the way that the economy, politics and society are integrated around a particular mode of capitalist development. It is important to note that these different factors include not just institutional and formal arrangements – technical systems of production, legal rules, strategies of economic and social organisation – but the norms, conventions and social ideologies that support them. In the regulation approach, the reproduction of capitalism depends on a network of factors, from the organisation of production to the operations of government to the socialisation of families.

Viewed in this way, Fordism appears 'less as a mere system of mass production and more as a total way of life' (Harvey 1990: 135). Gramsci's work of the early 1930s is particularly prescient on this point. He links Fordism with a larger culture or ideological system that he terms 'Americanism'. Fordist innovations on the production line may have been geared to economic efficiency in the first instance, but in an extended sense they sought to create 'a new type of worker and of man', based on a form of work that was 'inseparable from a specific mode of living and of thinking and feeling life' (Gramsci 1971: 302). The organisation of production was critical to wider patterns of social and cultural organisation, which served in their turn to reinforce the industrial paradigm by reproducing the 'human complex' of the productive system in a stable, 'well-adjusted' form (ibid.: 303). 'Hegemony', in this account, 'was born in the factory' (ibid.: 285).

The hegemony of 'Americanism' as a mode of capitalist production and reproduction would be secured by the terms of the post-war settlement. The entrenchment of Fordist systems across advanced capitalist economies after 1945 took place against a backdrop of expanding world trade and investment activity. As we saw in Chapter 2, the economic insularity of the inter-war period was reversed by the international trade regime opened up under the General Agreement on Tariffs and Trade. This structured liberalisation of trade between the major industrialised economies underpinned post-war growth in domestic Fordist systems. The rise of mass production and the expansion of mass consumer markets within national economies were therefore tied into an international framework in which trade was managed via GATT, and monetary policies backed by the stabilising role of the dollar as reserve currency. The reproduction of capitalism could be understood not simply in terms of national systems of economic and political regulation, but of an international regime which both fostered and set the boundaries of inter-state exchanges.

The crisis of Fordism

The model looks foolproof, but the Fordist settlement did not hold. Neat as the internal logic may be, by the mid-1970s cracks had appeared in the Fordist machine. These were the results of both external and internal pressures. Harvey (1990: 140) again provides a symbolic date for the crisis of Fordism – 1973, and the onset of the world recession prompted by the oil crisis of that year.

A number of factors may be used to account for this 'crisis' of Fordism. The first of these is the increasingly international character of economic relations from the early 1970s. Fordism was an industrial system firmly based on national economies, centring on the link between domestic production and consumption. Fordist production was primarily (although not solely) about production for domestic markets. Production for international markets operated largely through foreign subsidiaries or via conventional export methods on trade terms brokered under GATT. The spread of multinational corporations in the latter part of the twentieth century, as well as the emergence of new economic competitors, undermined these established arrangements. Multinationals, in the first instance, as the forerunners of an emerging global economy, put into question the very coherence of 'domestic' markets. Where ownership and management, supply and labour sources, production processes, distribution and consumer markets are dispersed across transnational space, the idea of what is a domestic and what a foreign market becomes less stable. In the latter decades of the twentieth century, transnational production of this kind would greatly outstrip export trade as the principal means of reaching 'foreign' markets (Held and McGrew 2003: 26). The spread of multinationals, moreover, went together with the rise of new economic competitors: initially West Germany and Japan, followed by newly industrialising economies in Southeast Asia. The entry of these new players transformed an export system in which Fordist economies had been used to trade with each other, and with their allies, ex-colonies and client states on various special terms. The original GATT agreement had been signed in 1947 by 23 states; in 1995 its successor body, the World Trade Organization, was founded with a membership of more than 130. The entrance of new competitors into the world market changed international patterns of trade and investment. In particular, it marked a break between domestic production and domestic consumption, as imported goods became more available and more attractive to consumer markets. Trade barriers of various kinds might be used (and still are) to deter the import of foreign-made goods, but the limits within which national economies could protect themselves in this way would become gradually tighter, more artificial, and less viable.

These external pressures added to the internal problems that had become apparent within Fordist production by the early 1970s. The economic problems of this period in part were due to the rigidity of mass production systems which were slow or simply unable to adapt to changing economic and social conditions. It might be said that Fordist production got better and better at what it did (that is, more efficient in producing standardised mass goods with fewer workers), but proved simply unable, when it was needed, to do much else. The ongoing rationalisation of Fordist production processes gradually depressed the need for industrial workers. Advances in technology, notably in computerisation and robotics, helped to increase productive output while requiring fewer bodies to work on the production lines. Growing unemployment, however, meant falling consumer demand – the virtuous circuit of mass production and mass consumption was broken at the point where large-scale production could be sustained by a shrinking industrial workforce. At the same time, these problems of over-supply at home were made worse by increasingly competitive import markets from abroad. One answer to such effects of over-capacity is to diversify the goods produced within an economy, but sclerotic mass production systems were not fit for this kind of purpose. As consumer markets became more segmented from the late 1960s, there remained the problem that large-scale production was geared to standardisation. As Henry Ford is famously quoted as saying of the Model T Ford, you could have any colour: as long as it was black.

These problems in the field of economic accumulation were accompanied by crises in the field of political regulation. As unemployment asserted itself as a stubborn structural problem in the early 1970s, greater economic and social demands were made on welfare budgets and on governments. In a number of national settings serious unemployment coexisted with high inflation and low or no economic growth. This was a combination (termed 'stagflation') which conventional economic wisdom held shouldn't happen, and which Keynesian styles of economic management seemed unable to handle. The historic settlement between capital, labour and the state which had helped to reproduce the Fordist regime appeared less and less capable of delivering social stability and economic growth. On the one hand, then, the crisis of Fordism can be seen in slow motion in the stagnant growth and institutional inertia which gripped advanced market economies in the 1970s. On the other, it has its climactic moment in the shock of the oil crisis of 1973, as Arab states moved to boycott supply to Western economies in the context of the Arab-Israeli war, and OPEC imposed dramatic price hikes.

From a regulationist perspective, the crisis of Fordism represents a crisis not simply in a certain approach to industrial production, but in a definite mode of capitalist accumulation and political regulation. These economic and political arrangements were based on a complex of institutional structures, including corporatist arrangements between government, organised capital and organised labour; production by national companies largely geared to domestic markets; and a fairly substantial economic role for the state. The early lines of 'post-Fordism', then, were visible in the weakening of corporatist consensus – especially the exit of capital not only from three-way bargaining but from any primary attachment to domestic investment; the internationalisation of corporate investment, ownership and operations; and the rolling-back of state intervention into the economy. In this light, Fordism (and whatever replaces it) is not simply a question of how things are produced in an economy, but stands for a regime of economic accumulation bound into a system of political regulation and social coordination. One does not have to accept Gramsci's (1971: 285) claim that, under Fordist conditions, the 'whole life of the nation' comes to 'revolve around production' to argue in this context that structures of production are integrated into broader systems of social and political organisation.

After Fordism

Accounts of the crisis of Fordism tend to agree on the factors that helped to break down this regime. It is not so clear, however, what was to come 'after' Fordism. A number of theorists have questioned the coherence of any distinct 'post-Fordist' regime of accumulation (see Harvey 1990; Hirst and Zeitlin 1991; Jessop 1992), and to an extent what came after the crisis of Fordism was simply the long-drawn-out death throes of mass industrial production – the staggering decline of manufacturing industries over various waves of redundancy, restructuring and reprieve; the entrenchment of unemployment and steady deskilling; the drip-feed to heavy industry provided by government defence spending, especially in the United States; and more and more jobs in services – junk or otherwise. While mass production was in decline in North America and Western Europe, what is more, it was growing in a number of newly industrialising economies, although generally outside of any stable compact between industry, workers and the national state, and in the absence of the labour conditions and protections that Fordist workers gradually had secured.

Piore and Sabel (1984) analyse the uneven transition from Fordism around what they call the 'second industrial divide'. Their version of the first industrial divide, to re-cap, referred to the gradual displacement of craft production by mass industrial production from the early twentieth century. The second industrial divide marks the move away from large-scale manufacture towards more flexible techniques of production. The authors describe this as a shift to 'neo-Fordism' or 'flexible specialisation'. They date such a shift from the late 1960s, as changing technologies, new forms of economic competition, and the reorganisation of labour processes together came to undermine Fordist arrangements. A move towards small- and medium-scale production, with an emphasis on product diversity and flexible organisation, offered one solution to the industrial stagnation of the early 1970s. Production and labour would become more 'flexible' and more 'specialised': responsive to changing conditions of both supply and demand, geared to greater product diversity, and open to ongoing innovation. The intense rationalisation of Fordist production, with its massive output of standard goods and its constant pressure on marginal unit costs, would be supplanted by the lean production of smaller batches of customised goods. Cost-efficiency through economies of scale would give way to more flexible economies of scope.

Despite the broad periodisation of these different 'industrial divides', Piore and Sabel do not see flexible specialisation as simply displacing mass production at the centre of economic organisation. Flexible production co-existed with enduring mass productive forms, as in the model of neo-Fordism where large-scale production systems incorporated more flexible techniques and workplace structures. The Japanese car and electronics industries, for example, with their use of flexible methods for producing high-volume commodities, can be taken as a primary instance of neo-Fordist production (Castells 2000: 169–72; Lash and Urry 1994: 65–81; Tomaney 1994). Indeed, Bob Jessop (2003) suggests that, rather than using the categories of flexible specialisation or post-Fordism to capture such changes, we might better refer to the emergent system in terms of a corporation that has the same symbolic resonance which Ford had for the mass production complex: 'Toyotaism' maybe, or 'Sonyism' or 'Gatesism'. The move towards technological innovation and flexible production, in these terms, is certainly not the property of the smaller or leaner enterprise: it remains quite compatible with the mega-corporation.

While the analysis of Fordism describes a large-scale system of production, consumption and regulation, the axial principle of flexibility and the gradations of scale which are built into various accounts of post-Fordism can make it difficult to analyse such a system in a broad-brush way. Lash and Urry (1994: 84) offer a useful shorthand, characterising Fordism in terms of low diversity, high-volume production; neo-Fordism as diversified quality, medium-batch production; and post-Fordism in terms of advanced services and high-technology production. How do these changes in the nature of goods and the way they are produced link with wider aspects of economic and social organisation? To simplify, we can define some of the typical features of post-Fordism in contrast to those of Fordism as follows:

Fordism	post-Fordism
mass production	flexible or 'batch' production
standardised products	diversified products
assembly-line production	computer-controlled production
heavy industry	clean technology
corporate hierarchies	horizontal networks
semi-skilled worker	polarisation of skills

national economy   international economy
industrial centres   new industrial districts
mass consumption   differentiated markets

This basic comparative scheme begins with aspects of production but opens out onto wider organisational, spatial and social issues. These might be outlined on three levels: first, changes in production and labour processes; second, shifts in the spatial organisation of economic activity; and third, new patterns of consumption.

Changes in production and labour processes

Changes at the level of production and work mark the principal differences between Fordism and post-Fordism. Whereas Fordism was based on high-volume production of fairly standard goods, post-Fordism stands for flexible production of more diversified goods. Flexible production centres on the manufacture of goods in smaller batches, of different kinds and on tighter time-scales ('just-in-time' production). Such flexibility has been enabled by new productive technologies as well as by changes in the way production is organised. The new capacities and fine calibrations of computerised design and production mean that small-batch and customised product runs can be as time- and cost-efficient as the old mass assembly line. While in certain cases large-scale production systems could be adapted along neo-Fordist lines to incorporate these changing technologies and to organise labour on a more flexible pattern, it also became common for large producers to out-source aspects of the manufacturing process to a network of subcontractors operating at smaller scales. In this way, changes in production technologies were linked to changes in corporate hierarchy and workplace organisation. 'The shift from standardized mass production to more flexible production methods', as Hirst and Thompson (1999: 6) suggest, went together with a move away from 'the large, nationally rooted, oligopolistic corporation as the unchallengeably dominant economic agent towards a more complex world of multinational enterprises, less rigidly structured firms and the increased salience of smaller firms'.

The reorganisation of production through subcontracting networks created a kind of dispersed assembly line which integrated firms of different size and at different points along the supply, production and distribution chain. This not only reorganised production processes but also had the potential to redistribute economic power. Piore and Sabel (1984), for instance, argued that flexible specialisation had the capacity to increase workers' skill levels and offer them greater autonomy over the labour process. Their theory of flexible specialisation was based on a model of customised goods or parts produced by skilled workers, especially in smaller or medium-sized firms, and aided by high-spec design, production and information technologies. It was closer to older versions of craft production than to the inflexible, repetitive and progressively deskilled labour of work-ers on the lengthy assembly lines typical of Fordist production (see also Hirst and Zeitlin 1991; Storper and Scott 1992; cf. Braverman 1974). We will come back to look more closely at this issue of the post-Fordist labour process; first, it is worth looking at the way these changes in production operated in space.

Shifts in the spatial organisation of economic activity

The Fordist system of production was based on a certain model of spatial organisation. Lash and Urry (1994: 17) write that the

> old Fordist, organized capitalist core was characterized by a set of pro-ducer networks clustered around a heavy-industrial hub of the motor, chemicals, electrical and steel industries. Finance, services and distribu-tion functions were either subordinate to, or driven by, this industrial production function.

It follows that processes of industrial restructuring since the 1970s have also involved forms of spatial restructuring. First, major industrial centres have experienced both decline and dispersal, as production functions have dimin-ished or have been redistributed across more extended spatial networks. The finance, research, service and distribution functions which were once inte-grated into large producers have been progressively 'hollowed out' of these corporations, forming a complex of independent producer services operat-ing through various subsidiary, subcontracting and market relations. These formerly 'subordinate' sectors in knowledge and research, finance, property and services, have become central to the post-industrial economy. A new spatial core in this way can be seen to cluster around producer and business services, financial services, information and communications (see Sassen 1994, 2001). Post-Fordism therefore denotes not only a shift in the organ-isation of production, but an economic and spatial shift from production to services. Indeed, it is in these service and communications industries that forms of flexible specialisation tend to be most advanced, as information technologies and 'immaterial' labour are adapted to patterns of networking, contracting-out, customised outputs, and so on.

While economic space can partly be mapped around these post-industrial sectors, producer networks continue to shape a post-Fordist economic geog-raphy. A number of theorists have analysed the emergence and re-emergence of regional economies under post-Fordist conditions, based on high-tech and media clusters (various silicon valleys or corridors), high-performance manufacturing regions, or craft-based industrial districts (Amin 1994: 22; see also Sabel 1994; Scott 1988; Storper and Scott 1992). If the crisis of Fordist production could be charted around the decline of such industrial centres as the Midwest rustbelt of the US, the Ruhr in Germany, Turin in

Italy or the Basque country in Spain, it followed that post-Fordist restructuring could be traced around new industrial spaces in California's Bay Area, Baden-Württemberg in Germany, the Third Italy, or on Spain's Mediterranean coast. These post-Fordist economic geographies appear quite diverse, including advanced technopoles such as Silicon Valley itself, or the more linear ribbons along the Salt Lake City-Provo corridor or Massachusetts' Route 128; the clustering of mature industries and research infrastructure, as in Baden-Württemberg; networks of small to medium enterprises, such as in Jutland in Denmark; or craft-based districts like Emilia-Romagna in Italy. What these different models share is the horizontal integration of firms, an emphasis on skill and innovation, and perceived competitive advantages deriving from co-location and dense economic and social networks.

Other critics have pointed up the uneven geographies of post-Fordism shaped by different histories of capitalist development and modes of state regulation (see Peck and Tickell 2002). A sanitised version of post-Fordism as all clean technology, quality circles and niche production can underplay the extent to which economic restructuring worked through processes of de-industrialisation that decimated industries, workforces, towns and regions (see Bluestone 1982; Crump and Merrett 1998; Harrison 1988). Patterns of decline and growth are also subject to reversal: a number of older industrial areas, such as the West Midlands in Britain and parts of the US Midwest, have undergone recoveries, while both Silicon Valley and Route 128 have been through their own periods of downturn. While the shift towards greater flexibility may have redistributed production across economic space, it has also produced distinct re-concentrations of economic power. In contrast to a dispersed geography of new industrial districts, Lash and Urry (1994: 12) argue that a post-Fordist core has consolidated around the urban centres which house the headquarters of major corporations and their networks of business and communication services. If this 'information-saturated, service-rich, communications-laden core represents a major shift from the older order's central cluster of Fordist industries', it also results in new and often stark geographies of economic power and exclusion. These can be traced between the urban command centres of the new core, and sites of low-cost production and service work, often in developing economies. Other places do not even make it onto the economic map, remaining outside the networked loops of information and chains of commodity production. And blunt patterns of polarisation are also evident *within* core cities, between different classes of post-Fordist labour: what we might call the 'service-rich' as opposed to the 'service-poor' in the fields of work and consumption.

New patterns of consumption

Changing forms of consumption provide a clear connection between productive restructuring and wider social and cultural shifts. Fordist production

was geared to mass consumption in fairly undifferentiated consumer markets. This was not simply a cultural assumption: the expectation of stable
and uniform consumer preferences was *built into* a system where massive
amounts of capital were sunk into fixed assets (factories, machinery, distribution networks) which were designed to produce standard goods on a large
scale. As Aglietta (1987) argues, a Fordist aesthetic of functional design can
be seen as an effect of technical constraints in engineering, semi-automated
production, and long production runs. There was little room for innovation
in design or flexibility in output. In Aglietta's view, both the geography of
Fordist consumption (based on the clear separation of home and workplace,
and the growth of the suburbs) and its primary commodities (automobiles,
standardised housing, and all the associated mod cons) were directly related
to the organisation of mass production.

This loop between mass production and mass consumption proved
unsustainable. By the 1970s, large-scale Fordist systems had saturated existing consumer markets in contexts where the rigidities of mass production
could not respond quickly and flexibly to changing patterns of consumer
demand (Slater 1997: 189). This structural problem became particularly
acute with the entry into the market of new international competitors, as
consumer commodities from Japan and from newly industrialising Asian
economies became more available in foreign markets. Consumer imports
helped to diversify patterns of demand, but the problem faced by a number
of capitalist economies in the 1970s was not so much a welter of frustrated
niche consumers as it was the capacity for over-production in mass industrial systems. Indeed, there is an argument to be made that changes in production shaped changes in consumer demand, rather than vice versa. Just as
Fordist production promoted standard consumer choices, so the shift
towards more diversified production needed to find diverse consumer markets. If these did not already exist, it would be necessary to invent them
through the creation of needs that is the speciality of advertising and marketing. Slater (1997: 190–1) points out that Fordist marketing aimed to trade
on product differentiation (whatever it is that makes Pepsi different from
Coke), but tended to assume that markets themselves were fairly undifferentiated. Mass consumer markets were simply segmented around standard
demographic variables such as age, income, occupation, gender and region.
Post-Fordist marketing, in contrast, targets consumers less as teenagers,
white-collar workers or suburban housewives than in terms of distinct lifestyles, identities or market niches. These do not correspond in any simple
way to standard sociological categories, but rather draw on a complex of
consumer practices, elective identities and cultural associations (ibid.: 191).
Indeed, the work of marketing, design and advertising can be seen not
merely as identifying or accessing these cultural segments, but as helping to
constitute them. The expansion and diversification of consumer demand is
in this sense both an economic and a cultural effect. Such an effect is particularly visible within 'late' post-Fordism, in a technological or immaterial

economy which has the capacity to produce an array of new, customised or re-engineered goods and services ahead of any market (or even any use) for them. The production and positioning of consumer markets and of niches within them is not only a post-Fordist phenomenon, of course, but it is arguable that an emphasis on continual innovation and product diversity cranks up the intensity and sharpens the inventiveness of contemporary market-making (see Barry and Slater 2003).

Post-Fordist problems

Post-Fordism, considered in these terms, is more than the blasted landscape that emerges from the crisis of Fordism. It describes not only the restructuring of production, but also points to forms of corporate, spatial and consumer restructuring. However, there are a number of analytical problems with the concept of post-Fordism that raise critical questions concerning its application to contemporary economic conditions. These include the central focus on production; the variable effects of labour flexibility; the Fordisation of services; and the export of both Fordist and post-Fordist modes of exploitation to developing economies. The first of these issues is the primacy given to production in accounting for socioeconomic change. Harvey (1990: 147) rejects the category of post-Fordism, referring instead to the economic shifts that have taken place since the 1970s as a move towards 'flexible accumulation'. The design of new and more flexible production systems, that is, is only part of the story of economic restructuring. Harvey contends that theories of post-Fordism focus too tightly on questions of production, underplaying the role of ever more flexible finance capital in driving economic changes. Shapeshifting, footloose and increasingly electronic, the deregulation of finance capital from the 1970s created new sources of wealth, patterns of exchange and economic power (ibid.: 160–5). A focus on technical or organisational changes in production overlooks the extent to which the dispersal and reintegration of production and exchange processes has been premised on mobile money. While theories of post-Fordism concentrate on shifting circuits of productive capital, circuits of finance capital have been at least as critical to the reorganisation of economic space. An extended concept of flexible accumulation, what is more, is able to take in the different domains that have been subject to flexible restructuring beyond specialised production. The notion of flexibility equally applies to the reshaping of labour markets, industrial relations and work processes. It is not only products, but workers, that have become 'flexible'.

The notion of labour flexibility is open to contrary readings. Certain theorists saw in a shift to post-Fordism the scope for alternative forms of industrial organisation, enskilling and worker autonomy. Piore and Sabel (1984) viewed the second industrial divide as potentially reversing the centralisation and concentration of economic power that marked the high modern period of industrial production. It re-staged the choice between mass production and craft production as models not only for how things should be made, but for how workers, industries and economic power might be organised. The contrast between mass and craft production was also a contrast between large-scale industries and monopoly corporate powers, on the one hand, and specialised enterprises and dispersed economic control, on the other. New industrial districts, the spread of horizontal networking and subcontracting, the renaissance of the small and medium-sized firm, the specialisation and re-skilling of productive work – all had the potential to disperse economic power across space and between social actors (see also Sabel 1994; Tomaney 1994). In this way, new or revived forms of flexible and craft production might also open up new or revived forms of industrial democracy.

Flexibility, however, plays in different ways. Applied to production, it signifies a capacity for adaptation, monitoring and self-correction, diversified output, frequent technical innovation, and short time-frames. When applied to labour, these same factors can go with effects of casualisation and weakened job security, heightened surveillance, lack of control over or expertise within the labour process, erratic hours and constant deadlines. Ten years prior to Piore and Sabel's account, Harry Braverman (1974) had argued that more and more work in contemporary capitalist economies involved deskilling, routinisation and alienation. The restructuring of production, or the shift from manufacturing to services, was less relevant to critical socioeconomic analysis than the way that capitalist labour processes systematically deskilled workers and degraded worker autonomy. It is worth recalling at this point Gramsci's much earlier version of Fordist labour processes. Citing Frederick W. Taylor's notorious claim that it might be possible – using correct techniques of scientific management – to train an 'intelligent gorilla' to undertake routine industrial work, Gramsci argued that such a statement simply expressed the larger purpose of the Fordist-American system. This was aimed, he went on (1971: 302), at

> developing in the worker to the highest degree automatic and mechanical attitudes, breaking up the old psycho-physical nexus of qualified professional work, which demands a certain active participation of intelligence, fantasy and initiative on the part of the worker, and reducing productive operations exclusively to the mechanical, physical aspect.

For Gramsci, this marked the perfection of the industrial process. However, automatic and mechanical attitudes are not only inculcated (if they are) on a Fordist assembly line. The routinisation of service work also tends to militate against any incursion of 'intelligence, fantasy and initiative' into the labour process. Indeed, the mass production of services is a third critical counterweight to theories of post-Fordism. The accounts of 'McDonaldization' offered by Ritzer and others point to the intense Fordism of mass

service industries, while Head has written of the role of 'the customer relations factory' and the 'digital assembly line' in organising the labour process
within the new economy (see Head 2003; Ritzer 2002b; Royle 2002). These
effects of Fordisation in service sectors are replicated in the growing outsourcing of routine service work to developing economies (see the discussion
in Chapter 1). The latter represents a contemporary mode of the 'peripheral
Fordism' (Lipietz 1986) under which high-volume industrial production was
shifted to developing regions where labour and other costs were lower. The
crisis of Fordism in the core in this sense was off-set by the export of Fordism to newly industrialising countries. In these contexts, the typical Fordist
worker was more likely to be a low-paid female than a unionised male.
David Harvey (1990: 153) characterises transnational production in
terms of the 'enhanced capacity of multinational capital to take Fordist
mass-production systems abroad, and there to exploit extremely vulnerable women's labour power under conditions of extremely low pay and
negligible job security' (see also Dicken 2002; Mies 1998; Munck 2002).

This is not to say that Fordism has the monopoly on labour exploitation.
Arguments for flexible specialisation as promoting worker autonomy and
skills are challenged by growing insecurity and routinisation in advanced
economies (see Bourdieu 1998b; Heery and Salmon 1999a). Such arguments
become problematic when taken outside the more privileged sectors of the
'new' core; even more so when considered in transnational contexts. In this
way, post-Fordism involves both new patterns of casualisation and some
more familiar patterns of labour exploitation. Sweatshop production, for
example, can be seen as post-Fordist on the model of networks of small-scale
enterprise working flexibly to meet short orders. The contrast between the
high-tech worker in Silicon Valley and the sweated worker in an off-shore
factory represents what Trigilia (2002: 217) calls the 'high' and the 'low
road' to flexibility. A prominent example of the low road has been the route
taken by certain major multinationals in the apparel and footwear industry,
outsourcing production to contract factories where labour conditions
become someone else's problem. As seen in previous chapters, the commodity chains which link a prestige sports shoe with a sweated worker increasingly have been pieced together (see Frankel 2001; Fung *et al.* 2001; Klein
2000), sometimes by corporations themselves. In 2005 Nike published a list
of the 700 factories with which it contracted to produce finished Nike-
branded products as of 1 April that year (see www.nikebiz.com). The report
detailed 124 'active contract factories' in China, 73 in Thailand, 35 in South
Korea, and 34 in Vietnam. Nike and the factories making its products
employ 650,000 workers globally, 200,000 in Chinese contract factories
alone. An audit of Nike's contractors in 2003–4 found evidence of poor
employment practices or actual abuses in over one-quarter of its factories in
Asia. Between 25 and 50 per cent of the plants in this region restricted
workers' access to toilets and to drinking water; a similar percentage did not
allow workers at least one day off per week. More than 50 per cent of

factories employed workers for over 60 hours per week, with wages below the relevant legal minimum in one-quarter of all sites. The gains from flexibility, it seems, are entirely to the corporation: there would appear to be little 'flexibility' in a seven-day working week. It should be noted that in this context Nike is not, strictly speaking, the employer but the *buyer* of the finished product. Labour standards in this sense become a set of 'compliance issues' between buyer and subcontractor. Such a set-up does not fit easily into any clear-cut model of Fordism, neo-Fordism or post-Fordism. Rather, it draws in a complex mix of corporate control, subcontracting networks, mass commodity production, highly aestheticised design and lifestyle marketing: all premised on a kind of pre-Fordist 'absolute surplus value' squeezed out of workers by low wages and long working hours.

Conclusion

Theories of Fordism describe a mode of mass industrial production that was tied into a system of economic accumulation, political order and social reproduction. In this way, they assume that the meaning of production goes beyond technical processes and material outputs to take in forms of workplace organisation, corporate structures, patterns of consumption, modes of regulation and spatial arrangements. The concept of Fordism provides a shorthand for a larger system of economic and social coordination. There is something of a mismatch between this analysis of Fordism as an integrated system of production, consumption and regulation, and more partial accounts of post-Fordism. The latter can be seen as less concerned with a wholesale shift in economic and social organisation than with a diverse set of changes in how production and work are organised. Such a contrast is partly due to the uneven and inconsistent ways in which post-Fordist features have developed. It is also due to the air of coherence Fordism gains when viewed as an ideal-type or historical artefact. In practice, Fordist systems of production varied across different spatial and temporal settings. This is also the case for economic organisation 'after' Fordism. Trigilia's notion of the high and low roads to flexibility is extremely useful in pointing to the contradictory modes in which production and labour have been restructured along 'flexible' lines. The Nike case offers an exemplar here, as advanced transport, communications and design technologies, as well as networks of subcontracting relations distributed across space, are deployed in processes of mass commodity production by highly exploited workers. Against such a background of off-shoring and subcontracting, post-Fordist production can be understood as part of an extended system of accumulation and regulation which produces very different grades of flexible worker; which polarises skills between high-tech and routine production; and which offers deeply uneven gains from flexibility or mobility.

5 Knowledge, information, signs

The shift from Fordism to post-Fordism involves a set of changes in the organisation of production in late capitalist economies. These changes concern not only the 'how' of production – the way in which goods are made, but also the 'what' of production – the nature of products themselves. The discussion below centres on this second element, the distinctive kinds of goods which are produced in contemporary economies. In particular, it considers the expanding economic role of knowledge, information and signs: as aspects of the labour process, as components of production, and as commodities for consumption.

There are a number of conceptual cues for such an analysis. The first comes from theories of 'post-industrial' economy and society, represented here by the classic work of the US sociologist Daniel Bell. For Bell, the emergence of post-industrial society can be traced from the 1960s, based on the restructuring of capitalist production, new advances in technology, and changing patterns of work. His account points to: the transition from manufacturing to services; the growth of the professional and technical labour force; and the intensification of knowledge across the spheres of work, research and innovation, managerial control and policy formation. These economic trends went together with a shift in social power which gave enhanced status and influence to a new 'knowledge élite'. Bell emphasises the role of knowledge as an attribute or capacity of certain social actors – as a privileged form of human capital – as well as its role in shaping a broader post-industrial culture. A second perspective, which was considered in Chapter 2, focuses on knowledge in the more abstract form of information. Theories of information society add two important dimensions to the debate over the place of knowledge in the economy: the growing importance of information technology in socioeconomic life, and the nature of information as a commodity. Knowledge is not just an individual or corporate asset; it can also be seen as the key feature of advanced production technologies, and as a distinct economic product in its own right.

The central part of the discussion considers more recent ideas about the role of symbolic goods in contemporary capitalist economies. This expands on the brief discussion of Lash and Urry's work in Chapter 2, examining more closely their treatment of an 'economy of signs'. The authors consider the economic production of signs in two ways: in terms of knowledge or informational goods, and in terms of aesthetic or cultural goods. Such immaterial goods are key items of contemporary consumption, but also enter into processes of design, production and exchange. For Lash and Urry, these sign commodities are central to a contemporary mode of 'reflexive accumulation' which is characterised by increasing cognitive and symbolic work on the part of both producers and consumers. Workers, like the technologies they utilise, are called upon to be self-monitoring in respect of their labour process, while consumers' choices are mediated by a sometimes complicated mix of information and aesthetic content. This can, at least on one reading, be seen to promote enhanced worker expertise and heightened consumer discrimination. A more critical take on the notion of non-material commodities is found in George Ritzer's treatment of the proliferation of 'nothings' in contemporary economic life. He argues that economic exchange, particularly in globalising sectors, increasingly is based on forms of 'nothing' – goods, places, jobs and services that lack any real distinguishing substance of their own. If the accounts considered earlier in the chapter point to the growing economic importance of knowledge, services and symbolic distinction, Ritzer's version suggests that work, exchange and consumption can just as easily be understood in terms of mindless routine, de-personalised function, and uniform 'choice'.

The penultimate section of this chapter focuses on the relation between economy and culture. This is an issue that runs through the perspectives considered below, and which is particularly critical to Lash and Urry's analysis. Its relevance here is somewhat distinct from economic sociology's assumption that economic action and relations are always more or less embedded in cultural contexts. Rather, this approach to the late modern economy suggests that cultural goods, practices and meanings are becoming more integrated into economic processes – as commodity forms, as aesthetic components of production, as forms of work, and as elements of consumer behaviour. The extended import of changes in production, however, goes beyond the growing 'interpenetration' between economy and culture. The final part of the discussion reviews some of the key changes charted in Chapter 4 and in this chapter: not only in terms of what kinds of goods are being produced and how, but in relation to an extended set of impacts in the fields of consumption, knowledge, work, space and culture.

Post-industrial society: the economic role of knowledge

Daniel Bell's argument in *The Coming of Post-Industrial Society* (1973) is concerned with a broad contemporary shift from industrial to post-industrial modes of economic organisation. Advanced economies can be seen as 'post-industrial' in that structures and relations of industrial production, while still present, are no longer primary in shaping social and economic forms (see also Touraine 1971). Sociology may have developed as the study of industrial societies, but the transition to post-industrialism involves new economic arrangements, class identities and social relations. Whereas the industrial period was typified by heavy industry, factory production and manufacturing technologies, post-industrial society is broadly characterised by service industries, white-collar employment and information technology. Post-industrial societies – and Bell takes his text from the US case – are increasingly dependent on a service economy in which large numbers of workers are not engaged in the production of goods but in the exchange of services. Services both take a greater share of gross domestic product in these economies, and also represent a greater share of employment.

The main factor behind this shift is the axial role of knowledge in the post-industrial economy – from increased automation and technical skill in the workplace, to the development of new technologies of production and communication. Of course, knowledge has always played a crucial role in economic life: workers' skills are vital to processes of production; innovation is key to economic progress; the mental labour (or 'knowledge work') of lawyers, doctors, teachers or clerks has been going on for a long time. What Bell identified, however, was a change in the way that knowledge was conceived and valued as an economic object, and the growing economic share that such knowledge work took. The shift from industrial to post-industrial society saw the central role played by the production of industrial goods give way to the exchange of knowledge. Moreover, Bell's argument is not simply concerned with the content of production and work, but with the organisation of social and economic power. The enhanced economic value of knowledge produced critical changes in social structure, seen in the emergence and growing status of certain 'knowledge classes'. These strata included new kinds of knowledge workers, from computer programmers to management consultants or financial advisors, as well as older traders in knowledge such as lawyers, professors and other white-collar professionals. A post-industrial division of labour develops around the production and dissemination of knowledge, as the number of white-collar, service and professional workers outstrips the number of manual workers in the occupational structure. This alters not only the organisation of work but also the distribution of power. Post-industrial economies offered greater economic rewards and social influence to 'knowledge élites' – members of a professional class engaged in the high-level production and control of knowledge. In this way, command over knowledge becomes a significant basis for social and economic power in its own right, as distinct from the ownership of capital or established forms of political power.

The role of knowledge forms one key strand within the post-industrial thesis; a second is the expanding economic role of culture and consumption. Theories of post-industrialism developed in a context of increasing affluence in capitalist societies, fuelled by the economic growth of the 1950s and

1960s. The 'affluent society' described by J. K. Galbraith (1998) seemed to point to a profound change in economic and social organisation. Post-war affluence may have been unevenly spread, but for large numbers of people in liberal capitalist societies economic life was no longer taken up with hardship, struggle or scarcity – if still hard at times, it was a world away from the chronic insecurity of pre-twentieth-century history. Disposable income was a new economic reality that generated new social and economic issues. It was not simply a question, that is, of how people made their money, but of how they spent it. Bell and other analysts remarked on the way that growing affluence, at least for significant parts of the population, resulted in altered forms of consumer demand: away from basic goods to more diverse consumer items; from durable products to services; and from household consumption to cultural and leisure goods. These changing patterns of consumer demand were also addressed by theories of post-Fordism, specifically in terms of their links to changes in production (see Chapter 4). Bell's work, in contrast, points to the relation between changing consumption and new forms of post-industrial work. Alongside the category of the knowledge élite, active in the production and control of knowledge, Bell would develop the concept of the 'cultural mass'. This stratum takes in those involved in the economic distribution of cultural goods and services – not so much

> the creators of culture but the transmitters: those working in higher education, publishing, magazines, broadcast media, theater, and museums, who process and influence the reception of serious cultural products. It is in itself large enough to be a market for culture, purchase books, prints and serious music recordings. And it is also the group which, as writers, magazine editors, movie-makers, musicians, and so forth, produce the popular materials for the wider mass-culture audience.
>
> (Bell 1978: 20)

The cultural mass in this way provided the consumer market for its own output at the 'serious' end of the cultural spectrum, as well as producing cultural goods for mass market consumption. This distinction between high (or middle-brow) culture and mass cultural consumption may be a dubious one in value terms, but these lines of differentiation within the cultural field, and the role of such cultural intermediaries in brokering cultural exchange, remain important topics within the study of contemporary cultural economies (see Bourdieu 1984; see also du Gay and Pryke 2002a).

The idea of the post-industrial has become commonplace in social and economic debate. Given its received character today, it is instructive to think about Bell's argument in the intellectual context of its time. On one level, his analysis challenged existing accounts of social and economic change – in particular, Marxist theories concerning the transition from industrial capitalism to (industrial) socialism. Bell suggested that capitalism in fact was undergoing another sort of transition, to a system in which industrial structures played a lesser role and where economic and social power was being reconfigured. Class relations were no longer organised around industrial production: it followed that these older class relations would not be the basis for radical social transformation nor for any future form of economy and society. The rise and rise of the knowledge class, as a class fraction which stood outside the traditional relation of production between capital and labour, had scuppered the Marxist line. Bell's position was a liberal one, but similar arguments were also advanced by sociologists on the Left. Alain Touraine, working in France, asserted that the primary conflict within post-industrial society was not between capital and labour, but between the dominant 'structures of economic and political decision-making and those who are reduced to dependent participation' (1971: 9). The new ruling class in post-industrial society was a technocratic class with particular command over knowledge and bureaucratic power. Touraine advances a more baleful account of the post-industrial condition as one of living in a 'programmed society' in which knowledge functions take primary importance, but are subject to serious capture and control.

On another level, Bell's work was not saying anything particularly new. The shift to a service economy and the growth of the professional middle classes were well-established features of post-war capitalist societies, especially the United States (see Mills 1951). Bell's contribution was to encapsulate this shift, but not exactly to 'forecast' it, as his book's title claimed. Moreover, post-industrial restructuring took rather different forms in different national and institutional contexts. Even in the US, a significant proportion of services remained geared to manufacturing activity (see Cohen and Zysman 1987). A distinct service sector has proved difficult to define, particularly as it has expanded and become more complex. Harry Braverman (1974: 360), for instance, defined services in terms of work 'offered directly to the consumer', in which 'production and consumption are simultaneous', and no enduring product is exchanged. It is arguable, though, that a significant proportion of contemporary service activity is concerned with the production and exchange of goods. Is the fast food restaurant industry, to take a key example, best understood in terms of the provision of services or the mass production of food?

The post-industrial thesis, moreover, only really runs in respect of advanced capitalist economies. Castells (2000a: 220) argues that de-industrialisation in North America and Europe was offset by the growth of industrial output and jobs in newly industrialising economies, such that during the period between 1970 and 1997 'new manufacturing jobs elsewhere largely exceeded the losses in the developed world'. The description of economic and employment shifts in the United States could not and did not provide a more general model of economic change. Bell's account, however, remains influential in highlighting certain features that would be crucial to later socioeconomic analysis – most notably the social and economic primacy of knowledge and information. In this sense, his work can be seen not merely as commenting on the passing of industrial society, but as signalling the emergence of 'information society'.

Information society

At the centre of Bell's thesis is the role of knowledge in post-industrial society. Forms of knowledge – expertise, information, ideas, innovation – have greater importance not only within economic processes but also in terms of a wider cultural framework. Bell argues that the broad culture of post-industrial societies is shaped by knowledge – in the expansion of education and skilled employment, in the growth of media and cultural consumption, in the heightened influence of experts in management and policy spheres. Such an argument is critical to theories of information society. The concept of information society takes up the focus on knowledge which is at the core of the post-industrial thesis. Bell's work on technical and expert élites – on knowledge workers – highlighted the social relations of knowledge production. Later approaches to information society stress two other important elements of the production of knowledge. These are, firstly, the expanding role of information and communications technology, and secondly, the commodification of knowledge as a product. Whereas Bell directs our attention to the social organisation of knowledge, information theorists emphasise the importance of knowledge as a technical and a commodified form.

Manuel Castells remains the foremost sociological theorist of information society. His object of study is the network organisation of 'informational capitalism'. As we saw in Chapter 2, Castells characterises the late modern period as an 'information age', in which key economic and social interactions are mediated by flows of capital, information and symbols through electronic networks. Information has always been crucial to operating in markets, but Castells argues that it assumes even greater importance in contemporary capitalist economies. Castells' work since the late 1980s has concerned itself with 'the historical emergence of the space of flows, superseding the meaning of the space of places' (Castells 1989: 348). Shaped by a dominant mode of 'informationalism', production, consumption and exchange are increasingly disconnected in physical space, but highly integrated in electronic time. The dispersal of economic processes under conditions of globalisation places a premium on the rapid transmission and circulation of information across different economic sites, from the stock exchange or research laboratory to corporate headquarters, branch offices and factory floors. As production and organisational activities are distributed across physical space, information and communications technologies re-integrate these elements into a coherent process. Castells' interest is in the information network as a socio-technical form – it constitutes the basic 'morphology' of contemporary societies (2000a: 500). Networks of information, that is, are not simply technical matters: they provide the template for the organisation of social and economic life, and for the geography of social and economic power.

In tandem with this focus on information as a socio-technical form, theories of information society also analyse it as a commodity. Information circulates through networks in more or less commodified ways. For Mark Poster (1990), late modern societies are organised by a 'mode of information' which has scope for both intensely commodified and relatively free information exchanges. Information is a highly distinctive kind of economic commodity. Although it can be controlled and even monopolised, information is not prone to scarcity in the same way as other goods. We can all, at least in principle, consume the same image, listen to the same music or read the same message. The increasing scale and speed of electronic reproduction, furthermore, has the capacity to subvert the restrictions of private property, state regulation, corporate secrecy and individual privacy. Poster's argument has real currency in a context in which the Internet has made information accessible in vast amounts, at rapid speed, and often at little or no cost. The privatisation of the Internet, and the marketisation of information within it, has not advanced at such a rate as its critics might have anticipated. State and market regulation is always incomplete, corporate secrets are not watertight, the claims of private property do not always trump those of the electronic commons. As Castells (2000a: 6–7) points out, the development of the Internet may have been closely tied to military technologies, but it has also facilitated the mobilisation of resistance movements. Similarly, while Internet technology greatly expands the market in information, it also allows for the circulation of open-source software, free downloads and free access to information.

Even so, on the other side of this argument stands the monopoly control over information by massive corporate publishers (such as Bertelsmann), media and telecommunications companies (AOL Time Warner or News Corporation), and software giants (Microsoft is really the only game in town). In these cases, the command of information through network technologies helps to reproduce and entrench existing economic relations. There is ample evidence, too, that the 'pure' production of information is gradually more commodified, not only in the competition between private research sectors in various silicon valleys, but also in the market-style 'reforms' of universities on a competitive and entrepreneurial basis (see Harvey 1990: 159–60). At a more general level, social actors have differential access to information content, information skills and information technology. Indeed, Daniel Bell was alert to the way that knowledge scarcities could create social and economic divisions within post-industrial societies. While an élite of knowledge workers may have a significant degree of control in relation to knowledge and information, low-grade work can be further de-skilled and casualised by the shift towards 'informationalism'. The call-centre employee is, after all, perhaps more symbolic of the contemporary information worker than the media baron or software entrepreneur.

The 'economy of signs'

Lash and Urry's work provides a meeting point between these post-industrial approaches to knowledge and information, and the post-Fordist approach to production considered in the previous chapter. They draw on these different perspectives in developing their account of a late capitalist 'economy of signs'. The authors accept much of the substance of post-Fordist theory, but criticise it on four grounds (see Lash and Urry 1994: 60–1). First, the analysis of post-Fordism remains centred on manufacturing processes, and underplays the role of the service sector in contemporary economies. Second, it gives insufficient emphasis to the role of information and knowledge within economic processes, both as an element of production and as a form of work. Third, post-Fordist theory tends to assume the economic primacy of production over consumption. Fourth, it generally fails to recognise the 'extent to which culture has penetrated the economy itself, that is, the extent to which symbolic processes . . . have permeated both consumption *and* production' (1994: 61). We can reverse the terms of these criticisms to reveal the bare bones of Lash and Urry's own analysis. That is, their account emphasises: (1) the economic shift towards services; (2) the role of knowledge and information within economic life; (3) the economic importance of consumption practices; and (4) the symbolic or cultural content of both production and consumption.

The authors propose that contemporary economies of 'signs and space' are constituted through flows of 'capital, labour, commodities, information and images' (1994: 12). Objects, images and people circulate more quickly over greater distances – examples could be taken from the movements of share prices on trading screens or television images via satellite, to the routes of migrant labour or global tourists. Such processes are 'structured', Lash and Urry argue, less and less by the social and economic frameworks of nation states, and more and more by the network format of information and communication flows (1994: 6). Such 'structured flows' of information and images can be analysed on a macro-scale in terms of the anatomy of globalisation (see the discussion in Chapter 2). They can also be analysed within specific processes of production and consumption using a concept of 'reflexive accumulation'. What does this new category add to existing accounts of socioeconomic accounts: to the various jargons of post-industrialism, post-Fordism or flexible specialisation? The key term here is 'reflexivity'. Theories of reflexivity have been widely taken up within the social sciences since the early 1990s to consider questions ranging from the status of scientific and political authority to the nature of late modern self-identity (see Beck *et al.* 1994; Giddens 1991). Lash and Urry apply this concept to the specific case of economic processes and practices. Their notion of reflexive accumulation emphasises three factors in the analysis of contemporary economies: (1) the function of reflexive knowledge in production; (2) reflexive modes of consumption; and (3) the role of non-material goods.

Reflexive production

The first key element of reflexive accumulation is the role of knowledge and information within production processes. This is nothing new so far – such a point is familiar from accounts of post-industrialism or post-Fordism. Information and communications technology play an increasing part within design and manufacturing processes. Micro-electronics, computer-controlled production and computer-aided design mean that technical and information networks are threaded through chains of production. What Lash and Urry stress, however, is the *reflexive* way in which knowledge operates within these production systems. They develop this concept on two levels: cognitive reflexivity refers to the processing of information, while aesthetic reflexivity refers to the processing of symbolic content. In both cases, reflexivity implies a kind of feedback effect – the capacity to monitor and finely calibrate economic processes through a continual loop of information. Cognitive reflexivity, or information-processing, is central to the technical organisation of production and the regulation of work. Such cognitive labour is undertaken by both human and technical actors, reproduced through research, design and technical expertise, and programmed into advanced manufacturing technologies. This underlines the extent to which social labour in the economy of signs is undertaken by, or integrated with machine 'labour' (see Barry and Slater 2003). It is particularly evident in the feedback effect through which new productive technologies are geared to self-monitor and self-correct within very fine margins. Knowledge loops of this kind are typical of emergent technologies in computerisation, robotisation, and in nano- and bio-technologies. Meanwhile, and as we will see below, the role of aesthetic reflexivity (or symbol-processing) within production is most pronounced in the contemporary import of design and the styling of goods, shaping not only the function but the look of things.

Taken in these terms, the ideas of reflexive production and work refer to fairly advanced levels of technology and expertise. However, modes of reflexivity are also apparent in more ordinary workplace settings. Numerous types of worker are required to be self-monitoring in respect of their own labour process, and this cuts in different ways. On the one hand, it can be viewed in terms of increasing autonomy, self-management or smart teamwork in post-Fordist workplaces (see, for example, Piore and Sabel 1984; Tomaney 1994). On the other, it is visible in the lengthening reach of audit and permanent evaluation into the workplace, particularly but not only in the public sector (see Bourdieu 1998a; Power 1997). Such conventions of self-appraisal and technologies of monitoring introduce a kind of higher Taylorism into people's working lives, as work processes are divided, dissected and measured as a set of more or less meaningful 'outputs'. The lower Taylorism, too, has not disappeared and indeed seems to be more pervasive than ever: as substantial numbers of service workers undertake their tasks by telephone or computer, the capacity to monitor, record and feed back information about their performance is similarly enhanced. Many kinds of service labour in this sense can be managed as a form of piecework, measured down to the number of calls or even the number of keystrokes. Recent innovations in this domain include the use of satellite and radio technology, originally developed for military logistics, to track workers' movements and location via wireless computer systems that can be worn in specially adapted vests or on fingers, arms or wrists. Wired workers in supermarkets, warehouses or distribution centres can be directed to collect and shelve goods on a just-in-time basis. These 'wearable warehouses' do away with the need to take paper inventories, and are designed to reduce worker error and prevent theft. The technology also offers wider potential to monitor the productivity of manufacturing and clerical workers, both by measuring repetitive assembly tasks or keystrokes on a wordprocessor, and by tracking workers' position on the factory or warehouse floor.

Reflexive consumption

Current modes of accumulation, to take up Lash and Urry's second component, are also increasingly 'reflexive' on the side of consumption. Reflexive consumption is based upon customised consumer patterns, niche marketing and product diversity. Aesthetic reflexivity is particularly important in this context, as actors process a welter of symbolic or cultural codes in making consumer choices. Lash and Urry argue that this aesthetic dimension is not merely producer-driven: that is, it is not solely the business of industrial or graphic designers, advertisers or marketers. They also point to the kind of 'demand-side semiotic work' done by consumers in the quest for forms of aesthetic distinction (1994: 15). This effect is not confined to the competition for status through structured codes of consumption, but is also seen in the heightened individualisation of late modern consumer style. Social class, cultural background or other kinds of group membership may be less likely to provide the contemporary consumer with their cues, as greater emphasis is placed on the crafting of the individual self through consumption and lifestyle choices. Acts of consumption, that is, allow individuals to reflect upon (and to reflect outward) questions of identity. Consumer choices are worn as individual marques, rather than badges of membership. Reflexivity refers here not only to aesthetic sensibilities but to the degree of 'knowing-ness' with which people consume, including through ironised or 'anti-brand' forms of marketing and consumption. None of this necessarily means, of course, that people look any more different from each other than they used to (nor does it guarantee that you'll be able to find anything you like while out shopping); it does, though, tend to increase the rhetoric as well as the range of consumer choice.

There is a difficult balance to be struck here between a more culturalist approach which wishes to take consumption (and consumers) seriously in terms of reflexive social practice, and an economic analysis which is alert to the ceaseless march of commodification. The most alternative or subcultural modes of consumption tend to lose their critical edge in market contexts where, as Thomas Frank (1998) observes, hip has become 'the official capitalist style'. Meanwhile, a parasitic industry has emerged in which an array of makeover experts, personal trainers, style and image consultants – even 'personal shoppers' – promise to help the befuddled consumer through the mess of choices available to them. Economically and culturally trivial as these personal services may be, they trade on the idea that the modern consumer needs particular kinds of expertise just to go to the shops. The field of consumption, it seems, has become so specialised, so mysterious, so arcane, so fraught with potential gaffes, that you need an expert to help you buy a pair of jeans (although see Gronow and Warde 2001, on the pervasiveness of 'ordinary consumption'). These banal manoeuvres are part of a larger cultural shift in advanced liberal societies in which individuals are positioned as a kind of entrepreneur of themselves, making choices and realising value in an extended private sphere (see Rose 1991). This takes the argument over reflexive consumption somewhat outside Lash and Urry's frame, going beyond the typical realms of consumer culture to the new consumer ethos that attaches to privatised spheres of health care, pensions and savings. In these contexts, social actors are positioned as consumers in ways that require them to negotiate often complex forms of information. Different modes of reflexive consumption, then, may be primarily aesthetic or cognitive in character, requiring the consumer to process an array of either symbolic or information content, or both.

The field of service employment geared to the emergent 'needs' of reflexive consumers has grown apace: from media workers and ad-people, to software designers or financial advisors, and on to life coaches and psychotherapists. As might be gathered from this list of occupations, the thesis of reflexive accumulation can offer a rather élitist discourse of economic life (see also Featherstone 1987). The other side of the story, however, is less privileged. Modes of reflexive accumulation, Lash and Urry (1994) suggest, have the potential not only to integrate large numbers of people into its networks of information and images; they also exclude vaster numbers of people from circuits of communication and control. The economy of signs in this sense is characterised not only by the integrating logic of information and symbolic 'flows', but by more stark lines of exclusion. A dual logic of economic inclusion also produces intense social and economic polarisation around service industries themselves (see also Waldinger and Lichter 2003). The post-industrial middle classes – in financial and professional services, in communications, design, media and culture – generate demand both for each other's labour and for low-grade service work in such sectors as retail, leisure and catering, private security, domestic work and other personal services. As Lash and Urry (1994: 165) point out, these 'new advanced-services middle classes . . . provide a market not only for one another, but also for the casualized labour of the new lower class'.

Non-material products

Lash and Urry stress, thirdly, the place of non-material products in the reflexive economy. Late modern consumption can be seen as highly semiotic in nature, not only in the sense that the symbolic content of goods or services informs consumer choice, but also in the extent to which individuals are actually consuming *signs* in the form of media products, informational goods, and immaterial consumer items. The objects that circulate within current economies of signs and space are increasingly light on material content. A greater economic share, Lash and Urry (1994: 61) suggest, is taken by the production and exchange of services, images and information. Some critics have termed this the 'weightless' economy, coordinated through advanced technologies and composed of intangible services and 'goods' that lack a stable physical form (see Coyle 1999; Leadbeater 1999). What is produced and consumed are not so much material objects as weightless signs. The production and processing of signs include 'the zeros and ones of computer programmers, the careful clauses of lawyers, the subtle images of graphic artists, or the models of research scientists' (Muirhead 2004: 32). The older idea of mental labour gives way in this context to a newer concept of 'immaterial labour'. Partly this is simply one of the regular refurbs that theoretical jargon undergoes, but the shift in language also marks a shift in focus from the labour process (mental labour or knowledge work) to the immaterial nature of the product.

Lash and Urry divide non-material goods into two kinds, which follow the distinction between cognitive and aesthetic reflexivity (1994: 4, 15). 'Post-industrial goods', firstly, are based on knowledge or information. In this sense they comprise largely cognitive content. This might involve services based on expertise and innovation – an individual's technical skill, a consultancy's strategic know-how, an accountant's advice, an engineer's assessment or a lawyer's mediation. Post-industrial goods also circulate as commodified or 'alienated' forms of information – shares and other financial goods, software programmes, patents and other kinds of intellectual property. This category of non-material goods, or what we might call 'sign commodities', derive from the theories of post-industrial society developed by Daniel Bell and others. They represent commodified or capitalised knowledge.

The second type consists of what Lash and Urry call 'postmodern goods'. These are based on aesthetic or symbolic content, on forms of signification. Such goods include cultural and media commodities: film, video and television content; downloadable images and music. Such commodities, of course, are not exactly 'weightless'. Consumers need the hardware to be able to access the sign content, but advances in the necessary technology continue the trend to ever lighter and more portable cameras, audio and visual gear, personal stereos and computers, on which to produce, exchange and transmit the immaterial content. The tendency for items such as these is towards the point of disappearance – the hands-free mobile telephone, the digital camera the size of a cigarette packet, the audio player which is even smaller. Why go lap-top when you can have palm-held? The materiality of these objects diminishes as their virtual capacity increases: mobile phones of twenty and even ten years' vintage appear comically large. Knowledge or symbolic content is the key value-added in these kinds of goods, as evidenced by the virtual iron law of gadget-shopping which decrees that the smaller an item is, the higher its price. The matter – the plastic stuff of these kinds of technology – intrudes less and less on the message. Of course, it should be said that the trend is not necessarily downward for other kinds of goods, even those that mediate cultural content – televisions, like cars, seem only to be getting bigger.

This analysis of the semiotic nature of postmodern goods extends beyond obviously aesthetic objects such as music videos or digital images to highlight the way that more and more material goods, from refrigerators to running shoes, are marketed in terms of their aesthetic or symbolic content. The design intensity of contemporary production processes, the fetishisation of the brand, and the heightened aesthetic claims of some kinds of advertising, mean that the consumption of material goods is increasingly 'about' the consumption of signs. The material item, as a functional thing, can be rather residual to the consumption process. When a fridge can have its own Internet connection, when sports clothing takes to the street, when people who have never played basketball buy Air Jordans, the function of certain items has been cut fairly far adrift from their sign value. As Lury (1996: 191) asserts, cultural goods have come to provide 'a model of consumption for other goods'. She calls this the 'stylization' of consumption (1996: 51); Featherstone (1987) refers more broadly to the 'stylization' of life. The commodification of information and images in this way takes place within more general processes of cultural commodification.

Of course, there is nothing very novel in the idea that economic exchange has to do with the circulation of signs, symbols, aesthetic values and cultural signifiers. Various theorists of consumer culture, from Veblen (1934) to Bourdieu (1984), have viewed consumption in terms of the symbolic competition for social status. In this sense, material goods (as well as non-material goods, whether chamber music recitals or football matches) are always part of an 'economy of signs'. In his classic essay on 'Advertising: the magic system', Raymond Williams (1980) traced the way that advertising serves to imbue dumb products with powers and associations quite unrelated to their material form or to their actual function. For Williams, as for Marx, the fetish character of commodities is a key feature of capitalist exchange. In Williams' account, it is the work of advertising to invest objects with their 'magical' properties – to give various kinds of cigarettes, mineral waters, electronic gadgets or branded clothing their transforming powers, such that one who smokes or drinks or wears them receives the secret of cool, sophistication, currency or style. It is all to the capitalist good, of course, that such magic wears off. A single dose is never enough: you need to keep consuming. This is not a question of being materialistic, William suggests (1980: 185). If we really were *materialistic* about consumption, we would drink beer because it quenched our thirst – not because it was 'reassuringly expensive' (at one end of the taste spectrum), or 'what mates do' (at another). The 'taste' of beer, that is, is as much a symbolic as a sensory matter. Following Williams, consumers are not simply interested in material objects *as* material objects, but as an array of signs and their meanings.

Williams' treatment of advertising is a mid-twentieth-century update on Marx's account of commodity fetishism, highlighting the role of an exemplary modern industry in the ideological work of capitalist exchange. The economy of signs, however, refers to a more extended process. It is not simply that advertisers add on meaning, fix aesthetic hooks into otherwise fairly undistinguished products, but that the process of making meaning and creating signs is at work from the earliest stages of production. In Lash and Urry's account, aesthetic or cultural factors are not only relevant to practices of consumption, but also to the production process. This is obviously true in the case of aesthetic goods and services, but is also evident in the production of more conventional goods. The economic role of culture, that is, goes beyond the framework of values, trends and associations which steers consumer choice. It shapes the way that products are conceived, designed, made and used.

It is worth returning, here, to our discussion in the previous chapter of Michel Aglietta's treatment of the commodity aesthetic of Fordism. As Aglietta (1979: 155) argues, 'since consumption is a material process, it is located in space; it has a specific geography and object-network'. In his account of Fordism, this spatial organisation was based on the separation between workplace and home, and the growth of the suburbs as the primary site of consumption. The network of relations between individuals and between objects was mediated by mass commodities – the car, the suburban home and its contents. A similar argument might run in relation to newer economies of signs and space, which also possess their own geography and object-network. This is a geography where the separation between home and workplace has become less clear – given increasing urban gentrification and the vogue for live/work spaces, telecommuting or telecottaging, the growth of freelance labour and cultural work, and the wiring of the workplace into the electronic world outside. So too, the signal commodities of this economy are electronic, aesthetic and informational goods which form the direct link between production and consumption. To put Aglietta's argument simply: the Fordist worker made cars on an assembly line, he then bought one of these cars from a suburban car-yard so that he could drive to work and make more of them. The emblematic Fordist object – the motor-car – mediated a geography based on the spatial separation of home, work-place and sites of mass consumption. The Microsoft worker, meanwhile, produces software that enables her to 'work from home', in the nice catch-phrase of the time; she can even consume other immaterial goods (music, images, information) while she's at work. As an exemplary post-Fordist object, the personal computer collapses the spatial distance between work and home, and the temporal separation of work and consumption.

These arrangements also link to certain models of time. Fordist time, at least in principle, was regular and regulated – oriented to the long produc-tion run, the standard working day and working week, shift-work and over-time, annual holidays, the clear demarcation between work time and leisure and consumption time. In the post-Fordist economy, time is less organised: it is typified by just-in-time production; the constant deadline; the 24-hour working day; the 24/7 working week; the dissolving boundary between working and non-working time. Shift-work and overtime lose their meaning (and often their monetary value) outside a concept of the 'normal' working day. In increasingly competitive job markets for freelance workers and cor-porate high-flyers, time off has become something like industrial 'down-time' under the old Fordist system, when the technology sits idle and no value gets produced. Bell (1973) had warned of the problem of time scarcity in the post-industrial economy. It is not simply that time is scarce or 'sped-up' in this context: it is de-differentiated (see also Thrift 2002b). The dis-organisation of productive and working time is also reflected on the side of consumption. Lash and Urry (1994: 16) speak of the 'video paradigm' which is characteristic of the economy of signs, 'where attention spans are short, and events jumbled out of narrative order via re-wind, fast forward and channel hopping'. This is another spin on the ideas of time–space com-pression and distanciation we saw in earlier discussions, as the broad seg-mentation of time into tranches of work and non-work activity is displaced by fragmentary bits of time, as the lines drawn between work and play become hard to discern.

From non-material products to 'nothings'

There is a danger that such an approach to the symbolic or 'immaterial' economy may slide into a fairly breathless account of élite economic practices, cutting-edge technology and hip cultural style. A more pessi-mistic argument about the role of non-material products in contemporary economic life is to be found in George Ritzer's (2004) work on *The Globalization of Nothing*. For Ritzer, the production and consumption of non-material goods and services is not primarily a matter of highly skilled knowledge work, design intensity, or informed aesthetic distinctions. His argument here continues the line he developed in his earlier accounts of the 'McDonaldization' of society (see Ritzer 1993, 2002a), targeting the creeping rationalisation and homogenisation of social and economic life. Ritzer contends that contemporary economic exchange, particularly under conditions of globalisation, is increasingly premised on the production and circulation of 'nothing' – 'social forms that are comparatively devoid of distinctive substantive content' (2004: xi). These may include material objects or physical locales, but such 'nothings' are easily substitutable, and easily replicated across different sites. They do not necessarily remind either worker or consumer of exactly where they are. In contrast to the reflexive model of consumption outlined above, 'nothings' are suited to those instances of consumption when the objective is, precisely, *not* to have to think.

Ritzer divides these forms of 'nothing' into four types: non-places, non-things, non-people, and non-services. Non-places, firstly, refer to such sites as the shopping mall, chain hotel, fast-food outlet, café franchise, theme park or airport departure lounge. These are uniform spaces which lack any particular or local sense of place. One uses and experiences such non-places in standard ways, regardless of whether they are situated in Beijing, Brasilia or Boston (see also Augé 1995). Non-things, secondly, include global brands in clothing, coffee or mass-produced foods. These are material goods, to be sure, but the object is secondary to or subsumed by the brand, lacking any real distinguishing quality as a thing in itself. Non-people, thirdly, are required by those jobs that take a growing employment share in contemporary economies. These are 'junk jobs' in low-grade or highly routine services and manufacturing, in call centres and other non-places (see also Ritzer 2002b). Real people, of course, fill these jobs, but the nature of the work tends to limit skills, over-regulate the labour process, and render the worker invisible. Non-services, fourthly, are exemplified by various types of self-service, including automated teller machines, automated telephone systems and Internet shopping. Here there is not even a non-person on the other side of the counter or telephone line. In fact, the 'service' is largely performed by the consumer themselves, via a technological rather than a social exchange. The shift to e-commerce, automated and self service suggests that the human factor in many service exchanges is at least secondary, and often wholly dispensable.

Ritzer argues that it is these forms of 'nothing' – uniform, mass-produced, routine, disembodied – which are generated in increasing numbers in contemporary capitalist economies. They are especially suited to the modes of electronic exchange, branding, outsourcing, licensing, subcontracting and dispersed production that characterise the global economy. Ritzer rejects the notion that the consumption of 'nothings' (McDonalds burgers, mall shopping, franchised reality TV) is somehow coded as lower class. Indeed, they are well adapted to the 'speeded-up' and 'stretched-out' experience of those actors who are looped into global networks – drinking their branded coffee while managing their on-line bank account in an international transit lounge. In contrast, local 'somethings' – good, services or places that retain a distinctive, substantive or embedded quality – are harder to find, harder to make and harder to sell. Such a thesis might be seen as unduly melancholic, sentimental or nostalgic. It is not clear, after all, that old-style 'Moms and Pops' cafés made better coffee or better employers than the super-chains that displaced them. Ritzer's account is certainly intended as a polemic. It would be hard to contest, though, that his argument grasps a critical feature of global economic production and exchange. This is not to deny that local or national economies also deal in 'non-things' or employ 'non-people'; however Ritzer's point is that the globalising economy has both the capacity and the tendency to produce and circulate such 'nothings' on a greatly expanded scale. The commodity aesthetic at work here, it might be argued, is also one that produces its own object-network and its peculiar geography. It is mediated everyday by countless foot-soldiers clutching their Starbucks take-out, an emblematic object dislocated from any particular place but reproduced throughout the space of flows.

Culture and economy

The accounts offered by Lash and Urry, or by Ritzer, emphasise the cultural contexts and content of contemporary economic life. Economic sociology – from Veblen or Weber onwards – has long had a critical concern with the relation of economy to culture (see DiMaggio 1994; Swedberg 1991). At the same time, the 'cultural turn' which has taken place in social analysis over the last two decades has in part been understood as a turn *away* from the economic. The contention here is that an expanding interest in cultural questions within the social sciences has gone together with deepening scepticism and growing indifference towards older economic arguments. It has become a truism of contemporary analysis that other relationships and processes are at least as important as economic factors, and often more so, in the formation of social identities and the reproduction of social inequalities (see Chapters 6 and 7). It is not only or even primarily in the realm of the economic that we form our relations to ourselves and to others, create meaning, act out our social fate or encounter the workings of power. No-one, it seems, would argue otherwise now. The critique of economism, however, has left some unresolved problems – one being a tendency to dismiss economic explanations altogether (so that *any* argument about class, for example, can appear as 'reductionist' or simply out-dated); another being the inability to recognise or properly account for economic issues when they do arise. Such problems seem especially pronounced in debates over the relation between economy and culture. If we are now agreed that the cultural is not simply an effect of, or an alibi for, economic arrangements, it is less clear how we are to think about the relation between the two.

The question of the link between economy and culture has recently received new emphasis. Indeed, there are signs that the latest twist in the cultural turn may be a move back towards economic concerns. Such a trend is evident across a number of fields, with growing critical interest in economic and cultural globalisation, in the creative and cultural industries, in branding and intellectual property, in cultural work and the socioeconomic role of the 'creative' classes. This array of themes can be seen as part of a larger project to rethink the relation of culture to economy 'after' the cultural turn (see Ray and Sayer 1999). As Lash and Urry's work suggests, a concern with cultural processes does not simply displace economic issues from the field of inquiry; it may, however, pose different problems and demand fresh lines of analysis. In this context, Slater (2002: 75–6) cautions that 'the appropriate methodological response is not an "additive" one, a matter of adding traditional questions of political economy to a fundamentally cultural analysis, or an argument about the increased centrality of cultural industries in contemporary economy'.

This caveat reveals a persistent nervousness that, in any encounter between economy and culture, one or the other will appear as merely supplementary. Between the twin errors of economic reduction on one side and cultural triviality on the other, there remains uncertainty as to the terms on which economic and cultural analysis should meet. It is now some time since Stuart Hall (1988: 28) asserted that the distinction between economic and cultural change had become 'quite useless. Culture has ceased to be, if it ever was, a decorative addendum to the "hard world" of production and things, the icing on the cake of the material world.' Cultural factors after all are not restricted to matters of consumption but also bear on the side of production – in the design of goods and the styling of services – and on that of distribution – in the way that products are conceived for, positioned in or even themselves create markets (see Lash and Urry 1994; du Gay and Pryke 2002b). The making of meaning, the production and exchange of signs, runs through different stages of the economic process. These are important arguments and they look right, but they also raise a problem: the sense of the term 'culture', as it applies to these various economic moments, can become diluted – even meaningless. It is hard and may be foolish to insist on any 'stable distinction between material and cultural life' (Butler 1998: 36), but it is also difficult to specify just what is cultural about particular economic practices or objects when culture is apparently to be found everywhere in the economic process.

Such lines of definition may have blurred because critics now tend to view economic forms through a cultural lens, or it may be that contemporary capitalist economies really are more 'cultural' than they previously were. Lash and Urry (1994: 61) argue for a substantive economic shift over recent decades, noting the 'extent to which culture has penetrated the economy itself, that is, the extent to which symbolic processes . . . have permeated both consumption *and* production'. The result, they suggest, is the 'effective de-differentiation of culture and economy' (ibid.: 8), not only as analytic terms but as spheres of social practice. It is not simply that economic processes *look* different in the wake of the cultural turn: they are different. Their account represents one very influential approach to the study of economic life as this becomes more and more 'culturalised'. Writers such as du Gay and Pryke (2002b), in contrast, are less convinced that the economy has taken some substantive cultural turn of its own, preferring to examine economic arrangements and objects as cultural products in themselves. Their version of cultural economy traces the discursive feints and expert knowledge which put economic realities together. Rather than asking whether the economy has become somehow more cultural, this kind of analysis asks how economic objects – markets, firms or commodities, say – are defined and economic verities are secured as an effect of certain intellectual and expert cultures (see also Barry and Slater 2003; Callon 1998). These different approaches to the cultural analysis of the economy are based on different senses of the term 'culture': as a set of specific practices, images and things that are more or less amenable to commodification; and in a broader, anthropological sense of how systems of economic meaning and habits of economic behaviour are produced and exchanged. It involves, we might say, a split between 'substantive' and 'formal' modes for cultural analysis of the economy – one concerned with the practical role of cultural objects and processes in economic life, the other with the language, techniques and representations through which economic knowledge is reproduced and economic objects are realised (cf. Polanyi 1992; Sahlins 1972). Neither has the final say on how cultural explanations might be brought to economic problems. The first approach – as exemplified by Lash and Urry's work on the economy of signs – can be too generalised and self-consciously innovative, overstating the importance or the novelty of cultural goods and practices in contemporary economies. The second version of cultural economy – focusing on the discursive constitution of economic realities – can be too sophistic, offering a neat commentary on economics and its fellow travellers in advertising, marketing, finance and business.

Culture is a notoriously flexible concept, and this is no less true in accounts of the relation between economy and culture. Depending how you put it, the cultural aspects of economic life might refer to the aesthetic, expressive or symbolic dimensions of production and consumption; to matters of custom or habit; to processes of communication; to values, norms or meaning (see Warde 2002). In an ironic inversion of the economic approach to human behaviour in which any social action can be read as a matter of rational choice (Becker 1976; Becker and Murphy 2000), it seems that everything economic might now be viewed as an effect of cultural practice. It may be true, but ultimately it means very little, for critics to 'conclude that because economic practice is meaningful, it is thereby cultural' (Warde 2002: 185). It is impossible to think of a type of social action that wouldn't fit this bill. Is it really the case, then, that the distinction between economy and culture has become 'quite useless'? Hall's argument was directed against the old authority given to economic arguments in critical accounts of social change. The 'de-differentiation of culture and economy', however, has now become a fairly standard critical gesture, and one which is worth questioning. If we consider the broad series of shifts which have taken place in capitalist economic organisation since the second half of the twentieth century, it is evident that the role of cultural processes in economic life has been altered and in some respects enhanced. It is not so clear, however, that distinguishing cultural from economic changes is a 'useless' or artificial exercise. Of course, if we follow the anthropological sense of the term, then economic arrangements are always an element of a broader human culture (see Polanyi 1992). But if we take a restricted sense of the cultural – as a more or less well-defined sphere of practices and objects – it becomes possible to look with a little greater precision at the linkages between economic and cultural change.

Summary of key changes

The last two chapters have considered a range of theories which centre on the changing nature of production in contemporary economic life. Rather than seeing production merely as a technical sphere of economic activity, these accounts stress the wider social contexts in which production systems are embedded and products are made. In this sense, theories of Fordism and post-Fordism, post-industrial and information society, reflexive accumulation and the economy of signs, offer a larger set of perspectives on socioeconomic change since the mid to late twentieth century. They also build upon the approaches to economic globalisation considered in Part I. The final section of this book considers the impact of these diverse changes on individual and collective economic identities, and on patterns of social and economic division. Before turning from more structural accounts to these questions of individual and group effects, it may be worth reviewing some of the key shifts the preceding discussions have identified in the formation of contemporary economies. These can be detailed in a schematic way across a number of social and economic domains:

1 Production

- A decline in primary industries (both extractive and manufacturing) within advanced capitalist economies since the 1950s.
- New international division of labour (NIDL); relocation of production and assembly functions to newly industrialising economies.
- Deconcentration of industry from old industrial centres; emergence of a fragmented space economy based around new industrial districts, industrial parks and export-processing zones.

- Permanent innovation in technology; intensified role of knowledge and information in production processes.
- Shift towards flexible production based on specialised design and customised output.

2 Consumption

- Increasing importance of consumption as an economic driver.
- Expansion of production and services geared to consumer markets.
- Consumption patterns arguably more highly individualised (Lash and Urry), *or* more standardised (Ritzer).
- Privatised consumption of public and collective goods.
- Intensified links between consumption choices and the formation of individual identities.

3 Knowledge

- Knowledge increasingly commodified as an economic product.
- Ascendancy of 'knowledge élites' in the form of professional, managerial and high-level technical workers.
- Control over knowledge linked to economic and social power.
- Enhanced role of information technology in production, consumption and exchange.
- Heightened role of reflexivity in production, consumption and labour processes.

4 Work

- Decline of mass labour in semi-skilled industrial jobs.
- Growth of service sector.
- New international division of labour.
- Polarisation between high-skilled and low-skilled jobs in both production and services.
- Erosion of the distinctions between working and non-working time, work and consumption.

5 Space

- Globalisation of capital, production, consumption and some labour markets.
- Shift from national economies to international economy in respect of both market and regulatory processes.
- Decline of industrial centres; growth of new industrial districts and global cities.

- Electronic communications and advanced transport technologies coordinate economic exchanges within a 'structure of flows'.
- New core–periphery relations based on integration into or exclusion from global networks.

6 *Culture*

- Growing commodification of culture.
- Interpenetration of culture and economy.
- Enhanced role of design, aesthetics and styling in production processes.
- Increasingly cultural content of both material and immaterial goods.
- Centrality of the cultural as a field of both consumption and work.

These factors can be seen to add up to the 'disorganisation' of the economic, social and spatial arrangements which structured advanced capitalist economies during the middle decades of the twentieth century (see Offe 1985a; Lash and Urry 1987). The distinction between 'organised' and 'disorganised' forms of capitalism – like the distinctions between industrial and post-industrial societies, the first and the second industrial divide, or Fordist and post-Fordist economies – is a useful analytic device for tracing processes of socioeconomic change. It describes a set of strong social and economic *tendencies* which vary, often quite substantially, over time and space. Such tendencies are always incomplete, uneven, and subject to reversals. Ford's workers still make motor cars on assembly lines (although admittedly not many in Michigan); national governments still enact economic policies; a significant amount of consumption remains at subsistence level or even just 'ordinary' rather than specialised; sweatshops may be viewed as features of both pre-Fordist and post-Fordist economic arrangements. What these broad schemes capture, though, are some of the crucial trends which have disorganised and re-organised capitalist processes since the latter decades of the twentieth century. They are especially pertinent, from a sociological standpoint, in tying economic changes into a broader set of social, cultural, political and spatial shifts. The chapters that follow will trace the effects of these shifts in the formation of economic identities and the reproduction of economic divisions.

Part III

Social identities and economic divisions

6 Class

The arguments developed so far have been concerned with a set of broad structural changes within contemporary economies. These final two chapters consider the impact of such large-scale processes at the level of social agents. How have recent shifts in economic organisation and systems of production remade economic divisions and social identities? The starting point for this discussion is the concept of class. While class has been a primary category of social analysis, sociologists have become sceptical about its salience as both an objective economic location and a subjective social marker. This chapter therefore examines attempts to rethink class analysis in light of the major socioeconomic changes described in the previous sections.

The discussion begins with neo-Marxist and Weberian approaches to class developed during the 1970s and 1980s to address a new set of economic and social conditions: first, the fragmentation of an industrial working class; and second, the expansion of middle-class groupings. In this sense, the analysis of post-industrial society had identified not only a shift in economic organisation from production to services, but a related shift in structures of social and economic power. More recent debates have gone on to question the validity of class as a meaningful economic measure and as a basis for self-understanding or social solidarity. It has become a truism of contemporary sociological thought that other social categories are at least as important as class, and often more so, in the formation of social identities and the reproduction of social inequalities. However, if class no longer has primacy in thinking about social differentiation, there is still a need to account for those divisions which are primarily economic in character. Although economic factors continue to shape social relations and identities, they do so in ways which frequently go beyond the established terms of class analysis. Changing patterns of work, and the tightening link between consumption and social identities, have weakened notions of class based on relations of production. This chapter outlines efforts to analyse such changes in class formation, or alternatively to explain economic divisions and social identities outside the framework of class.

These arguments can read rather differently when placed in an international setting. In the later part of the discussion, we examine class formation in the context of global economic networks. The discussion is focused on accounts of a transnational capitalist class (TCC) composed of different economic, political, professional and commercial fractions. While a number of critics have argued that it is difficult to identify coherent classes *within* societies, these analyses suggest that class interests are crucial to the organisation of the international economy. Such debates over international class formation, however, can be somewhat lopsided. Key theorists have described the formation of a transnational capitalist class whose networks and interests extend across national borders; it is harder, however, to speak of an integrated working class in the same manner. Although labour is distributed across transnational production processes, these networks are not always visible, and transnational labour is not clearly constituted on the basis of common interests. Indeed, one of the measures of class power under global conditions may be the relative coherence of capitalist class interests in contrast to the relative disconnection of less privileged class groupings.

Neo-Marxist accounts

The classical Marxist approach holds that class relations in capitalist society can be understood in terms of a central division between the bourgeoisie or capitalist class – those who own the means of production – and the proletariat or working class – those who produce surplus value through their labour. Other class fractions exist, but the relation between capital and workers is the core class relation under capitalism. As capitalism expands, this class division becomes more pronounced, while other classes (remnants of the aristocracy, the petty bourgeoisie and the peasantry) become less relevant. The development of capitalist economies over the twentieth century put this Marxist analysis into serious question, both in terms of objective class positions and of subjective class identities. Most notably, the emergence of the service economy diminished the economic and social weight of a blue-collar working class engaged in industrial production. The related growth of the middle classes, meanwhile, interposed a new mass class between capital and labour. This expanding middle class was highly differentiated in terms of their working conditions and rewards, their autonomy over the labour process, and their relative control within organisations. Such a fragmented class profile, as well as the fact that they were not directly involved in production, made it difficult to fit white-collar labour into a standard class framework. As Daniel Bell and other critics noted, the primacy of knowledge functions in a post-industrial economy meant that economic and social power were redistributed around new class fractions. From a Marxist standpoint, the historic divide between labour and capital was blurred by the increased status and power of professional, managerial and expert workers.

The expansion of the middle classes – not only (or even mainly) in high-grade knowledge and management roles, but also in more routine white-collar work – poses serious analytic problems for the Marxist bipolar model of class. Debates over these changing class structures became very charged during the 1970s, contemporary with the analysis of post-industrial society. For some Marxist critics, the white-collar or knowledge worker remained part of the working class, on the grounds that they still sold their labour in return for a wage, and lacked real control over the labour process (see Mallet 1975). For others, such as Nicos Poulantzas (1973, 1975), these fractions formed part of a new petty bourgeoisie, different from the old class of small entrepreneurs and shopkeepers in earning a salary rather than being self-employed, but sharing similar political and ideological positions (see also Westergaard and Resler 1975). This class of 'mental labour' tended to embrace ideologies of individualism and the aspiration to bourgeois status; they assumed supervisory and surveillance functions in respect of the working class; and were concerned with the circulation rather than the production of commodities. The problem that arose here for class analysis, and even more so for class politics, was that such a thesis could appear to signal the 'end' of the working class altogether (see Bauman 1982; Gorz 1982). Indeed, Erik Olin Wright (1978) argued that, under Poulantzas' definition, by 1970 around 70 per cent of US waged workers would have to be classified as members of the petty bourgeoisie. Other capitalist economies would soon catch up, as the shift from manufacturing to services accelerated. In 1950, for example, Britain was amongst the most working-class societies in the developed world, measured in terms of the proportion of its workforce (approximately half) employed in extractive and manufacturing industries. By 2005, 70 per cent of Britain's economic output was in services.

Wright himself made a more qualified argument concerning the position of the new middle class. Its members occupy 'contradictory class locations', particularly insofar as managerial workers take on some of the command and control functions of capital. At the same time, he contends, they remain excluded from real economic power in the form of capitalist ownership (Wright 1978; see also Carchedi 1977). Both ownership and control are crucial to the organisation of class relations under capitalism. Wright argues that class analysis must therefore take into account relations of both exploitation and domination. For capitalists and for workers, class positions remain quite straightforward in this respect. Capital has control over investments and the accumulation process, over the physical means of production, and over the labour power of others. Workers generally have little or no control over any of these factors. Managers, technocrats and supervisors, meanwhile, have different degrees of control over various aspects of these processes, including forms of legal ownership and command over investment and allocation decisions. Wright's analysis in this way is able to admit the significant social and economic power of certain managerial and professional strata, as well as changing patterns of capitalist ownership under which salaried executives may also own substantial capital shares (see also Wright 1985, 1997). He groups top corporate executives in with the traditional capitalist class of owners, while segmenting into different layers a corporate middle class which sits in contradictory locations between the capitalist and working classes (see also Braverman 1974). As for class politics, the position of these contradictory class fractions will only be determined in specific instances of social struggle: there is, as it were, no last instance in which class relations become self-evident as a basis for political action.

Wright's approach remains a very useful one for thinking about the degrees of autonomy and control possessed by managerial and technical workers under late capitalism. As the economy becomes more highly differentiated, such contradictory locations are likely to proliferate. Take the owner of a fast-food franchise, Wright suggests: are they a member of the petty bourgeoisie or a functionary for corporate capital? Or a university professor with a large research centre, grants and employees: are they a 'semi-autonomous employee' or a small employer? In his earlier work, Wright maintained that the large majority of service and white-collar workers had little autonomy over their labour process, let alone access to other forms of status or control. In this sense, they should be understood as working class (Wright 1978: 82–3). Here, he can be seen to take up Harry Braverman's (1974) argument that the growth of white-collar employment as a proportion of the overall labour force had gone together with a creeping 'proletarianisation' of white-collar work. Such an analysis retains real relevance over three decades later, in the era of 'McJobs' and an increasingly polarised service economy (see Ritzer 2002b; Royle 2002). Wright's later work maintains that 'the middle class is not simply a residual category of locations that do not comfortably fit the categories of "capitalist" or "worker". Rather, middle class locations in the class structure are those that are linked to the process of exploitation and domination in contradictory ways' (1997: 23). The dual focus on exploitation and domination helps to account for the class situations of those middle-class actors who have command over organisational assets as well as over the labour process of others. Indeed, Wright's analysis over time has produced increasingly more stratified models of class based on three core attributes: the ownership of capital; control over organisational resources; and skills or expert credentials (see Wright 1985, 1997). The category of credentials, it might be noted, adds a Weberian inflection to Wright's broadly Marxist approach. Taken along these lines, classes can be divided in a different way. Using the criterion of control, for instance, produces a structural split between those who own capital, those who manage organisational assets, those who supervise others' labour, and non-managing employees. The fact that this last category would include both unskilled labourers and many professional workers points to how different subclasses can be grouped together in various ways. Using the measure of credentials, in contrast, will produce alternative groupings from a definition based on access to managerial control (see Milner 1999: 101). The development of Wright's work, which has provided the basis for a large-scale comparative study across 15 countries, has therefore been towards greater complexity and contingency in the definition of class positions (see Wright 1997).

This focus on linked processes of exploitation and domination remains central to the critical analysis of class. In a recent neo-Marxist account, Stanley Aronowitz rejects the common-sense definitions under which social scientists regularly define class positions according to occupational grades or income criteria: 'What distinguishes the working class is its lack of relative power over the terms and conditions of employment' (2003: 26). Of course, the use of class proxies (such as income, occupational status or education) within empirical social research serves a different purpose from arguments concerning class power in social theory. However, Aronowitz has a point in contending that such depoliticised definitions of class have become very prevalent within social debate more generally. In his account, a divide between manual and mental labour – now re-branded as material and immaterial labour – does not undercut the argument about workers' relative lack of power. Such power is relative because 'unions do make a difference': indeed, 'immaterial workers' may be as likely as any to deploy union tactics, as walk-offs by Boeing engineers in the US or BBC employees in the UK attest (ibid.: 26, 16). Even quite privileged spheres of white-collar work, then, might be assimilated into this version of class exploitation. Aronowitz (ibid.: 10) 'proposes to define the class divide according to the line of power, which includes but is not limited to questions of ownership and control of the key means of material and immaterial production'. This line divides between a power bloc made up of certain class alliances – 'the most decisive sectors of capital, the national and international political directorate' and their camp followers (ibid.: 11) – and a diversity of 'social formations', including waged workers, the new class associated with new social movements, women, blacks and ethnic minorities. These social forms are not reducible to distinct class identities or to a single 'economic class formation', but rather cross-cut economic with social and cultural factors. In this way, Aronowitz seeks to bring together a Marxian analysis of ruling-class power with a social movement approach that does not give primacy to economic identities. This can be a rather uneasy accommodation, resulting in an ironic position where there is a more or less distinct ruling class defined by the interests of capital, but no subordinate class. Such a position bears comparison with the approaches to class and élite power in the international economy, considered later in the chapter.

Weberian analysis: market position and status

For Max Weber, modern capitalism is by definition a class society – market processes necessarily produce class divisions. However, class represents just one form in which power is distributed, together with status groups and political parties (Weber 1978). These three forms can be seen to organise economic, social and political relations respectively. Weber accepted the broad terms of Marx's definition of class as an economic relation between capital and wage labour: capitalism requires a class of propertyless workers who must sell their labour on the market. However, he rejects Marx's theory of surplus value as the key to capitalist exploitation, preferring a marginalist approach to the market as the central – and in principle neutral – mechanism ordering economic exchange. It follows that Weber saw class neither as so central to social processes, nor as so tied to social conflict. This is because classes do not constitute social groups in themselves, but simply describe a set of market locations, defined by the ownership of property and relative degrees of market power. Class situation derives from market position. Class therefore refers to 'all persons in the same class situation' (Weber 1982: 69): the sum of individuals who share common life chances, given by their position in labour, property and commodity markets. Under this scheme, capitalist markets can produce numerous class fractions based on differentials in income and property-holding. 'In principle', Weber (1982: 69) writes, 'the various controls over consumer goods, means of production, assets, resources and skills each constitute a *particular* class situation'. Weber focused on three broad class types: property classes, based on ownership of property; commercial classes, based on earning and spending power in the market; and social classes, which define the range of class positions within which individual and generational mobility typically occurs (1982: 69). In spite of the potential for markets to produce many different class positions, Weber's own account of the capitalist class structure in fact is quite consistent with Marxist categories. Weber sets out four major social classes which group together people who share common class situations. These are the working class, the petty bourgeoisie, the intelligentsia or specialists, and the privileged classes. The last two categories are particularly interesting, given the way that class analysis has more recently been challenged by the shift from manufacturing to services and the growth of the new middle class. Weber (1982: 71) includes among the class of 'propertyless intelligentsia and specialists' a range of 'technicians, various kinds of white-collar employees, civil servants – possibly with considerable social differences depending on the cost of their training'. He also notes that the privileged classes derive their position not only from property but from education. In this way, Weber points towards the changing structure of social power around the growing importance of knowledge and expert credentials in economic life.

In Weber's analysis, economic class positions do not necessarily translate into forms of social organisation. A number of conditions must hold if members of an economic class are to constitute themselves as a coherent social agent. They must first be able to identify their immediate opponent in direct conflicts of class interest. Second, a large number of people must share a common class situation. Third, it must be practically possible to coordinate the group, for example within the same physical space. Fourth, class organisations require a leadership oriented towards clearly understood goals

(Weber 1982: 72). While class groupings may, on these terms, mobilise on the basis of common interests, equally they may not act in pursuit of shared economic and political objectives – partly because class relations are shot through by other power relations based on status groupings and party solidarities. In Weber's account conflicts between status and ethnic groups have been at least as prominent as class struggles in processes of social change, particularly in non-capitalist contexts. Weber defines class in capitalist societies as an economic relation based on ownership of property and on market position, writing that ' "classes" are clearly the product of economic interests, bound up with the existence of the "market" ' (Weber 1978: 45). Class position determines people's economic life chances through the ownership of property and the capacity to generate (and spend) income. Status, in contrast, is a 'social evaluation . . . based on some common characteristic shared by many people' (1978: 48). These social evaluations do not derive simply from such economic factors as wealth or income, but involve shared 'styles of life', social networks, hereditary positions, political standings, and practices of consumption. Status confers social honour or prestige founded, in principle, on non-market hierarchies. While status may be related to class position, it is not simply determined by it. As Weber points out, for instance, money is not in itself a status qualification, although it may help you attain one. 'In practice' he accepts, 'status differentiation goes together with monopolisation of cultural and material goods and opportunities', and with the closure of these opportunities to outsiders (1978: 52). He goes on:

> One might say, therefore (with a certain amount of oversimplification) that 'classes' are formed in accordance with relations of production and the acquisition of wealth, while 'status groups' are formed according to the principles governing their consumption of goods in the context of specific 'life-styles'.
>
> (1978: 54)

The common recognition of status hierarchies means that these groupings tend to constitute self-identified social groups in a way that classes generally do not. Class, in sum, is an economic category, while status is a social category.

Contemporary economic arrangements appear well suited to a Weberian analysis of class as an effect of the market, rather than being grounded in relations of production. If neo-Marxist accounts were confounded by the shift in advanced economies from industrial production towards services, a neo-Weberian approach suggests that class is not simply given by people's location within relations of production, but by their position in various markets: their market power or market capacity. In particular, an emphasis on the capacity of education or technical credentials to command income in labour markets and goods in consumption markets can help to account for the privileged class situation of certain middle-class professionals and managers. A range of Weberian approaches to social stratification tended to dominate US and British sociology in the middle decades of the twentieth century, in both theory and empirical analysis (see Bendix and Lipset 1966; Dahrendorf 1959; Goldthorpe 1980; Lockwood 1958; Parkin 1974, 1979; Parsons 1949; Parsons and Smelser 1956). Other critical accounts have drawn on both Marxist and Weberian perspectives: two key figures to consider in this context are the British sociologist Anthony Giddens and the French sociologist Pierre Bourdieu.

Class structuration: Giddens

Although Giddens (1981) rejects the idea that his is a neo-Weberian approach to class, his account in *The Class Structure of the Advanced Societies* takes up some of Weber's central arguments to critically analyse capitalist class relations. 'Weber's work', he suggests (1981: 296), 'raises questions that must be confronted': among them, ' "the market" as a medium of class formation' and 'the social and political significance of the "new middle class" '. Following Weber, Giddens argues that capitalism is the model form of a class society, given that it is fundamentally organised around markets. It is only under capitalism that labour and commodity markets are *built into* the system of production. Exploitation and commodification through the market are at the centre of capitalist accumulation. Class therefore assumes greater significance as capitalist markets in labour, commodities and property develop. Like Weber, Giddens makes a distinction between class in terms of market position, and class as a form of group identity: a distinction, that is, between economic and social versions of class. While he agrees with Weber that classes do not form self-evident social groups, he does not accept that they are no more than a set of objective market positions or an aggregate of shared life chances. Giddens remains committed to the analysis of class identities, and to the systematic patterning of class relations under capitalism. His critical extension of Weber's work is the attempt to account for how economic class locations translate into social classes – the link, that is, between positions in the market and class as a structured social system (1981: 105).

In these terms, the constitution of class goes beyond an aggregate of particular market positions. Class is systematically structured and reproduced as a social form. What Giddens terms 'class structuration' works through different processes: (1) closure of mobility chances; (2) the division of labour; (3) the organisation of authority within the enterprise; and (4) patterns of distribution. Classes are constituted, firstly, via effects of social closure, which restrict people's mobility and access to resources (see also Parkin 1974, 1979). For Giddens, the question of mobility is basic to class formation, and the social distribution of 'mobility chances' is decisive for the structuring of class relations. The degree of closure around different market capacities shapes class relations and works to reproduce class positions across generations. Giddens identifies three principal forms of market capacity in this context: ownership of property; education or technical credentials; and labour. This notion of market capacity denotes the assets individuals bring to market exchanges, and therefore their relative market power. In crude terms, the three main market capacities – property, credentials, and labour – characterise the basic class structure of upper, middle and working classes. While closure is never total, Giddens argues that effects of mobility closure serve to reproduce distinct class positions and to restrict intergenerational mobility.

The social structuring of class relations is reinforced by the division of labour at work, and by systems of authority and control within the enterprise. Both of these factors are especially important for understanding the position of the new middle class. The divisions between manual skills, the 'general symbolic competence' required for routine clerical work, and the 'specialised symbolic skills' of technical and expert labour correspond to different forms of labour market power (Giddens 1981: 186). The organisation of authority at work, furthermore, positions members of the new middle class in contingent ways, at times inside and at times excluded from management structures. Giddens' intervention was a critical contribution to debates over how the new middle class and post-industrial work might be incorporated into class analysis. Even so, this extended way of understanding class position could already be seen in more standard empirical approaches to class. The social grade system used from the 1950s to define class in Britain defined class categories (from A to E) not only on the basis of occupation but also in terms of qualifications, income and level of responsibility. The division of labour between different work functions in this way was correlated with market capacities in the form of educational credentials and earning power, as well as with structures of managerial authority.

Giddens identifies a further component of class structuration: the influence of what he calls 'distributive groupings'. This is a critical reworking of Weber's approach to status. Weber saw status as deriving from social evaluations of honour or prestige, and reproduced through common lifestyles, social networks, and shared practices of consumption – what he called 'privileged modes of acquisition' (Weber 1982: 72). Giddens takes these arguments further by looking at how class situation may also be expressed and reproduced through practices of consumption. Modes of consumption, that is, are not merely expressive of status but serve to reinforce class as a social structure. In market societies, consumption is an economic category which is deeply shaped by class. The consumption of economic goods, then, produces certain 'distributive groupings' which reproduce and demarcate class divisions. Patterns of neighbourhood segregation, for instance, indicate that class structuration is not only determined by what happens in labour markets (see also Saunders 1990). Class positions are also reproduced in other markets, whether for housing, education or for consumer goods.

The systematic structuring of class relations is linked to particular forms of class identity. In this context, Giddens draws a distinction between 'class awareness' and 'class consciousness'. Class awareness is based on the recognition of shared values and attitudes, linked to a common style of life (1981: 111). It does not necessarily entail any sense of class allegiance, or any recognition of the existence of other classes with alternative attitudes or beliefs. In this sense it is quite consistent with the '*denial of the existence or reality of classes*', typical of middle-class values of individualism and meritocracy (ibid.: italics in original). Class consciousness, in contrast, involves the recognition of class differentiation and class identity. It takes various forms, from simple registers of class difference to a 'conflict consciousness' (more common, he thinks, in the working class) to a heightened – and rare – 'revolutionary consciousness'. Giddens' arguments in this domain are clearly influenced by Marxist thought. His reworking of Weber's analysis, however, adds a number of insights to debates over class in advanced capitalist contexts. Capitalism, firstly, remains the exemplary form of 'class society'. Class, secondly, is based on market position, which includes but is not confined to social relations of production. The distribution of chances or capacities in other markets (such as the housing market) also structures class relations. The key market capacities, and therefore the major determinants of class position, are ownership of property, educational credentials, and labour. Effects of closure around these capacities – inequalities in wealth, inequitable access to education, demarcations between different skills – limit mobility between class positions and reproduce class relations over time. Finally, as class exists not only as an economic fact but as a structured social system, it generates forms of class identity and consciousness, even if this is rarely 'revolutionary' in character. Giddens argues, contra Weber, that class-based politics has been an important force for social change in liberal societies. Moreover – and contrary to a standard Marxist analysis – he holds that it is wrong to downgrade more mundane forms of 'worker resistance as secondary and unimportant because it does not promise the imminent demolition of the capitalist mode of production' (1981: 311). These continuing struggles over rights and conditions of work demonstrate the practical articulation between economic class locations and social class identities.

Class and capital: Bourdieu

One of the most significant attempts to re-draw earlier sociological models of class is found in the work of Pierre Bourdieu. His analysis is deeply informed by both Marxist and Weberian approaches, but in itself seeks to move beyond these frameworks (see Milner 1999: 137; see also Bourdieu 1993). For Bourdieu (1987: 9), class cannot be reduced to either objective or subjective definitions: to either an 'analytical construct' or a 'folk category'. Bourdieu's work mediates between the two positions. Classes, as Weber argued, do not constitute self-evident social groups, but neither are they

simply abstract ideas. Rather they are objects and outcomes of social struggle, as people try to 'define their social identity' at the level of public representations and discourses (1987: 11). Bourdieu's own critical intervention is
to develop an analysis of class as this is reproduced through cultural practices. He defines class in terms of the possession of various forms of capital:
not only economic, but also cultural, social, and symbolic capital (see
Bourdieu 1987, 1997). These forms of capital are all critical determinants of
class membership and social status. Economic capital is the most obvious
category in play here, referring to property, income and financial assets.
However, Bourdieu insists that social analysis should address the distribution of capital in its different forms, particularly in the way these interact to
reproduce social advantages and inequalities. The other modes of capital
that Bourdieu identifies require a little more unpacking. Cultural capital,
firstly, refers to knowledge, credentials, expertise, taste or discernment. This
form of capital accumulates through the distribution, consumption and
reproduction of cultural goods, values and hierarchies, and is closely linked
to education. Cultural capital takes three forms. It is *embodied* in modes of
expression, taste preferences, bodily disposition and presentation. It is
objectified in the shape of cultural goods, and it is *institutionalised* in the
form of qualifications and credentials, honours or awards.

Social capital refers to the benefits that accrue from the membership of
social groups. It is, in turn, both practiced and socially instituted. The practical reproduction of social capital works through exchanges within social
networks, as actors draw on their contacts to access financial resources,
information or inside knowledge, employment opportunities, goods,
favours or services in kind. It is socially instituted in such forms as family
names, old school ties, political parties, social clubs or professional associations. Bourdieu argues that the accumulation of social capital relies on both
individual and collective 'investment' strategies. It can be measured in two
ways: by the extensiveness of an actor's networks, and by the capacity to
mobilise resources through these networks. Such resources – the 'profits' of
group membership – may be material (services or goods), or symbolic (prestige, social status). Symbolic capital, finally, crosses over these other forms
of capital, referring to the recognition and representation of social status
and hierarchies of distinction. It circulates in systems of meaning and signification which normalise social and economic differentials. In this sense, the
credential as a *sign* – the formal qualification or professional title – is as
much a capital asset as the expertise it is meant to denote. The neo-Weberian
theorist Frank Parkin (1979: 55) captures this point neatly when he suggests
that formal credentials can be seen as much as measures of 'class-related
qualities and attributes' as guarantees of any effective skill.

For Bourdieu, classes in contemporary societies are characterised by their
command over various forms of capital: economic, cultural, social and
symbolic. He asserts that social action – including those practices, such as
cultural consumption or education, 'purporting to be disinterested or

gratuitous' – can be understood as a set of 'economic practices directed towards the maximizing of material or symbolic profit' (1977: 183). The influence of Weber is quite visible, here, particularly his argument that status privileges can be used to monopolise economic assets and to close off social and economic opportunities to outsiders. Indeed, Bourdieu (1993: 136) cites Weber's relevance for a 'radical materialism' that seeks to analyse the economic determinants of apparently 'disinterested' behaviour in such fields as art, culture or religion. Bourdieu's own work counters both a simple economism which sees all forms of capital as reducible to economic factors, and an overly cultural approach which stresses the symbolic dimensions of social exchange while ignoring its material conditions (see Bourdieu 1997).

Class, in these terms, may be analysed not merely as an economic category but as a wider system of meaning and practices. Bourdieu captures this idea with the concept of 'habitus', a framework of social and cultural conditioning which shapes people's perceptions and actions. Habitus is 'a system of *dispositions*, that is of permanent manners of being, seeing, acting and thinking, or a system of *long-lasting* . . . structures of perception, conception and action' (Bourdieu 2002: 27; see also Bourdieu and Wacquant 1992). Common schemes of acting and thinking are typical of groups who share similar positions in social space. They constitute 'a set of acquired characteristics which are the product of social conditions and which, for that reason, may be totally or partially common to people who have been the product of similar social conditions' (2002: 29): in this sense, modes of habitus tend to be shared by people who occupy the same class position. Habitus both guides and is reproduced through everyday practices, norms and values, bodily conduct and taste cultures – from accents to political opinions to sexual mores or ethical habits. It therefore refers to the complex of ways through which class is produced both materially and culturally. Bourdieu (1977: 85) argues that class must be understood in relation to both 'a system of objective determinations' and 'the class habitus, the system of dispositions (partially) common to all products of the same structures'. This theory of class constitution is worked out empirically in Bourdieu's classic work on *Distinction*, a detailed study of cultural tastes and practices in three urban centres in France in the 1970s. Bourdieu begins by mapping different social classes in terms of the social distribution of various forms of capital. He identifies three major class groupings – the dominant class, the middle class, and the popular class – subdivided into various class fractions (Bourdieu 1984: 16–17). These class locations can be correlated with different 'zones of taste' which shape cultural preferences and consumption. In this way, even the most 'disinterested or gratuitous' practices – listening to music, say, or watching sport – are tied to forms of cultural and symbolic capital. Social differentiation operates not only on the basis of structural economic factors, but through symbolic associations within the realm of culture. Such modes of class distinction compound social inequalities with symbolic judgements – 'peremptory verdicts which, in the name of taste, condemn to ridicule, indignity, shame, silence ... men and women who simply fall short, in the eyes of their judges, of the right way of being and doing' (Bourdieu 1984: 511).

Bourdieu's work on this level can be read as a critical rethinking of Weber's distinction between class and status. Weber had contended that capitalist societies were characterised by class relations derived from the market rather than by status relations. As capitalist markets developed, societies should become more clearly organised along class lines while status distinctions became less prominent. Market logics, after all, do not recognise status hierarchies or questions of honour: just the colour of your money. This argument, however, overlooks the way that economic relations are structured by and help to reproduce social evaluations, most notably via forms of discrimination based on race, ethnicity or gender. It also understates the extent to which class and status interact within contemporary capitalist societies. In Bourdieu's term, the two are barely separable: 'Position in the classification struggle depends on position in the class structure' (1984: 484). Struggles over classification, what is more, are part of the struggle through which groups seek to identify themselves in class terms. Bourdieu is close to Weber when he argues that classes exist only 'on paper', as formal categories, unless and until they manage to organise themselves through forms of social identification and political mobilisation. The relation between class as an economic division and class as a social identity is a question of practical organisation and political struggle.

Changing formations of class and work

These various reworkings of Marxist and Weberian theory aimed to address changes in production, work and stratification in late capitalist economies while retaining class as a central category of analysis. The expansion of the service sector, the gradual decline of industrial production, and the growth and diversification of the middle classes posed new challenges for – but did not invalidate – both class analysis and class politics. Other critics, however, have questioned the continuing relevance of class as a means of understanding social divisions and identities (see Laclau and Mouffe 1987; Pakulski and Waters 1996; Waters 2000; cf. Crompton *et al.* 2000; Day 2000; Lee and Turner 1996a). Giddens' own account of class under advanced capitalism would alter quite notably over time. In later work he argued that, while capitalist societies continue to be divided around economic class, social class identity has greatly diminished (see Giddens 1994). Market relations have only intensified as more and more aspects of contemporary life come under the sway of the market, but this does not mean that class consciousness has become any more pronounced. On the contrary, in advanced capitalist societies class consciousness has come to seem old hat – disappearing as traditional working-class occupations disappear, diluted by the aspirational rhetoric of market populism, pacified by a centrist politics that goes 'beyond left and right'.

Giddens' argument in *Beyond Left and Right* challenges several aspects of his earlier approach to class. While contemporary capitalism continues to stratify individuals around different market positions, he suggests that class has become less connected to 'communal experience'. Even the basic recognition of shared life chances has weakened. The category of class therefore needs to be rethought in a number of ways:

1   Class positions tend to be experienced more in terms of 'individual biography' and less in terms of 'collective fate' (1994: 143). The various constraints and opportunities that derive from people's social and economic locations are less likely to be understood in terms of class. The basis for class identity has eroded as collective narratives or solidarities give way to wider effects of individualisation. It follows that the link between economic class and social class, which had been critical to Giddens' earlier work, is now much harder to make.

2   Relations of production and work are less relevant to social identities and divisions, while consumption has become more crucial. As Giddens (1994: 143) puts it: 'The individual relates to the class system not just as a producer but as a consumer. Lifestyle and taste . . . become as evident markers of social differentiation as position in the productive order'. While he hangs onto the language of 'class' here, Giddens' argument is closer to a neo-Weberian account of status as a social position that is reproduced through consumption practices (see also Turner 1988). Consumption is increasingly integral to the formation of social identities, while modes of social differentiation refer less to economic positions than to symbolic associations.

3   Class problems are less likely to be shared across generations. In contrast to his earlier arguments concerning the reproduction of class positions over time, Giddens suggests that class is no longer experienced as a sort of generational legacy. The various injuries associated with class tend to come 'laterally', from current market processes, rather than as an intergenerational effect (ibid.: 144). The contemporary class problems which individuals experience – job insecurity, lack of affordable housing, welfare retrenchment – in this sense may be quite different from those of their parents' generation.

4   Social mobility through the market, both upward and downward, means that class has become less of a 'lifetime experience'. In contemporary market contexts the closure of mobility chances between class positions tends to be less rigid. Class locations therefore may alter not only between generations, but even within individual biographies.

5   Exclusion from the labour market is a significant basis of economic inequality and insecurity. It follows that class analyses which are based on market position or on the social relations of production both

overlook a major line of division in contemporary societies. Inclusion and exclusion in respect of work is just as relevant to the analysis of inequality as are people's relative positions within processes of production and exchange. The idea that class derives from people's degrees of market power overlooks the fact that large numbers of people are simply excluded from employment, property or consumer markets.

Taken together, these factors suggest that class patterns have been restructured in complicated ways while class consciousness has gone into (possibly terminal) decline. The point remains, however, that capitalist markets continue to extend and entrench: expanding across geographical space and into previously non-market sectors, notably that of public services. In advanced capitalist economies, labour and property markets tend to be highly competitive and increasingly stratified. The contest for market position can be intense and individuals' market power very precarious. In such a heightened market system, a Weberian concern with market position still offers real insights into social divisions and inequalities. This kind of analysis suggests that, while class may be less clearly based on people's relationship to the means of production, it is very evident in their relationship to the means of distribution. The distribution of social and economic goods, whether via the market or the state, continues to be stratified around class. Members of the new and the old middle class have a privileged relation to labour, property and investment markets – and the middle classes have always had a privileged relation to the state and public provision. In postindustrial labour markets, access to knowledge and expert credentials becomes a major determinant of market power. Patterns of ownership have also changed radically in late capitalist societies, as more members of the middle class own real estate, stock options and share capital, especially through pension funds. Middle-class strata are also well-positioned in relation to state services, especially in the domain of education (see Ball 2003; Bourdieu 1996; Devine 2004; Halsey *et al.* 1997).

Indeed, there is a case to argue that some contemporary capitalist societies are growing more class divided around the kind of market capacities and credentials Giddens and others have identified (see Crompton *et al.* 2000; Lee and Turner 1996b; Perrucci and Wysong 2003; Westergaard 1995). For example, recent research comparing rates of intergenerational mobility within North American and European societies has indicated that mobility is significantly lower in Britain and the United States than it is in Canada or the Nordic countries (Blanden *et al.* 2005). Such findings tend to counter conventional views of the United States as a high-mobility culture; in this context, what is more, inequalities of class and race overlap, as patterns of mobility appear more restricted for black Americans than for white Americans (see Bowles *et al.* 2004). Intergenerational mobility has shown a marked decline in Britain since the late twentieth century, against a backdrop of rising inequality (see also Hills and Stewart 2004; Thompson 2004).

Tracking parents' and children's income over time, Blanden *et al.* suggest that their cohort of men born in 1958 were more likely to leave their parents' income class than men born in 1970. Education may be promoted as the primary impetus for social mobility, but this research shows that access to educational credentials continues to be stratified in quite stark ways. In spite of government efforts over more than two decades to promote education as the basis for equality of opportunity, particularly through the expansion of higher education, children from more affluent families are still over-represented at university, while those from low-income backgrounds remain severely under-represented (see also Ball 2003; Devine 2004). The percentage of children from the wealthiest quarter of all families who had completed a degree by the age of 23 rose from 20 per cent at the beginning of the 1980s to almost half by the end of the 1990s. Over the same period, the number of graduates from the poorest quarter rose just three points from 6 to 9 per cent (Blanden *et al.* 2005).

The uneven distribution of educational credentials produces real differences in labour market power (see Leicht 2005). In this context, it is highly questionable how far work has diminished in importance as a ground for economic divisions and social identities. It may be true that the growth of the service economy and the increasing role of consumption have seen a shift away from production as *the* fundamental economic relation: it does not follow, however, that work has been wholly displaced as a 'key sociological category' (Offe 1985b). Debates over the social and economic primacy of work have gone through various cycles since the 1980s. Within social theory, they stem in particular from 'post-Marxist' arguments that production and labour could no longer be seen as the fundamental basis of social organisation (see Laclau and Mouffe 1987). The decentring of production disrupted traditional class structures and an associated politics of class, as evident in the decline of labour movements and of class-based electoral politics (see Bauman 1982; Gorz 1982). Such arguments went together with a commitment to alternative modes of analysis concerned with inequalities and identities formed along lines of gender, race or ethnicity; and with social movements that went beyond class politics. In these terms, Claus Offe (1985b) questioned the status of work on two levels. On an objective level, work could no longer be seen as the primary structure of social organisation. On a subjective level, work was no longer central to individual identities. Offe's argument rests on several core assertions that appear more widely in debates over work. First, the growing differentiation of work functions, especially evident in the shift from industrial to service work, has made it difficult to speak about 'work' in generalising terms. Second, the social structural importance of work has weakened as the spheres of leisure, consumption, education and personal life become more separate from the domain of work. Third, individuals increasingly seek meaning and satisfaction outside of work, especially through consumption practices. Work identities are therefore less significant as a basis for individual self-definitions.

Finally, the differentiation of work functions and growing dis-identification from work as a source of selfhood have both weakened the capacity for work to provide a frame for collective action, particularly in class terms. Overall, Offe traced a broad shift in social organisation from 'work society' to a consumer or culture society; the gradual displacement of production by consumption as the key socioeconomic domain (see also Bauman 1998; Offe 1984). This 'crisis of work society' meant that social analysis had to give up its lingering fixation on labour and production as the basis of social structure, and to shrug off any residual Marxist hangover. In the same move, it put into serious doubt the relevance of class analysis based on categories of work or relations of production.

Offe's argument captures the main elements of a wider critique of 'productivism' in social theory, as well as core doubts over the relevance of work in contemporary contexts. There are, however, grounds for questioning his approach. Offe's primary contention was that the growing differentiation of work functions meant the concept of work no longer held together as a coherent category. Different kinds of work were just *too* different to be meaningfully compared. There is nothing especially new, however, about the differentiation of work. Segmented labour markets are typical of capitalist economies, and one can argue that this process of differentiating work and workers has been critical to capitalist control over the labour process. The major line of division, in Offe's account, was that between production and service work, as well as internal gradations within the field of services. He argued that the shift to services made it difficult to measure workers' productivity or efficiency in any standard way, and in this sense harder to rationalise managerial control over the labour process. As we have seen in previous chapters, however, service work has proved very amenable to reflexive methods of work surveillance, audit and self-regulation. These individualising modes of control have dual effects, imposing 'over-investment in work' by individual workers while at the same time serving to 'weaken or destroy collective references and solidarity' (Bourdieu 1998c: 97–8). This latter point may indeed undermine the links between work and class identities, but it does not decrease the centrality of work to social organisation. Offe's larger argument about a systemic shift from production to consumption, meanwhile, obscures the way that the production of consumption goods and services is central to contemporary processes of economic accumulation. Consumption, that is, is not simply about what people do when they are not working: increasing numbers of people are employed in the 'production' of consumption.

More recent social theory can appear rather ambivalent about the role of work in contemporary capitalist societies. Manuel Castells, for example, represents a common view when he asserts that individuals 'increasingly organize their meanings not around what they do but on the basis of what they are, or believe they are' (2000a: 3). Personal identity becomes more important as forms of social collectivity – whether organisations, institutions or class affiliations – lose their relevance as sources of meaning. Elsewhere, however, Castells contends that the 'process of work is at the core of social structure', and that *'paid working time* structures social time' (Castells 2000a: 216, 470; see also Muirhead 2004). In her analysis of contemporary cultural economies, meanwhile, Angela McRobbie (2002a, 2002b) makes the critical argument that work in fact has become more central to people's self-understandings (see also du Gay 1996). Her account supports Bourdieu's treatment of the way personal over-investment in work can go together with a weakening of collective references, suggesting that the individual's investment in work has come to replace any notion of the social as a source of security, politics or meaning. In largely un-unionised sectors where terms of employment are often *ad hoc*, where a high premium is placed on personal enterprise, and where would-be creative workers are subject to 'permanently transitional' jobs, the social frameworks offered by trade unions, labour regulations, equal opportunity policies or any collective kinds of politics tend to be absent (see especially McRobbie 2002b; see also Capelli 1999).

It is particularly pertinent to consider the growth of cultural work in this context. Daniel Bell (1978) identified the 'cultural mass', involved not only in the production but the distribution of cultural goods and services, as an increasingly important segment of the post-industrial economy. The role of cultural sectors in advanced capitalist economies has greatly expanded in the intervening period. These trends in cultural production and exchange sit in an interesting relation to the putative economic shift from production to consumption. Arguments that advanced economies were undergoing a transition from *Arbeitsgesellschaft* to *Kulturgesellschaft* – from 'work society' to 'culture society' – did not always foresee the extent to which culture would become colonised *as work* (see Offe 1984; Schwengel 1990; see also Beck 2000b; McRobbie 1999). Work in the creative or cultural sectors of the economy can blur the differences between work and non-work, the professional and the private self, work ethic and consumer style. It may be outdated to talk about the realm of necessity as distinct from the realm of freedom – and simplistic to treat as economic those things we do because we have to, and the cultural as those things we do because we want to – but fudging these distinctions can offer practical means for regulating workers in the cultural economy. Conventional ways of thinking about work do not always apply to jobs which confuse the separation of leisure from labour, consumption from production, creativity from drudgery. Discourses of creativity can help to normalise flexible labour processes, as the open-ended nature of creative work lends itself to long or erratic working hours, casualisation, demanding deadlines and constantly changing briefs. In this setting the linkage of cultural work to ideas of self-expression provides a basis for more or less willing self-exploitation on the part of workers, while the aura of the creative workplace helps to mask or dilute power relations between management and staff (Nugent 2004). An emphasis on personal creative style, furthermore, can offer a new means of reproducing rather standard lines of discrimination based on gender, ethnicity or age (see Sennett 1998). This complex of factors – the uncertain boundaries of work, the flexible associations of creative labour, the premium placed on individual talent – tends to promote over-investment in work while potentially undermining any sense of collective enterprise. Moreover, the aesthetic appeal of certain kinds of creative labour can overshadow the real world of work for large numbers of people engaged in the production of consumption. A growing body of critics have analysed the underside of work in the creative economy, focusing, for example, on casualised and sweated labour in the fashion industry (Bonacich and Applebaum 2000; Klein 2000; McRobbie 1998; Ross 1997), or the actual exploitation of 'virtual' workers in new media domains (Head 2003; Ross 1998).

How then might we think more systematically about the organisation of work in contemporary capitalist economies? One influential scheme comes from Robert Reich's (1991) work on the 'three jobs of the future'. Reich's model takes on the changes associated with post-industrialism, while continuing to see work structures as decisive for economic and social organisation. His analysis is based on emergent patterns in US labour markets, but the broad analytic categories he develops have wider relevance to other economic settings. These categories are understood in two ways: in terms of the division of work within the domestic economy; and the relation of these different grades of work to international economic processes. Reich argues that US labour markets in the twenty-first century will be characterised by three major spheres of work: symbolic-analytic work, routine production, and in-person services. Symbolic analysts include scientists, technicians and other academics; engineers and architects, executives and business consultants, high-level workers in media and culture. Their work deals in knowledge, information and symbols, with the kinds of cognitive and aesthetic goods that drive Lash and Urry's economy of signs. They represent the advantaged minority in current labour markets (Reich put them at about one-fifth of all US workers in 1990) – educated knowledge workers who are well positioned in relation to international economic networks, and potentially have access to international labour markets.

Routine production workers, meanwhile, are employed in semi-skilled labour in manufacturing, processing, distribution and administration. This category groups together production and service workers – such work is defined, therefore, not so much by the nature of the product as by the nature of the labour process. It is repetitive, relatively low-skilled and routine: these employees work on assembly lines and factory floors, in back offices and call centres. Reich put their number at around one-quarter of the US labour force at the start of the 1990s. In-person service workers, finally, are engaged in direct service provision. These workers wait tables or drive cabs; work as janitors, hospital orderlies, car-park attendants or security guards; they provide care for children, the chronically ill or for old people. This category, on Reich's reckoning, accounted for around one-third of all US workers by 1990. The remaining 20 per cent of US workers were distributed across other occupational categories, from farmers to craftspeople or small businesses. While these sectors will continue to employ people, Reich's argument is that the major labour market divisions of the twenty-first-century economy are likely to settle around his three broad spheres of employment: knowledge and symbolic work; routine production and service functions; and personal services.

Reich arrives at this model by grouping together different work functions into a set of overarching categories. These categories are broad and uneven, to be sure. Not all symbolic-analytic workers are well positioned in domestic labour markets, let alone in the global economy. The gradual downgrading of teaching, for example, or the casualisation of many cultural workers, tends to undercut more heightened accounts of the social and economic privileges of knowledge work (see Frank 2000). However, Reich sketches a general view of a divided labour market which seriously advantages certain categories of work – and therefore certain workers – over others. In particular, these three spheres of work involve different relations to globalising economic processes. The skills associated with high-grade symbolic-analytic work tend to be mobile; such workers frequently operate within international labour markets, or are engaged in the exchange of information and symbolic goods across international networks. Routine production workers, in contrast, are particularly vulnerable to economic restructuring and relocation, downsizing and retrenchment. The routine nature of such work means that it is relatively easy to transfer it from workers in one site to different workers in another. Such transfers of routine work are seen in the outsourcing of semi-skilled production or telephone services to lower-cost markets, whether inter-state or overseas. Finally, while personal service workers are often the least secure in contemporary labour markets – most likely to be low-paid, casualised, non-unionised and untrained – jobs of this kind are produced in growing numbers, and appear set to take an expanding employment share in twenty-first-century economies. It is notable in this connection that demand from symbolic-analysts for a range of personal services, from domestic workers to waiters, tends to create high volumes of work in this sphere.

Reich's model of changing structures of work has quite clear implications for differentials of economic reward and security in contemporary labour markets. However, this analysis is not developed in distinct class terms. A more recent account by Perrucci and Wysong (2003) considers the US employment structure as the basis for a 'new class society'. Their work can be clearly linked to that of Bourdieu, as they define class in relation to the possession of different forms of capital: consumption capital (or income); investment capital (wealth); skill capital (education or human capital); and social capital (networks). They divide class in the United States into two basic camps, the 'privileged class' and the 'new working class'. While this is a very familiar model, such a class divide is not based simply on ownership or non-ownership of property. Rather, these class categories involve uneven distributions of different types of capital. As such, they can be further divided into various class fractions (see Perrucci and Wysong 2003: 27–9).

The privileged class has extensive command over various forms of capitals, in respect of property and income, expertise and credentials, and social networks. It is constituted by two significant groups:

1   A 'superclass' of old-style capitalist owners, which accounts for around 1–2 per cent of the US population.
2   A credentialed class which is less clearly defined by investment or property wealth, but commands considerable amounts of income capital, skill capital and social capital. This fraction includes high-level managers and CEOs, accounting for around 13–15 per cent of the population, and élite professionals, numbering around 4–5 per cent. Although the class position of these groups may not be based on the possession of investment capital, they are able to mobilise other forms of capital – especially credentials – to gain access to this kind of wealth, accruing property and investments. In this way they bear out Bourdieu's (1987) argument that different forms of capital may be converted into each other.

Taken together, this 20 per cent represent the 'privileged class' in contemporary US society. This top fifth of the population, the authors argue, saw an increase in its share of national wealth between 1980 and 1999. The remaining four-fifths, in contrast, saw their shares decline over the same period (Perrucci and Wysong 2003: 54).

The other 80 per cent of the population, then, is characterised as the 'new working class'. It incorporates a number of different subgroups:

3   The 'comfort class' is made up of public sector workers in relatively secure employment (such as teachers, police officers or civil servants), small business-people, and skilled trades. This group tends to do fairly well in income terms, earning the average income and above. Wage-earners in this class are more likely to be in unionised sectors, and have relatively secure conditions of work. Overall, however, this grouping has fairly little access to investment capital. Perrucci and Wysong estimate they represent around 10 per cent of the population at the start of the twenty-first century.

The majority of the population are members of the 'contingent classes'. These include:

4   The mass of wage-earners – those working in clerical or sales jobs, in routine services or production. This group of workers has seen a

decrease in their job security in recent years, as well as in their relative earnings. Such workers may have reasonable levels of skill or credentials (Perrucci and Wysong note, for instance, that this category often includes college graduates), but are not able to convert this into significant levels of income. This class fraction accounts for something like 50 per cent of the US population.

5   A small number of self-employed workers experience a similar state of contingency or insecurity. This includes self-employed people with no waged employees or running a family business; they tend to bear a high degree of personal economic risk and have relatively low economic security. Perrucci and Wysong put this group at around 3–4 per cent of the total.

6   The excluded class, finally, is made up of the under-employed and unemployed, who experience acute economic insecurity, often in conditions of poverty. Members of this class have little access to any kind of capital; they may be very reliant on their social networks, but are largely unable to mobilise resources or opportunities through these networks. This excluded class accounts for as many as 10–15 per cent of the US population.

Beneath the broad two-class model, then, Perrucci and Wysong's analysis takes in a complex of factors that produce class differentials. Social class is based on a set of relations to different forms of capital; it is also defined by degrees of economic security. It is not only types of work but exclusion from work that determines people's position in this structure. In view of older arguments about the declining significance of both class and work, moreover, their argument is that these economic divisions have become more entrenched in the United States, as the distribution of wealth in the world's richest nation becomes increasingly lopsided. Contrary to any notion of the 'end' of class, US society can be understood in terms of the anatomy of a 'new class society' marked by pronounced inequalities. While Perrucci and Wysong may draw on an analytic language of class, however, it is not clear that these economic categories line up with recognisable social groups. The old problem of the relation between economic class and social class – between economic divisions and social formations – persists. It is a problem which becomes even more pronounced when set in an international context.

Class in a global context

Class analysis conventionally has focused on socioeconomic structures within national settings. International studies of class therefore have often been comparative – examining whether the French working class, say, is larger or more restive than its counterpart in the US. It is interesting to note, given the scepticism about class analysis amongst critics in many Western contexts, that class relations tend to appear much starker when viewed on a global stage. The work of world systems theorists such as Wallerstein, for instance, set relations of exploitation and structured inequality within the frame of a world capitalist economy, rather than within national boundaries (see Chapter 1). While class situations within specific societies (especially rich post-industrial societies) may appear highly complex, the appropriation of value and the formation of antagonistic class interests can seem plainer when viewed transnationally. One critical debate in this field concerns the formation of a transnational capitalist class. Sklair (2001) argues that globalisation should be understood as the effect of quite definite 'transnational practices' – the material practices of agents in specific institutional settings, and working through definite social networks. In this way, his approach grounds processes of globalisation in particular forms of agency and social alliances. The dominant agents in a global context together constitute a transnational capitalist class.

Sklair divides the transnational capitalist class (or TCC) into four fractions:

1   The corporate fraction consists of those who own and control transnational corporations and their affiliates in major banks and financial institutions (see also Bergesen and Sonnett 2001). This is the transnational capitalist class in its economic guise.
2   The state faction is comprised of globalising bureaucrats and politicians working through international institutions and transnational state networks.
3   The technical fraction is composed of globalising professionals, including élite lawyers, academics, economists and think-tankers. These experts, professionals and intellectuals provide ideological cover for international economic interests, as well as technical solutions for processes of transnational organisation and exchange (see also Robinson and Harris 2000).
4   The consumer or commercial fraction includes global merchants and distributors, as well as agents involved in international media and advertising.

These schematic distinctions, Sklair notes, are harder to make in practice. There are significant degrees of cross-over between various capitalist class fractions, given the corporate interests of numerous globalising politicians, or the role of TNCs in global media and advertising. However, discrete class fractions can be defined by the control of key resources. Transnational corporations command global capital circuits; a transnational political class is concerned with the distribution of political power; and the consumer fraction is engaged in the circulation of cultural meanings, primarily geared to the reproduction of an ideology of consumption. We might note that ownership alone is not the basis for inclusion in the transnational capitalist class: this is not simply or even primarily a class of capitalist owners. On what basis, then, do these different groupings hold together? Sklair argues, firstly, that these class actors share a set of economic interests geared to the reproduction and extension of existing transnational processes. Secondly, they divide between them core control functions in the global system, respectively in relation to economic organisation; domestic and international politics; and the 'culture-ideology' of global consumerism. Members of the transnational capitalist class, thirdly, tend to assume global as opposed to local perspectives in their fields of activity. It follows, fourthly, that these class actors adopt a more general cosmopolitan attitude, seeing themselves as internationals as much as national subjects. As Harvey (2003: 187) states, members of a transnational capitalist class are given to pay 'very little heed to place-bound or national loyalties or traditions'. Finally, these class actors share similar lifestyles, based on high degrees of mobility and élite consumption patterns.

Sklair's framework suggests that a transnational capitalist class can be analysed in terms of both structural economic positions and modes of social identification. The formation of this class identity goes beyond national affiliations or territories. Indeed, members of the TCC will often exploit transnational capitalist arrangements against the interests of national capital. The class fates of these actors are not determined by domestic economic processes. As Harvey (2003: 186) argues:

> Debt crises might rock Brazil and Mexico, liquidity crises might destroy the economies of Thailand and Indonesia, but rentier elements within all those countries could not only preserve their capital but actually enhance their own internal class position. Privileged classes could seal themselves off in gilded ghettos in Bombay, São Paulo, and Kuwait while enjoying the fruits of their investments on Wall Street.

The potential for conflict between international and national capitals also can produce cleavages within the transnational capitalist class – particularly between globalising politicians who must respond to domestic agenda and those economic agents of footloose global capital. These divisions are characteristic of competing capitals, however, and do not necessarily override the more basic mutual interests of different class fractions. Robinson and Harris (2000) argue that the TCC can be seen to form a global ruling class, whose collective interests dominate international social and economic arrangements (see also Van der Pijl 1998). Their anatomy of this dominant class includes the usual suspects in the ownership and leadership of TNCS, together with politicians, bureaucrats and professionals working within such institutions as the IMF or WTO, the OECD and G8 organisations, the World Economic Forum and peak associations of capital. It has its hangers-on amongst intellectuals in various think-tanks or in bodies such as the Ford and Carnegie Foundations, and in such academic settings as the Harvard Business School. Robinson and Harris follow Gramsci in describing this transnational élite as the 'ruling coalition' in a hegemonic system based on neoliberal consensus. Below the élite sits a shrinking layer of national middle classes who exercise little real power but – pacified with mass consumption – form a fragile buffer between the transnational élite and the world's poor majority. This hegemonic system, then, is based on the consensual integration of some and the coercion or exclusion of many more others.

A highly uneven model of integration and exclusion also informs Manuel Castells' analysis of global network society. Given the way that electronic flows have restructured economic exchanges and social relations, however, Castells is sceptical about the relevance of older class categories to the analysis of networks. He sees network power as forming around diverse transnational élites rather than distinct classes (2000a: 445). There is, therefore, no coherent transnational capitalist class. Castells' critical argument here is worth quoting at length. Under the 'new technological, organizational, and economic conditions' associated with a network society, Castells asks (2000a: 504), exactly

> who are the capitalists? They are certainly not the legal owners of the means of production who range from your/my pension fund to a passer-by at a Singapore ATM suddenly deciding to buy stock in Buenos Aires' emergent market.

The fragmentation of ownership makes it difficult to define a global capitalist class in terms of an identifiable stratum of owners. Neither can it be defined by structures of managerial control. Corporate managers command particular organisational resources and steer specific economic processes but have little extended control over rapid flows of finance capital or exchanges of information through electronic networks. Indeed Castells suggests that large-scale flows of information, goods and money escape the cognitive grasp, let alone the purposive control, of their putative managers. In certain contexts, to be sure, corporate managers remain key capitalist actors – this would be true, for example, in the case of the Japanese economy. In other contexts, older patterns of bourgeois ownership and control are in play, as in the Chinese foreign business networks which frequently are linked by family or social ties. In the case of the United States, he goes on:

> a mixture of historical layers provides to the capitalist characters a colourful array of traditional bankers, nouveau riche speculators, self-made geniuses-turned-entrepreneurs, global tycoons, and multinational managers. In other cases, public corporations (as in French banking or electronic firms) are the capitalist actors. In Russia, survivors of communist *nomenklatura* compete with wild young capitalists in recycling state property in the constitution of the newest capitalist province. And all over the world, money-laundering from miscellaneous criminal

businesses flows towards this mother of all accumulations that is the global financial network.

All of these may be capitalist players, but Castells (2000a: 505) argues that it does not make sense to speak of them as a coherent global capitalist class. Economic and political power is not organised around the actions of a dominant class, but through an integrated network of global capital. This network knits together diverse capitalist interests, but also distributes them across economic processes and geographical space. Different capitalist actors therefore do not hold together as either an economic or a social class – they do not share structural economic locations, nor do they act in concert to pursue common class interests. In Castells' version, the global network economy has realised the central logic of capital: to reproduce itself in an abstract form which, while it may be the product of human action, finally escapes human control. Over and above 'human-flesh capitalists' (and usually behind their backs), Castells' 'collective capitalist' takes the disembodied shape of financial and information flows speeding through electronic networks. This is, as he puts it, the 'mother of all accumulations': the generation of value from values, the making of money from money.

On the other side of the class equation, workers have not disappeared, and – contrary to certain predictions – the shift to an information economy has not produced mass unemployment. There are more jobs and more workers in the contemporary economy, partly due to the mass entry of women into the workforce in numerous societies. Castells' claim here is borne out by International Labour Organisation (2004) figures which set global employment in 2003 at a record 2.8 billion. Against this backdrop of more work, more workers, and expanding working classes, however, the social relations of production between capital and labour have been fundamentally altered. Capital, as Castells puts it, is global; labour is local. While capital is at once integrated and decentralised through networks, labour is both dispersed and increasingly divided. Castells raises some more telling questions in this regard:

> Who is contributing to value creation in the electronics industry: the Silicon Valley chip designer, or the young woman on the assembly line of a South-East Asian factory? Certainly both, albeit in quite substantially different proportions. Thus, are they jointly the new working class?
>
> (2000a: 506)

In economic sectors characterised by subcontracting, outsourcing and networking, it becomes difficult to demarcate the tasks of management, production, ownership and control. It is also hard to pinpoint exactly where value is being produced within these networks. Castells is right to say that both the privileged knowledge worker and the low-paid assembly worker are producing value within the 'same' production chain, but it seems nonsensical to think of them as occupying, therefore, the same class position. The implied gender distinction between the Silicon Valley designer and the young woman on the assembly line, moreover, is presumably not coincidental, as it marks one of the basic cleavages in a new international division of labour which concentrates large numbers of young female workers in foreign-owned and export sectors in developing economies (see Sklair 2002: 128–30; see also Mies 1998). Little of this maps onto a conventional Marxist model of the core social relations between classes. In Castells' account, labour and capital are not constituted by a structuring social relation within which one class can be said to produce value and one to appropriate it. Moreover, the class of producers is itself divided, dispersed and highly stratified. The ironic inversion brought about by the logic of networks is that faceless electronic capital is coordinated and integrated across space, while real human labour is increasingly fragmented and individualised (2000a: 507).

Other critics make similar arguments. While Sklair (2001) insists that it is possible to analyse a transnational capitalist class, he asserts that its very coherence and strength is a measure of the comparative weakness of transnational labour. Although some transnational trade unions, federations and workers' movements exist, neither corporations nor governments that want to bid for footloose capital will have much truck with organised labour. Class formation depends not only on one's position within relations of production, but on processes of self-representation, organisation and the recognition of competing class interests. In these terms, the TCC can be analysed in terms of economic class positions, and also as a social class with common (if not always entirely consistent) interests, value orientations and styles of life. The transnational working class, in contrast – given patterns of uneven development and the effects of different national politics – does not constitute a 'class for itself'. Global assembly lines separate workers through an exaggerated division of labour, while the gaps between design, development, production, assembly and distribution functions mean workers within an industry or even a corporation are largely unknown to, hidden from, or placed in competition with each other.

Conclusion

While the organisation of global production and exchange may undermine older class patterns, it is still the case that conditions of work and relations of exploitation are key points of contradiction and resistance within the global economy. Direct producers, as Sklair (2001) notes, continue to bear the brunt of economic crises. Doing away with class categories does nothing to alter the systematic production of economic inequalities and the reproduction of economic power. Sklair (2003) argues that widening social polarisation – together with environmental unsustainability – constitutes the critical threat to the contemporary global system (see also Amin 2003;

Munck 2002). Patterns of polarisation may not fall so clearly along standard class lines, but it follows that the critique of class leaves open the question of how one should analyse these social and economic divisions. The perspectives examined in this chapter have addressed class in terms of both objective economic structures and social identities. Class is also, however, a relational category. In this sense, it has been used not only to analyse the formation of specific socioeconomic groups, but also to account for the structural disparities between them. Reports of the 'death of class' may or may not be exaggerated (see Pakulski and Waters 1996), but relative inequalities endure. The discussion in the final chapter, therefore, takes up the question of how social and economic inequality might be analysed after the critique of class.

7 Inequality

The preceding discussion looked at how class has been put into question as a framework for analysing economic inequality and as a means of understanding social identities. While class may no longer be central to thinking about economic divisions, however, economic inequality clearly still exists: this chapter therefore examines how we might analyse social and economic inequalities 'after' class. It turns first to debates that trace social and economic divisions in advanced economies not along class lines but around a range of factors including economic insecurity and forms of social exclusion. The discussion goes on to set these issues of inequality and insecurity in a global context, focusing on the links between poverty, inequality and economic growth.

Recent approaches to economic inequality have seen a shift away from concepts of class – based on individuals' structural locations *within* an economic order – to notions of insecurity, as a condition where people have an uncertain or precarious relation to economic membership: that is, where they stand at least partly *outside* an economic order. Within European debates, this shift has been captured in the category of 'social exclusion', referring to the ways that economic and social marginality tend to overlap. In a US context, such arguments have been linked to theories of an impoverished 'underclass', a term used to denote the radical exclusion of vulnerable groups from the economic and social mainstream. In both cases, economic disparities stem not only from people's relative incomes, nor from their position within relations of production and work, but from their access to formal economic participation and their levels of social and economic protection. The argument in this chapter is that current economic arrangements produce pronounced (if not entirely 'new') patterns of inequality, which continue to structure contemporary societies in quite systematic ways.

The latter part of the discussion takes up the issue of inequality in a global context. Here, lines of economic division are severe. The discussion focuses on large-scale analyses developed by researchers in major international agencies, examining the contentious relation between growth, poverty reduction and levels of inequality. It looks at how different world regions are faring in relation to collective goals on poverty and development. The harsh disparities which characterise global economic relations can make theoretical and policy debates within advanced economies look almost trivial; however, the two parts of the discussion centre on common themes. The links between inequality, poverty and insecurity are critical to thinking about contemporary economic divisions in both national and international contexts. Degrees of inequality and of material deprivation vary sharply between the most and the least developed economies, but some of the key questions are the same. To what extent can poverty reduction be separated from decreasing inequality? Does it matter if the inequality gap widens so long as the poorest are protected? How does non-income poverty – exclusion, insecurity, incapacity – reinforce and reproduce economic and social divisions?

Inequality 'after' class

The shift away from class that occurred within critical analysis from the 1980s was partly a response to changing forms of social and economic organisation, but was also prompted by the claims of modes of inequality which sociology had been given to ignore or understate. An emphasis on class within social analysis had gone together with the relative neglect of inequality based on race or gender: racial or gender inequalities were frequently seen as secondary to class divisions, or appeared as effects of class structures. This conventional focus on class as the basis of social structure and the primary axis of social inequality has been roundly criticised for overlooking power relations which are not fundamentally about class, but rather centre on actual or ascribed identities of gender, race, culture, religion, or sexuality (see Bradley 1996; see also Phillips 1999a). Nancy Fraser (1995) has drawn a distinction in this respect between a 'social politics of equality', typically based on class, and a 'cultural politics of difference', associated with wider questions of identity. If class has been relegated from its primary analytic position, however, this does not mean that issues of economic inequality go away. Some of the most acute ways in which differences are socially marked, and personally and collectively experienced, are through economic structures. In this sense, criticisms of class from the standpoint of race or gender do not simply signal a move away from economic to cultural concerns, or from questions of inequality to those of identity. Inequality is still reproduced economically, and a focus on divisions other than class in fact can show up more severe economic disparities. Racial and ethnic differences frequently have been marked by forms of economic discrimination, domination and exploitation that are more vicious than class divisions, and which cannot be explained by recourse to class categories. So too, 'gender has exhibited far more pronounced inequalities of power and material rewards as well as offering more extreme examples of exploitation and brutal coercion than those occurring between classes' (Waters 2000: 49).

The critique of class therefore does not mean that economic inequality is no longer of analytic interest; in fact it can direct attention to starker forms of economic power and injustice. Too often, however, approaches to economic inequality have been seen as captive to a narrow 'distributive paradigm' that is over-determined by class, and which simply neglects forms of injustice which are not principally economic in character. Such an argument underlies a broad shift within social and political thought away from problems of inequality and redistribution and towards issues of difference and recognition (see Fraser 1997). It is interesting to note here the congruence between certain trends in social theory and current political orthodoxies of the centre-right and centre-left. There is a distinct family resemblance between academic debates over equality and the watered-down version of equality that has appeared in recent liberal and social democratic politics, linked to an explicit move away from a politics of distribution via fiscal and welfare programmes. In Anthony Giddens' (2000) work on *The Third Way and its Critics* the resemblance is deliberate, as the author seeks to make an intellectual case for the politics of what has been called the 'radical centre'. A central claim is that reducing poverty should take priority over reducing inequality. Giddens' argument sits against the backdrop of the British government's contemporary focus on poverty reduction – in a context where income inequalities had made Britain, by the turn of the century, one of the most unequal societies in Europe (see Townsend 2004). While in both theory and policy a concept of equality is retained, this is chiefly defined in terms of 'equality of opportunity'. Giddens' focus is on a new centrist politics in Britain, but his arguments have wider relevance for social democratic politics. Giddens contends that the politics of the left has always conceived equality in terms of 'equality of outcomes' – the attempt to even up economic disparities, particularly through state intervention into market processes. Such a conception lies behind policies to redress social and economic inequalities by way of redistribution, both through welfare transfers and by narrowing inequalities of income and wealth via taxation.

The move away from equality of outcome towards equality of opportunity has gone together with a growing policy focus on investments in human capital – through education, skills training, childcare provision, and so on – in contrast to the redistribution of economic capital. This repertoire of supply-side policy instruments was hardly invented by Blair's New Labour governments, but represents an increasingly standard approach for governments of both Left and Right since the 1980s. Such strategies, worked out at the level of policy, have quite clear affinities with neo-Weberian theory which sees people's capacities, including their skills and credentials, as determining their life chances in market societies (see the discussion in Chapter 6). The answer for governments, then, is to help people to develop these capacities. Social and economic outcomes might be shaped by the development of opportunities, rather than through direct interventions at the level of 'who gets what'. The distinction between equality of opportunity and equality of outcomes is therefore a distinction between enabling capacities and engineering consequences. Some of this, to be sure, is little more than semantics. Giddens might stress the difference between equalities of opportunity and of outcome, but in practice British government policy of the late 1990s and early 2000s sought to intervene at the level of 'outcomes' as well as fostering people's life chances. A commitment to reducing poverty in any reasonable time-frame cannot wait for the slow feed of social mobility through enhanced opportunities. Rather, government policy used strategies of intervention and redistribution – legislating for a minimum wage, cutting the lowest rate of tax, introducing tax credits for the working poor – in an effort to reduce levels of poverty at the bottom. A commitment to poverty reduction, however, does not necessarily decrease inequality in the absence of any checks on wealth accumulation at the top. The Office for National Statistics reported in 2004 that the richest 1 per cent in Britain (some 600,000 people) doubled its wealth to £797 billion between 1997 and 2003. Over the same period, the bottom 50 per cent of the population (30 million people) saw their share of national wealth drop from 10 to 5 per cent of the total. Reducing poverty, in this context, remained quite compatible with increasing inequality.

A major rationale for such an emphasis on equality of opportunity is the argument that non-income poverty is as critical to individual life chances as income poverty. In this extended sense, poverty is defined not solely on the basis of income, but in terms of a lack of basic capacities or capabilities – health, education and literacy, reasonable housing conditions, safety – which allow individuals to participate in social membership and to make choices in respect of their own lives (see Sen 1992). We will revisit this approach to non-income poverty in thinking about global inequality; in the present context, it is linked with debates over social exclusion in advanced economies. The relation between poverty and social exclusion reproduces the distinction between economic outcomes and social opportunities which has characterised recent debates over inequality. While poverty is an economic category defined by material deprivation, exclusion refers to a broader sense of being shut out from full social and economic participation (see Byrne 1999). It describes conditions of social deprivation which often overlap with, but are not simply identical to, economic disadvantage. This idea of social exclusion emerged from European policy debates of the 1980s, originating in France in particular, to refer to groups that stand in a marginal relation to core social and economic processes. In this way it does some of the same work as the notion of an 'underclass' in the United States, while aiming to avoid the latter's more negative connotations as well as its racial overtones.

Debates over the situation of an underclass in US society have been dogged by the conflation of economic, social and moral diagnoses (see Auletta 1982; Gans 1995; Jencks 1993; Massey and Denton 1993; Mingeone 1996; Wilson 1987). In an early work on the subject, Auletta (1982: xiii) noted that studies of poverty defined this excluded class in terms of '*behavioural*, as well as *income* deficiencies'. The sociologist Herbert Gans concurs, arguing that the characterisation of an underclass was based less on structural economic locations than on cultural or behavioural ascriptions. 'Such a behavioral definition', he says (1995: 2),

> denominates poor people who drop out of school, do not work, and, if they are young women, have babies without benefit of marriage and go on welfare. The behavioral underclass also includes the homeless, beggars, and panhandlers, poor addicts to alcohol and drugs, and street criminals. Because the term is flexible, poor people who live in 'the projects', illegal immigrants, and teenage gang members are also often assigned to the underclass.

Gans suggests that the very looseness of such definitions has allowed the underclass label to be applied indiscriminately, and in ways that too easily conflate poverty as an economic condition with antisocial, criminal or marginal behaviour. In this sense it re-hashes earlier debates over a 'culture of poverty' amongst low-income groups, based on the reproduction of certain patterns of behaviour and social and economic norms (see Lewis 1959, 1966, 1996; see also Moynihan 1969). Oscar Lewis' original work on impoverished families in Mexico, Puerto Rico and New York analysed specific cultures of poverty as adaptive strategies developed in contexts of systematic discrimination and structural economic disadvantage; however the concept proved amenable to later arguments that material deprivation in wealthy societies was somehow due to a cultural problem with the poor themselves. Lewis had argued that a culture of poverty was partly a response to poor groups' lack of access to mainstream institutions and agencies. This relation between low-income populations and public provision was conceived rather differently in later debates over poverty, welfare and the underclass. In the 1980s and 1990s, a number of prominent US critics argued that welfare policies reinforced a dependency culture amongst an underclass that was increasingly excluded from mainstream institutions and behavioural norms (see Jencks 1993; Murray 1995). Rather than ameliorating poverty and enhancing people's life chances, welfare provision served to entrench the very conditions and behaviours it aimed to address.

European debates over social exclusion generally sought to avoid the kinds of moral association that hung around the idea of an underclass; nevertheless some common themes are apparent. Policies to combat social exclusion in Britain from the late 1990s, for example, included community develop initiatives on housing estates, as well as projects to lower rates of truancy and teenage pregnancy. Each of these elements features in Gans' round-up of the behavioural definition of an underclass in the US. These problems of social exclusion, however, were represented in the British context principally as barriers to individual opportunity rather than in terms of behavioural failures. An emphasis on such factors as housing environments and exclusion from education is based on the premise that economic inequalities are not reproduced solely through differentials in income levels, nor does income alone determine individuals' life chances. Rather, economic divisions are cross-cut with social conditions in limiting opportunities and stunting capacities.

Such an approach to equality – based on reducing poverty, enhancing opportunity, and combating social exclusion – raises a number of critical issues. For one thing, it is not clear just how 'new' any of this is. Recent arguments for widening social inclusion can be seen to rework, without always acknowledging, older arguments for the role of welfare provision in securing basic social rights and extending social citizenship (see Marshall 1950; Titmuss 1968). In this sense, the politics of welfare is not only about economic protections but also about social membership. Furthermore, the distinction between equality of opportunity and equality of outcome does not stand up to scrutiny, particularly as a means of dividing off an old Left politics of welfare redistribution from a new centrist politics of market opportunity. Welfare politics have always been concerned with equalities of opportunity, treatment and access, rather than with equality of outcomes. It is arguable, for instance, that universalist principles in education provision were more consistent with equality of opportunity than are recent reforms in the direction of greater selection and differentiation in schools. Meanwhile, there are only limited cases of welfare provision where some principle of equality of outcome might hold, and these appear uncontroversial. Universalist principles in health care, as under the National Health Service in Britain, were indeed meant to promote (as far as they could) 'equality' of health outcomes irrespective of one's class or income, and it is very doubtful that Giddens or anyone else would want it otherwise. Outside of the health context, it is hard to think of an instance where welfare or redistributive politics sought to produce equalities of outcome. Strategies to offset the effects of income inequality, in particular, have not been geared to equal outcomes. Social housing, state pensions or welfare benefits – like the narrowing of income extremes through taxation – aim to decrease inequality or ameliorate its impact, rather than to level off social and economic outcomes.

The idea of 'equality of outcome' in fact is largely rhetorical, but it has definite effects: while the concept is analytically weak in itself, it can deflect attention from more substantive problems of inequality. When the politics of equality is defined so simplistically, any serious engagement with questions of income inequality is sidelined from debates over poverty and social exclusion. While no-one, to be sure, would argue with the goal of reducing poverty, it is less clear that poverty reduction and social inclusion can be so neatly separated from the goal of decreasing inequality. There is an argument to be made that the maintenance – and in some cases, the deepening – of economic inequalities is incompatible with efforts to widen social inclusion (see Phillips 1999b). In this view, it is not simply absolute poverty but relative inequalities that undermine social cohesion and divide social groups. In contexts of entrenched inequality, the danger is that the stably employed and relatively secure come to identify with the better-off, detaching their own concerns from those of the unemployed or insecure (see Galbraith 1992; Bauman 1998). Economic divisions are compounded by social distance and moral disengagement. An approach to equality based on promoting opportunities at the level of the individual, however, tends to side-step this broader question of the relation between social inclusion and reducing inequality.

Structures of inequality

Arguments that class categories are no longer the most obvious or accurate way to think about patterns of inequality do not mean that economic divisions are no longer structured in systematic ways. A number of recent analyses stratify contemporary societies around broad economic cleavages, based not simply on economic class locations but also on conditions of insecurity and exclusion. In this way they take up the critique of class-based models of inequality seen in the previous chapter, recognising that economic divisions are not solely organised around relations of production and work. The models considered below depict current patterns of stratification via broad schemes based on income, security and inclusion: the figures are approximate, therefore, but the lines of inequality they trace are more compelling.

Lash and Urry (1994) retain a class model to typify the economic divisions that are characteristic of advanced capitalist economies. One of the key challenges to conventional models of class has been the expansion of the service economy, and the related growth of the middle classes. The authors see this as a substantive shift in capitalist social structures, but argue that post-industrial economies produce both a mass middle-class grouping and also marked patterns of impoverishment, insecurity and exclusion. This is in large part due to the polarised nature of contemporary service industries, which generate both high-grade and very low-grade (poorly paid, insecure, unprotected and 'junk') jobs. They set out a basic model of social stratification along the following lines:

1   The top stratum is the relatively small capitalist class of owners. The rich, as ever, are always with us.
2   The mass class in advanced capitalist societies is the middle stratum of professional, managerial, administrative and service workers.
3   The working class, defined in conventional terms by their productive labour, is becoming smaller and is increasingly economically insecure. They are especially vulnerable to manufacturing downturns, downsizing, and the shift of productive jobs off-shore.
4   The bottom layer is occupied by a new lower class, defined by casual

and insecure work (if any), social marginalisation and poverty. This group tends to over-represent immigrant workers as well as women (see also Sassen 2001; Waldinger and Lichter 2003).

This can appear simply as a reworking of a quite standard class model, with the middle class (service labour) displacing the working class (productive labour) as the mass class in advanced capitalist societies. However, the interesting thing about this rather basic scheme is the depiction of a significant minority whose economic position is defined not by their work function but by their relative insecurity and exclusion from mainstream economic processes. Economic inequalities in this way are premised not only on relations of ownership and work, but on access to labour markets and security in work.

Indeed, Will Hutton (1995) sees insecurity as the central principle structuring contemporary economies. In his treatment of the 'thirty, thirty, forty society', Hutton jettisons the language of class to highlight patterns of relative economic security as the dividing line between different socioeconomic strata. Focusing on the British case, Hutton contends that the economy is broadly organised around:

1   Forty per cent who are stably employed and relatively secure: their workplaces are most likely to be covered by trade union agreements, they are more likely to have company or personal pensions and to have savings.
2   Thirty per cent who are relatively insecure: their work is casualised, their jobs are more likely to be unprotected, they may lack savings or pensions.
3   Thirty per cent are marginalised or excluded: this includes the unemployed or under-employed, those whose work is unprotected and low-paid, groups that live on state benefits or less.

Clearly this is a broad-brush depiction, and the figures are hit-or-miss. Hutton is less concerned with differentiating the very top layer of the economy than with divisions within the majority of the population. Byrne (1999), in contrast, goes for a ten, fifty, forty model, which distinguishes the most affluent from a stable majority and a substantial number whose economic position is relatively or profoundly insecure. This bottom forty per cent includes significant numbers of casualised workers, as well as groups who are simply excluded from mainstream economic participation. How the exact numbers carve up in such large-scale representations is less important than the lines of divisions these critics identify. In all cases, economic stratification does not simply follow income: rather, relative security becomes a key principle for understanding inequality (see Blau 1999; Gallie *et al.* 1998; Heery and Salmon 1999). Structures of inequality are based on income and wealth but also on economic security, legal and welfare entitlement, and economic inclusion in society. It is important to note, of course, that income and relative security will tend to overlap. Hutton points out that in increasingly flexible labour markets even very highly paid work can be insecure, but nonetheless the 'insecurity' of a freelance management consultant is not the same as that of casual cleaner. And while people's status within labour markets is crucial to their economic position, exclusion from the labour market altogether remains a primary source of inequality and insecurity (see also Bauman 1998; Wilson 1996).

While the discussion so far has focused on lines of economic division in advanced capitalist societies, such an emphasis on patterns of insecurity and conditions of exclusion has broader relevance. Robinson and Harris (2000), for instance, apply Hutton's conception of a 'thirty, thirty, forty society' in an international context. Whereas the secure 40 per cent of workers in core countries have protected conditions of employment and relative economic stability, they suggest that this proportion goes down to around 20 per cent in less developed economies. The middle 40 per cent in the core and somewhat less than a third in the capitalist periphery are in insecure work, lacking social protections and longer-term economic security. The bottom 30 per cent in the core are casualised or marginalised. This condition characterises more than 50 per cent in peripheral economies, structurally excluded from formal economic activity, radically unprotected, and – at an extreme – making up the ' "superfluous" population of global capitalism'. At this end of the scale, Robinson and Harris are concerned with acute insecurity and dire inequalities. While the framework of economic inclusion and exclusion, security and insecurity, can be applied to different international settings, the extremes of poverty and exclusion in the global system need to be considered in their own terms. It is to the question of global inequalities that the discussion now turns.

Global inequalities

There are sharp debates over patterns of global inequality, both in respect of how inequality should be measured and in terms of whether global inequalities are increasing or decreasing. Indeed, as one United Nations report has suggested, 'debates on global income inequality can indicate little more than how economists and statisticians can find many answers to seemingly the same questions' (UNDP 2003: 38). The preceding discussion of inequality in advanced economies centred on issues of security and exclusion in relation to labour markets, and this also provides a starting point for thinking about global inequalities. The International Labour Organisation estimated in its 2004 World Employment Report that a record number of people – around 2.8 billion – were employed globally in 2003, but nearly 1.4 billion were living on less than two dollars a day, with 550 million living on less than one dollar a day (that is, subsisting under the global poverty line). In this context, increasing access to work remains compatible with endemic poverty.

The relation between poverty reduction and decreasing inequality is especially vexed in a global setting. In contexts of sheer deprivation and chronic hunger, reducing poverty is clearly the most immediate priority. It is less clear, however, how far poverty reduction can or should be linked with efforts to decrease inequality, both within and between nations. An important intervention in this debate is that made by the World Bank researchers Dollar and Kraay (2002), who emphasise the role of economic growth in poverty reduction. They contend that the recent period of globalisation, dating from around 1980, has both promoted equality and decreased poverty. The authors track a long-term global trend towards greater inequality up to a peak in the 1970s; the trend since has been downward, chiefly due to the accelerated growth of two very large, very poor nations, China and India (see also Bigsten and Levin 2001). Against this background, Dollar and Kraay make two key assertions regarding inequality and poverty:

1   Increasing inequality from 1820 to 1975 can largely be explained in terms of the widening disparity between rich and poor countries, rather than growing equality gaps within countries – these tend to increase more slowly.
2   The proportion of the world's population living in poverty (on less than the purchasing power equivalent of one dollar a day) has declined over time but the number of poor grew in absolute terms up until 1980. While the world economy grew rapidly between 1960 and 1980, the number of people living in poverty increased because economic growth was concentrated outside the poorest countries and regions.

In these terms, patterns of inequality and poverty are somewhat separate questions. However, Dollar and Kraay suggest that both inequality and poverty are on downward trends. Since 1980 growth has been more widely spread across the world economy; consequently the number of people living in absolute poverty has diminished. Again, this is largely due to growth in China and India, which in 1980 included around one-third of the world's population but almost two-thirds of the world's poor.

For Dollar and Kraay economic growth is the key to taking people out of poverty, but to make a marked change to the global picture it is crucial that growth is not confined to those parts of the world that are already well-off. Poorer nations must have a share in economic growth, and the primary means to do this is through openness to international trade and investment. They are less interested, therefore, in nationalist or autarkic economic strategies than in the benefits to be gained from global integration. The authors argue that, during the period since 1980, the 'globalizers' amongst the less-developed countries have grown faster than 'non-globalizers' (and in many cases faster than developed economies). Those economies which have liberalised trade and attracted inward investment have seen the benefits in economic growth: Dollar and Kraay cite India, China, Vietnam, Mexico and

Uganda as cases in point. Such patterns are true not only for different national economies, but also for regions within national economies, as connected and 'disconnected' regions vary markedly in terms of growth. The problem of global inequality, then, is not so much that of growing inequality between the developed and the developing world, but of growing inequality within the developing world, based on varying access to global economic processes. Moreover, Dollar and Kraay argue that globalising measures do not in themselves promote inequality; rather inequality within economies tends to reflect domestic policies on such matters as taxation, education, employment protection and welfare. It follows that ensuring the benefits of globalisation – 'spreading the wealth', as the authors put it – requires a policy mix which limits protectionist measures by rich nations, and promotes sound domestic governance in developing economies. Trade openness at the international level should be matched by policy interventions to narrow inequalities at the national level.

This analysis has been influential, but also controversial. Most simply it is seen as advocating a 'trickle-down' approach to economic growth – a criticism that does not exactly square with Dollar and Kraay's emphasis on the importance of domestic policy interventions in ensuring that economic benefits are spread. A more complex argument concerns the structural relation between poverty and inequality. This is a problematic we have already seen in respect of advanced economies; it is one that becomes much more acute in a global context. How far can poverty reduction be separated from decreasing inequality? Should anti-poverty strategies centre on absolute poverty (the dollar a day measure) or relative poverty (degrees of inequality within societies)? There is evidence to suggest that more unequal economies do less well at translating economic growth into lower rates of poverty. A number of Latin American countries, for example, have seen growth without real reductions in poverty, and the region's largest economy, Brazil, maintains stark extremes of inequality (see Oxfam 2003; UNDP 2003: 37, 39). In key nations which have seen strong economic growth since the 1990s, such as Brazil, China, India and Mexico, the benefits have been unevenly distributed across regions and groups, while the richest members of those societies have benefited disproportionately. So too, in the nations which have done worst in promoting growth and reducing poverty, 'much of the burden is borne by marginalized groups – as in Burkina Faso, Mali and the Russian Federation' (UNDP 2003: 34). The argument here is not simply a moral but an economic one: economic inequality can be seen not only as unjust but as inefficient. Inequities in land ownership, in access to productive assets, income and market opportunities can impede economic growth and prospects for inward investment. Cornia and Kiiski (2001: 37) argue that high levels of inequality represent a barrier to growth in numerous developing and transitional economies (see also Barro 2000; Perotti 1996; cf. Knowles 2001). If reducing poverty and decreasing inequality do not always go together, moreover, increases in both poverty and inequality often do – as shown by mounting poverty and inequality in the former states of the Soviet Union (see Oxfam 2003; UNDP 1999: 3, 2003: 37–8).

Dollar and Kraay's case centres on a sustained downward turn in *global* inequality – that is, in the disparity between rich and poor nations. Inequality cuts, however, in different ways. Under one standard measure of equality, using the Gini coefficient, individual income levels appear to be slowly converging over time. This measure is weighted towards the median; it follows that as more people move off the bottom and towards the middle-income bands, overall income inequality narrows. In 2003, the world Gini coefficient stood at 0.66 (where 1 stands for complete inequality and 0 stands for complete equality – see UNDP 2003: 39). In line with Dollar and Kraay's analysis, such an indicator suggests that global income inequality has been decreasing since the 1970s. The Gini measure, however, does not capture so well the raw extremes of global wealth: in this context, the UNDP (2003: 39) asserts that 'in recent decades there has unquestionably been a widening gap between the incomes of the very richest and the very poorest'. In the early years of the twenty-first century, the richest 5 per cent of the global population commanded 114 times the income of the poorest 5 per cent, while the top 1 per cent had as much as the bottom 57 per cent. The 25 million wealthiest Americans, meanwhile, had an income equivalent to that of almost 2 billion of the world's poor population (ibid.). While absolute poverty may be decreasing at the very bottom, wealth is also massively increasing at the top:

> The world's 200 richest people more than doubled their net worth in the four years to 1998, to more than $1 trillion. The assets of the top three billionaires are more than the combined GDP of all least developed countries and their 600 million people.
>
> (UNDP 1999: 3)

Alongside these inequities in income levels may be set the unequal share of economic activity between nations. Richer nations continue to enjoy the lion's share of overall wealth, trade, investment and technology. By the end of the twentieth century, the fifth of the global population in the wealthiest countries had 86 per cent of world GDP to the bottom fifth's 1 per cent share; 82 per cent of the world exports to the poorest fifth's 1 per cent; and 68 per cent of foreign direct investment to the bottom fifth's 1 per cent. In light of Castells' arguments concerning the axial role of electronic networks in the global economy, furthermore, the world's richest nations had 74 per cent of the world's telephone connections (and 91 per cent of its Internet users), while the bottom fifth had only 1.5 per cent (all figures UNDP 1999: 3).

Moving from the level of global inequality to that of national inequality adds to this picture. Dollar and Kraay state that levels of inequality within nations tend to decrease only very slowly. Slow reductions in domestic inequality are one thing, however; growing inequality is another. Over the critical period identified by Dollar and Kraay, from 1980 to the end of the 1990s – when global inequality and absolute poverty figures were both reducing – inequality increased markedly *within* transitional economies in the former Soviet bloc, as well as in such advanced capitalist countries as Japan, Sweden, the United Kingdom, the United States, Canada and Australia (Cornia and Kiiski 2001; UNDP 1999: 3). Looking more closely at specific countries and regions tends to interrupt this steady narrative of widening growth, diminishing poverty and decreasing inequality. During the 1980s just four nations saw downturns in their human development index – a measure of life expectancies, levels of health and education, and basic living standards – while in the 1990s 21 nations witnessed such reversals (UNDP 2003: 34). This was in large part due to the HIV/AIDS crisis, but in the most severely affected nations the effects of the epidemic were compounded by a lack of economic growth, growing debt and falling commodity prices. In a large comparative review using data from 73 countries, representing 80 per cent of world population and 91 per cent of world GDP, Cornia and Kiiski adjudge that inequality increased during the 1980s and 1990s in 48 of the sample nations, and fell in just 9 (Cornia and Kiiski 2001).

Poverty, inequality, insecurity: challenges for human development

These trends provided the backdrop to the United Nations Millennium Declaration of September 2000, endorsed by 189 member states. The Declaration made a collective commitment to efforts to reduce poverty, improve health, support environmental sustainability, promote peace and protect human rights. It is highly debatable how far advances have been made on any of these fronts, but progress in reducing poverty at least is measurable. The 'road map' for realising this declaration is detailed in the form of eight Millennium Development Goals, the first of which is a goal for reducing the extreme poverty in which more than one billion of the global population lives (UNDP 2003: 15). The major target here is to halve by 2015 the number of people living under the global poverty line of $1 per day. A few years in, however, international agencies were projecting that the chances of reaching that goal varied markedly between regions and across nations: East Asia, Southeast Asia and South Asia had the best regional prospects, Latin America and the Caribbean were unlikely to meet the target, while sub-Saharan Africa was extremely unlikely to achieve it (see ILO UNDP 2003; World Bank 2005). At the national level dozens of countries were identified as priority cases, 'perilously off track to meet the Goals' (UNDP 2003: 15).

The outlook for East Asia looks strong, as the region manages to combine economic growth with poverty reduction. China is the crucial factor here – with 1.2 billion people, it has 70 per cent of the region's population, so trends in this country over-determine trends for the region as a whole. Indeed, conditions in China are decisive for global patterns of growth and poverty more generally. Arguments concerning the links between growth and poverty reduction therefore rest heavily on the case of China. Rapid growth in the Chinese economy is the defining global economic trend of the early twenty-first century. This represents as much the revival of an old economic power as the emergence of a new one: it took until the mid-1990s for China's rate of exports to regain their levels of the late 1920s. With GDP in 2003 still around only one-third that of Japan, China has vast growth potential. It also remains marked by extreme poverty and inequality. While the country has seen rapid economic growth, the distribution of its benefits is more uneven. The deepest inequality is between the minority living in Chinese cities and the 900 million peasants living on land that is increasingly subject to pollution and desertification due to massive programmes of urbanisation and industrialisation. In particular, there is a deep economic cleavage between the export zones of the Chinese coast and the rural interior, with substantial differences in poverty levels between coastal and inland areas (see UNDP 1999: 3, 2003: 34). While these entrenched disparities may weaken some of their more optimistic claims regarding global trends, such patterns also can be seen to bear out Dollar and Kraay's argument about the economic gap between globally connected and disconnected regions within the same country, as well as about the role of government policy in ensuring the effects of growth are distributed across a national population.

South Asia has also made significant progress from a very low base. The region has a massive population in total and a massive poor population, with one-third of its people still living in poverty and one-quarter of them going hungry (UNDP 2003: 34). India is the key to the region's progress, and has seen substantial economic growth, but there are doubts as to how far the benefits are being spread. Latin America and the Caribbean, meanwhile, are doing less well in reducing poverty. The 1990s saw low economic growth and increasing poverty in a particularly uneven region. While some nations have very sound human development indicators, overall the region had a higher proportion of its population living in hunger by 2000 than did East Asia. Again, progress is uneven across countries: Chile and Guyana bucked the regional trend to see growth in per capita incomes of around 5 per cent over the 1990s, and while levels of hunger trebled in Cuba over the decade it was massively reduced in Peru (UNDP 2003: 37).

The period since 1990 has seen striking trends for Central and Eastern Europe and the former Soviet states. The region has seen growing poverty and decreasing life expectancy, with the number living in poverty trebling to almost 100 million, or one-quarter of the total population (UNDP 2003: 37–8). By 2000 the region had lower average incomes than Latin America and the Caribbean. These patterns are underlined by the widening divide between those nations in Central and Eastern Europe that have headed towards membership of the European Union, and the 'CIS Seven' – Armenia, Azerbaijan, Georgia, Kyrgyzstan, Moldova, Tajikistan and Uzbekistan – which finished the decade with incomes approaching those of the least developed nations (UNDP 2003: 35). The most embedded problems remain, though, in sub-Saharan Africa. The region overall lacks any sustained economic growth, and while a handful of countries have seen increasing average incomes, one-half of the region's population lives in extreme poverty.

The emphasis in these analyses is on the linkage between economic growth and poverty reduction. On the one hand, this relationship can be quite straightforward: economic growth can reduce poverty by directly increasing household incomes. However, this is not an automatic effect of growth: it is more likely 'that economic growth reduces income poverty most when initial income inequality is narrow' (UNDP 2003: 17), while people can only share in economic growth where they have access to land and other assets, jobs, markets and credit. On the other hand, economic growth can also indirectly reduce poverty by increasing public revenues and allowing governments to invest in education, health and infrastructure. Such measures all promote skills and productivity levels, but they also have an impact on non-economic poverty. Anti-poverty measures may relate both to the distribution of private goods, and to the definition, distribution and quality of public goods: those goods held in common or public ownership, from water and air to hospitals or roads. This is to draw out the connection between income poverty and a broader 'human poverty' which limits people's capacities to make decisions in their communities and about their own lives due to poor health, sub-standard living environments or lack of education – that is, the lack of basic social and economic capabilities (UNDP 2003: 27).

Such arguments are indebted to Amartya Sen's work on inequality (see especially Sen 1992, 1999). Sen's core argument is that conventional approaches to inequality have focused too heavily on the distribution of commodities and capital, rather than on the share of capabilities or chances. He contends that strategies of economic development should aim to promote human capacities and not simply redistribute goods. Such capacities include individual human capital – knowledge, skills, abilities – but also shared forms of technical and informational capital – technology, information, intellectual goods. More broadly, a stress on capabilities takes in levels of health and education, standards of housing and environmental quality, community development and civil rights.

In contrast to certain of the contributions considered early in this discussion, leading debates on global equality emphasise the links between reducing poverty, decreasing inequality, and promoting human capacities. The distinction between economic and other forms of justice is in this sense a false one. The UN Development Goals are articulated as social and economic rights, and therefore tied up with wider human rights instruments and objectives (see UNDP 2003: 28; UNDP 2004). Moreover, problems of poverty and inequality are understood not merely in terms of income poverty, but also in respect of different kinds of insecurity. While uncertainties in employment conditions, labour market prospects and financial support are very significant in this context, insecurity is not confined to these economic forms. Rather, this problem can be defined in a number of ways (see UNDP 1999):

1   Financial volatility and economic insecurity, including the immediate and longer-term effects of financial crises and economic downturns.
2   Job and income insecurity, linked to restructuring and job losses as well as to more general effects of casualisation.
3   Health insecurity: the most obvious case is that of HIV/AIDS, but globalisation also means that other epidemics have the potential to travel faster and wider than in the past.
4   Cultural insecurity, the effects of which extend from the extremes of cultural genocide to monocultural policy-making and global trends towards homogenisation in media and cultural goods and images.
5   Personal insecurity, linked to crime and victimisaton – including problems of organised crime, sexual violence and sex traffic, vigilante and gun crime.
6   Environmental insecurity, a gathering crisis seen in depleted stocks, threats to biodiversity, and climate change.
7   Political and community insecurity, seen in war, civil conflict, state persecution and poor governance.

In all of these domains – from fears over personal safety to environmental degradation and organised violence – the costs of insecurity tend to be borne by the poorest groups in society. Situations of insecurity and risk in this way overlap with conditions of poverty, serving to reinforce existing structures of social and economic inequality.

Conclusion

Debates over inequality 'after' class in advanced capitalist societies have turned on a series of distinctions between economic and other forms of equality; between reducing poverty and narrowing inequalities; between income differentials, insecurity and exclusion. Setting these arguments in a more global context, however, tends to dissolve such lines of distinction. Inequality, poverty and insecurity interact in complex but legible ways to reproduce deep disparities both between and within nations. Furthermore, social and economic rights – those implied by politics to reduce poverty, promote human welfare and narrow inequalities – can be seen as continuous with wider cultural, political and human rights. To adopt the familiar maxim, famines do not happen in functioning democracies. This may be a truism, but it points to the fact that the stakes involved in arguments over inequality are much higher at a global level than they are in the most developed economies. In the latter setting, hair-splitting over equalities of opportunity as opposed to outcomes can appear as another of the luxuries of the better-off. It is fair to say that arguments over inequality are generally fraught by competing definitions, measures, focal points, and prescriptions. Still, there are more fundamental questions at issue than disputes over methodology or analysis. Sen (2002) criticises the idea that technical measures of (increasing or decreasing) inequality or of (increasing or decreasing) income are the acid-test of economic growth, or indeed of globalisation. They are neither easily comparable nor do they tend to be conclusive. The more relevant assessment, for Sen, is not the measure of existing distributions of wealth, but an evaluation of their *fairness* in comparison to alternative arrangements. Taking up a notion of justice as fairness in a global context is to underline the premise – of some politics and all economic sociology – that economic processes ultimately cannot be isolated from the social contexts within which they operate. Technical measures of economic inequality offer conflicting accounts of what nevertheless are objective conditions, but these real conditions are instituted through policy, structured by relations of power, and legitimised, reproduced or challenged by social actors.

Bibliography

Abu-Lughod, J. (1989) *Before European Hegemony: The World System A.D. 1250–1350*. Oxford: Oxford University Press.

Aglietta, M. (1979) *A Theory of Capitalist Regulation: The US Experience*. London: Verso.

Allen, J. (1995) 'Crossing borders: footloose multinationals', in J. Allen and C. Hamnett (eds) *A Shrinking World*. Oxford: Oxford University Press, 55–102.

Amin, A. (ed.) (1994) *Post-Fordism: A Reader*. Oxford: Blackwell.

Amin, A. (1997) 'Placing globalization', *Theory, Culture and Society* 14/2: 123–37.

Amin, S. (1977) *Imperialism and Unequal Development*. New York: Monthly Review Press.

Amin, S. (1997) *Capitalism in the Age of Globalization*. London: Zed Books.

Amin, S. (2003) *Obsolescent Capitalism*. London: Zed Books.

Amin, S., Arrighi, G., Frank, A. G. and Wallerstein, I. (1982) *Dynamics of Global Crisis*. London: Macmillan.

Amin, S., Arrighi, G., Frank, A. G. and Wallerstein, I. (1990) *Transforming the Revolution: Social Movements and the World-System*. New York: Monthly Review Press.

Ancelovici, M. (2002) 'Organizing against globalisation: the case of ATTAC in France', *Politics and Society* 30/3: 427–63.

Anderson, B. (1983) *Imagined Communities: Reflections on the Origin and Spread of Nationalism*. London: Verso.

Anheier, H., Glasius, M. and Kaldor, M. (eds) (2004) *Global Civil Society 2004*. Oxford: Oxford University Press.

Annan, K. (2003) 'The role of the state in the age of globalization', in F. Lechner and J. Boli (eds) *The Globalization Reader* (second edition). Oxford: Blackwell, 240–3.

Appadurai, A. (1990) 'Disjuncture and difference in the global cultural economy', *Theory, Culture and Society* 7/2–3: 295–310.

Appadurai, A. (1997) *Modernity at Large: Cultural Dimensions of Globalization*. Oxford: Oxford University Press.

Aronowitz, S. (2003) *How Class Works: Power and Social Movement*. New Haven: Yale University Press.

Aronowitz, S. and Gautney, H. (eds) (2003) *Implicating Empire: Globalization and Resistance in the Twenty-first Century World Order*. New York: Basic Books.

Arrighi, G., Hopkins, T. K. and Wallerstein, I. (1989) *Antisystemic Movements*. London: Verso.

Augé, M. (1995) *Non-Places*. London: Verso.

Auletta, K. (1982) *The Underclass*. New York: Random House.

Bairoch, P. (1996) 'Globalization myths and realities: one century of external trade and foreign investment', in R. Boyer and D. Drache (eds) *States Against Markets: The Limits of Globalization*. London and New York: Routledge.

Bale, K. (2000) *Disposable People: New Slavery in the Global Economy*. Berkeley: University of California Press.

Ball, S. (2003) *Class Strategies and the Educational Market: The Middle Classes and the Educational Market*. London: Routledge.

Barber, B. (1995) *Jihad vs McWorld: How Globalism and Tribalism are Reshaping the World*. New York: Times Books.

Barkawi, T. and Laffey, M. (2002) 'Retrieving the imperial: empire and international relations', *Millennium: Journal of International Studies* 31/1: 109–27.

Barro, R. (2000) 'Inequality and growth in a panel of countries', *Journal of Economic Growth* 5/1: 5–32.

Barry, A. and Slater, D. (eds) (2003) *The Technological Economy*. London and New York: Routledge.

Bauman, Z. (1982) *Memories of Class*. London: Routledge and Kegan Paul.

Bauman, Z. (1998) *Work, Consumerism and the New Poor*. Buckingham: Open University Press.

Beck, U. (2000a) *What is Globalization?* Cambridge: Polity.

Beck, U. (2000b) *The Brave New World of Work*. Cambridge: Polity.

Beck, U., Giddens, A. and Lash, S. (1994) *Reflexive Modernization: Politics, Tradition and Aesthetics in the Modern Social Order*. Cambridge: Polity.

Becker, G. S. (1976) *The Economic Approach to Human Behavior*. Chicago: University of Chicago Press.

Becker, G. S. and Murphy, K. M. (2000) *Social Economics: Market Behavior in a Social Environment*. Cambridge, MA: Harvard University Press.

Bell, D. (1973) *The Coming of Post-Industrial Society: A Venture in Social Forecasting*. New York: Basic Books.

Bell, D. (1978) *The Cultural Contradictions of Capitalism*. New York: Basic Books.

Bello, W. (2002) *Deglobalization: Ideas for a New World Economy*. London: Zed Books.

Bendix, R. and Lipset, S.M. (eds) (1966) *Class, Status and Power: Social Stratification in Comparative Perspective*. New York: Free Press.

Bergesen, A.J. and Sonnett, J. (2001) 'The Global 500: mapping the world economy at century's end', *American Behavioral Scientist* 44/10: 1601–15.

Biggart, N. W. (ed.) (2003) *Readings in Economic Sociology*. Oxford: Blackwell.

Bigsten, A. and Levin, J. (2001) 'Growth, income distribution, and poverty: a review', UN/Wider Discussion Paper 2001/129. United Nations University, World Institute for Development Economics Research, Helsinki. *http://www.wider.unu.edu/publications*.

Bishai, L. (2004) 'Liberal Empire', *Journal of International Relations and Development* 7/1: 48–72.

Blanden, J., Gregg, P. and Machin, S. (2005) *Intergenerational Mobility in Europe and North America*. Centre for Economic Performance, London School of Economics.

Blau, J. (1999) *Illusion of Prosperity: America's Working Families in an Age of Economic Insecurity*. Oxford: Oxford University Press.

Block, F. and Evans, P. (2005) 'The role of states in the economy', in N. J. Smelser and R. Swedberg (eds) *The Handbook of Economic Sociology* (second edition). Princeton, NJ: Princeton University Press, 505–26.

Bluestone, B. (1982) *The Deindustrializing of America: Plant Closings, Community Abandonment and the Dismantling of Basic Industries*. New York: Basic Books.

Blustein, P. (2001) *The Chastening: Inside the Crisis that Rocked the Global Financial System and Humbled the IMF*. New York: Public Affairs.

Bonacich, E. and Applebaum, R. (2000) *Behind the Label: Inequality in the Los Angeles Apparel Industry*. Berkeley: University of California Press.

Boot, M. (2003) 'Neither new nor nefarious: the liberal empire strikes back', *Current History* 102/667: 361–6.

Bourdieu, P. (1977) *Outline of a Theory of Practice*. Cambridge: Cambridge University Press.

Bourdieu, P. (1984) *Distinction: A Social Critique of the Judgement of Taste*. Cambridge, MA: Harvard University Press.

Bourdieu, P. (1987) 'What makes a social class? On the theoretical and practical existence of groups', *Berkeley Journal of Sociology* 32: 1–17.

Bourdieu, P. (1993) *Sociology in Question*. London: Sage.

Bourdieu, P. (1996) *The State Nobility: Elite Schools in the Field of Power*. Cambridge: Polity.

Bourdieu, P. (1997) 'The forms of capital', in A. H. Halsey, H. Lauder, P. Brown and A. S. Wells (eds) *Education: Culture, Economy and Society*. Oxford: Oxford University Press, 46–55.

Bourdieu, P. (1998a) 'The myth of "globalization" and the European welfare state', in *Acts of Resistance: Against the New Myths of Our Time*. Cambridge: Polity, 29–44.

Bourdieu, P. (1998b) 'Job insecurity is everywhere now', in *Acts of Resistance: Against the New Myths of Our Time*. Cambridge: Polity, 81–7.

Bourdieu, P. (1998c) 'Neo-liberalism, the utopia (becoming a reality) of unlimited exploitation', in *Acts of Resistance: Against the New Myths of Our Time*. Cambridge: Polity, 94–105.

Bourdieu, P. (2002) 'Habitus', in J. Hillier and E. Rooksby (eds) *Habitus: A Sense of Place*. Aldershot: Ashgate, 27–34.

Bourdieu, P. and Wacquant, L. (1992) *An Introduction to Reflexive Sociology*. Cambridge: Polity.

Bowles, S., Gintis, H., and Osborne, M. (eds) (2004) *Unequal Chances: Family Background and Economic Success*. New York: Russell Sage.

Boyer, R. and Durand, J-P. (1997) *After Fordism*. Basingstoke: Macmillan.

Bradley, H. (1996) *Fractured Identities*. Cambridge: Polity.

Braudel, F. (1984) *The Perspective of the World*. New York: Harper and Row.

Braverman, H. (1974) *Labor and Monopoly Capital: The Degradation of Work in the Twentieth Century*. New York: Monthly Review Press.

Brenner, R. (1998) 'Uneven development and the long downturn: the advanced capitalist economies from boom to stagnation, 1950–1998', *New Left Review* 229: 1–26.

Brenner, R. (2002) *The Boom and the Bubble: The US in the World Economy*. London: Verso.

Byrne, D. (1999) 'The dynamics of income inequality', in *Social Exclusion*. Buckingham: Open University Press, 79–108.

Callinicos, A. (2001) *Against the Third Way: An Anti-Capitalist Critique*. Cambridge: Polity.

Callinicos, A. (2003) *An Anti-Capitalist Manifesto*. Cambridge: Polity.

Callon, M. (1998) 'The embeddedness of economic markets in economics', in M. Callon (ed.) *The Laws of the Market*. Oxford: Blackwell, 1–57.

Capelli, P. (1999) *The New Deal at Work*. Boston: Harvard Business School Press.

Carchedi, G. (1977) *On the Economic Identification of Social Classes*. London: Routledge and Kegan Paul.

Carrier, J. G. (ed.) (1997) *Meanings of the Market: The Free Market in Western Culture*. Oxford: Berg.

Carrol, W. K. and Fennema, M. (2002) 'Is there a transnational business community?', *International Sociology* 17/3: 393–419.

Carruthers, B. G. and Babb, S. L. (2000) *Economy/Society: Markets, Meanings and Social Structure*. Thousand Oaks, CA: Pine Forge Press.

Carruthers, B. G. and Uzzi, B. D. (2001) 'Economic sociology in the new millennium', *Contemporary Sociology* 29/3: 486–94.

Castells, M. (1989) *The Informational City*. Oxford: Basil Blackwell.

Castells, M. (1999) 'Grassrooting the space of flows', *Urban Geography* 20/4: 294–302.

Castells, M. (2000a) *The Rise of the Network Society* (second edition). Oxford: Blackwell.

Castells, M. (2000b) 'Materials for an explanatory theory of the network society', *British Journal of Sociology* 51/1: 5–24.

Castells, M. (2000c) *End of Millennium*. Oxford: Blackwell.

Castells, M. (2004) *The Power of Identity* (second edition). Oxford: Blackwell.

Castles, S. and Davidson, A. (2000) *Citizenship and Migration: Globalisation and the Politics of Belonging*. London and New York: Routledge.

Chase-Dunn, C. (ed.) (1980) *Socialist States in the World-System*. Beverly Hills, CA: Sage.

Chase-Dunn, C. (1998) *Global Formation: Structures of the World-Economy* (second edition). Lanham, MD: Rowman and Littlefield.

Chase-Dunn, C. (1999) 'Globalization: a world-systems perspective', *Journal of World-Systems Research* 5/2: 187–215.

Chase-Dunn, C., Kawano, Y. and Brewer, B. (2000) 'Trade globalization since 1795: waves of integration in the world-system', *American Sociological Review*, 65/1: 77–95.

Cohen, J. and Rogers, J. (eds) (2001) *Can We Put an End to Sweatshops?* Boston: Beacon Press.

Cohen, R. and Rai, S. M. (eds) (2000) *Global Social Movements*. London: The Athlone Press.

Cohen, S. and Zysman, J. (1987) *Manufacturing Matters: The Myth of the Postindustrial Economy*. New York: Basic Books.

Cornia, G. A. and Kiiski, S. (2001) 'Trends in income distribution in the post-World War Two period: evidence and interpretation', UN/Wider Discussion Paper 2001/89. United Nations University, World Institute for Development Economics Research, Helsinki. *http://www.wider.unu.edu/publications*.

Cox, K. R. (ed.) (1997) *Spaces of Globalization: Reasserting the Power of the Local*. New York: The Guilford Press.

Cox, M. (2003) 'The empire's back in town: or America's imperial temptation – again', *Millennium: Journal of International Studies* 32/1: 1–27.

Coyle, D. (1999) *The Weightless World: Thriving in the Digital Age*. Oxford: Capstone Publishers.

Crompton, R., Devine, F., Savage, M. and Scott, J. (eds) (2000) *Renewing Class Analysis*. Oxford: Basil Blackwell.

Crump, J. R. and Merrett, C. D. (1998) 'Scales of struggle: economic restructuring in the US Midwest', *Annals of the Association of American Geographers* 88/3: 496–515.

Cumings, B. (2003) 'Is America an imperial power?', *Current History* 102/667: 355–60.

Dahrendorf, R. (1959) *Class and Class Conflict in Industrial Society*. London: Routledge and Kegan Paul.

Davis, J. (1992) *Exchange*. Minneapolis: University of Minnesota Press.

Day, G. (2000) *Class*. London: Routledge.

Della Porta, D., Kriesi, H. and Rucht, D. (eds) (2000) *Social Movements and the Globalizing World*. New York: St Martin's Press.

Devine, F. (2004) *Class Practices: How Parents Help Their Children Get Good Jobs*. Cambridge: Cambridge University Press.

Dicken, P. (1994) 'Global-local tensions: firms and states in the global space-economy', *Economic Geography* 70/2: 101–28.

Dicken, P. (2002) 'Trading worlds', in R. J. Johnston, P. J. Taylor and M. J. Watts (eds) *Geographies of Global Change: Remapping the World*. Malden and Oxford: Blackwell, 43–56.

Dicken, P. (2003) *Global Shift* (fourth edition). London: Sage.

DiMaggio, P. (1994) 'Culture and economy', in N. J. Smelser and R. Swedberg (eds) *The Handbook of Economic Sociology*. Princeton, NJ: Princeton University Press, 27–57.

Dobbin, F. (ed.) (2004) *The New Economic Sociology: A Reader*. Princeton, NJ: Princeton University Press.

Dodd, N. (1994) *The Sociology of Money: Economics, Reason and Contemporary Society*. Cambridge: Polity.

Dollar, D. and Kraay, A. (2002) 'Spreading the wealth', *Foreign Affairs* 81/1: 120–33.

Dollar, D. and Svensson, J. (2000) 'What explains the success or failure of structural adjustment programmes?', *Economic Journal* 110: 494–517.

du Gay, P. (1996) *Consumption and Identity at Work*. London: Sage.

du Gay, P. and Pryke, M. (eds) (2002a) *Cultural Economy*. London: Sage.

du Gay, P. and Pryke, M. (2002b) 'Cultural economy: an introduction', in P. du Gay and M. Pryke (eds) *Cultural Economy*. London: Sage, 1–19.

Dunkley, G. (2000) *The Free Trade Adventure: The WTO, the Uruguay Round and Globalism – A Critique*. London: Zed Books.

Dussel, E. (1998) 'Beyond Eurocentrism: The World-System and the Limits of Modernity', in F. Jameson and M. Miyoshi (eds) *The Cultures of Globalization*. Durham, NC. and London: Duke University Press, 3–31.

The Economist (1999) 'Frozen Tigers: the prospects for East Asian Economies', in *Economics: Making Sense of the Modern Economy*. London: *The Economist* Newspaper and Profile Books, 195–222.

Embong, A-R. (2000) 'Globalisation and transnational class relations: some problems of conceptualisation', *Third World Quarterly* 21/6: 989–1000.

Featherstone, M. (1987) 'Lifestyle and consumer culture', *Theory, Culture and Society* 4/1: 55–70.

Fevre, R. (2003) *The New Sociology of Economic Behaviour*. London: Sage.

Fine, B., Lapavitsas, C. and Pincus, J. (eds) (2001) *Development Policy in the Twenty-first Century: Beyond the Post-Washington Consensus*. London: Routledge.

Fisher, W. and Ponniah, T. (2003) *Another World is Possible: Popular Alternatives to Globalization at the World Social Forum*. London: Zed Books.

Fligstein, N. (2001) *The Architecture of Markets: An Economic Sociology of Twenty-First Century Capitalist Societies*. Princeton, NJ: Princeton University Press.

Foster, J. B. and McChesney, R. W. (eds) (2004) *Pox Americana: Exposing the American Empire*. New York: Monthly Review Press.

Frank, A. G. (1966) 'The development of underdevelopment', *Monthly Review*, September: 17–31.

Frank, A. G. (1998) *ReOrient: Global Economy in the Asian Age*. Berkeley: University of California Press.

Frank, T. (1998) *The Conquest of Cool: Business Culture, Counterculture and the Rise of Hip Consumerism*. Chicago: University of Chicago Press.

Frank, T. (2000) *One Market Under God: Extreme Capitalism, Market Populism and the End of Economic Democracy*. New York: Doubleday.

Frankel, S. (2001) 'Globalization, athletic footwear commodity chains and employment relations in China', *Organization Studies* 22/4: 531–62.

Fraser, N. (1995) 'From redistribution to recognition? Dilemmas of justice in a "postsocialist" age', *New Left Review* 212: 68–93.

Fraser, N. (1997) *Justice Interruptus: Reflections on the Postsocialist Condition*. New York and London: Routledge.

Fukuyama, F. (1992) *The End of History and the Last Man*. London: Hamish Hamilton.

Fung, A., O'Rourke, D. and Sabel, C. (2001) 'Realizing labor standards', in J. Cohen and J. Rogers (eds) *Can We Put an End to Sweatshops?* Boston: Beacon Press, 3–42.

Galbraith, J. K. (1992) *The Culture of Contentment*. Boston: Houghton Mifflin.

Galbraith, J. K. (1998) *The Affluent Society*. Boston: Houghton Mifflin.

Gallie, D., White, M. and Cheng, Y. (1998) 'The growth of job insecurity', in *Restructuring the Employment Relationship*. Oxford: Clarendon Press.

Gans, H. T. (1995) *The War Against the Poor: The Underclass and Antipoverty Policy*. New York: Basic Books.

George, S. and Sabelli, F. (1994) *Faith and Credit: The World Bank's Secular Empire*. London: Penguin.

Giddens, A. (1981) *The Class Structure of the Advanced Societies* (second edition). London: Hutchinson.

Giddens, A. (1990) *The Consequences of Modernity*. Stanford, CA: Stanford University Press.

Giddens, A. (1991) *Modernity and Self-Identity: Self and Society in the Late Modern Age*. Cambridge: Polity.

Giddens, A. (1994) *Beyond Left and Right: The Future of Radical Politics*. Cambridge: Polity.

Giddens, A. (2000) 'The question of inequality', in *The Third Way and its Critics*. Cambridge: Polity, 85–121.

Gill, S. (1995) 'Globalization, market civilization, and disciplinary neo-liberalism', *Millennium* 24/3: 399–424.

Gills, B. (ed.) (2001) *Globalization and the Politics of Resistance*. New York: Palgrave.

Gilpin, R. (2001) *Global Political Economy: Understanding the International Economic Order*. Princeton, NJ: Princeton University Press.

Goldman, M. (ed.) (1998) *Privatizing Nature: Political Struggles for the Global Commons*. London: Pluto.

Goldman, R. and Papson, S. (1998) *Nike Culture: The Sign of the Swoosh*. London: Sage.

Goldthorpe, J. (1980) *Social Mobility and Class Structure in Modern Britain*. Oxford: Oxford University Press.

Gordon, D. (1988) 'The global economy: new edifice or crumbling foundation?', *New Left Review* 168: 24–65.

Gorz, A. (1982) *Farewell to the Working Class*. London: Pluto.

Gowan, P. (1999) *The Global Gamble: Washington's Faustian Bid for World Dominance*. London: Verso.

Gramsci, A. (1971) [1934] 'Americanism and Fordism', in *Selections from the Prison Notebooks*. London: Lawrence and Wishart, 279–318.

Granovetter, M. (1985) 'Economic action and social structure: the problem of embeddedness', *American Journal of Sociology* 91/3: 481–510.

Granovetter, M. and Swedberg, R. (eds) (2001) *The Sociology of Economic Life* (second edition). Boulder, CO: Westview Press.

Gronow, J. and Warde, A. (eds) (2001) *Ordinary Consumption*. London: Routledge.

Guehenno, J-M. (1995) *The End of the Nation-State*. Minneapolis: University of Minnesota Press.

Guillen, M., Collins, R., England, P. and Meyer, M. (eds) (2002) *The New Economic Sociology: Developments in an Emerging Field*. New York: Russell Sage Foundation.

Gyngell, A. (2004) 'Lessons from parallel worlds', *The Australian Financial Review*, 3 September: 3–4.

Hall, R. and Biersteker, T. (eds) *The Emergence of Private Authority in Global Governance*. Cambridge: Cambridge University Press.

Hall, S. (1988) 'Brave new world', *Marxism Today*, October: 24–9.

Hall, T. D. (ed.) (2000) *A World Systems Reader*. Lanham, MD: Rowman and Littlefield.

Halsey, A. H., Lauder, H., Brown, P. and Wells, A. S. (eds) (1997) *Education: Culture, Economy and Society*. Oxford: Oxford University Press.

Haq, M., Kaul, I. and Grunberg, I. (eds) (1996) *The Tobin Tax: Coping with Financial Volatility*. Oxford: Oxford University Press.

Hardt, M. and Negri, A. (2000) *Empire*. Cambridge, MA: Harvard University Press.

Hardt, M. and Negri, A. (2004) *Multitude*. London: Hamish Hamilton.

Harrison, B. (1988) *The Great U-Turn: Corporate Restructuring and the Polarizing of America*. New York: Basic Books.

Harvey, D. (1982) *The Limits to Capital*. Oxford: Blackwell.

Harvey, D. (1990) *The Condition of Postmodernity*. Oxford: Blackwell.

Harvey, D. (1995) 'Globalisation in question', *Rethinking Marxism* 8/4: 1–17.

Harvey, D. (2000) *Spaces of Hope*. Berkeley: University of California Press.

Harvey, D. (2001) *Spaces of Capital: Towards a Critical Geography*. London and New York: Routledge.

Harvey, D. (2003) *The New Imperialism*. Oxford: Oxford University Press.

Head, S. (2003) *The New Ruthless Economy: Work and Power in the Digital Age*. New York: Oxford University Press.

Heery, E. and Salmon, J. (eds) (1999) *The Insecure Workforce*. London and New York: Routledge.

Held, D. (1991) 'Democracy, the nation-state and the global system', *Economy and Society* 20/2: 138–71.

Held, D. (1995) *Democracy and the Global System: From the Modern State to Cosmopolitan Governance*. Cambridge: Polity.

Held, D. (2004) *Global Covenant: The Social Democratic Alternative to the Washington Consensus*. Cambridge: Polity.

Held, D. and McGrew, A. (2002) *Globalization/Anti-Globalization*. Cambridge: Polity.

Held, D. and McGrew, A. (2003) 'The great globalization debate: an introduction', in D. Held and A. McGrew (eds) *The Global Transformations Reader* (second edition). Cambridge: Polity, 1–50.

Held, D., McGrew, A., Goldblatt, D. and Perraton, J. (1999) *Global Transformations: Politics, Economics and Culture*. Cambridge: Polity.

Herod, A. (2002) 'Global change in the world of organized labor', in R. J. Johnston, P. J. Taylor and M. J. Watts (eds) *Geographies of Global Change: Remapping the World*. Malden and Oxford: Blackwell, 79–87.

Hilferding, R. (1981) [1910] *Finance Capital: A Study of the Latest Phase of Capitalist Development*. London and Boston: Routledge and Kegan Paul.

Hills, J. and Stewart, K. (2005) *A More Equal Society? New Labour, Poverty, Inequality and Exclusion*. Bristol: The Policy Press.

Hines, C. (2000) *Localization: A Global Manifesto*. London: Earthscan.

Hirst, P. (1997) 'The global economy: myths and realities', *International Affairs* 73/3: 409–25.

Hirst, P. and Thompson, G. (1992) 'The problem of "globalization": international economic relations, national economic management and the formation of trading blocs', *Economy and Society* 21/4: 357–96.

Hirst, P. and Thompson, G. (1999) *Globalization in Question: The International Economy and the Possibilities of Governance* (revised edition). Cambridge: Polity.

Hirst, P. and Zeitlin, J. (1991) 'Flexible specialisation versus post-Fordism: theory, evidence and policy implications', *Economy and Society* 20/1: 1–156.

Hobson, J. A. (1988) [1902] *Imperialism: A Study*. London: Unwin Hyman.

Holton, R. J. (1992) *Economy and Society*. London: Routledge.

Holton, R. J. (1998) *Globalization and the Nation-State*. London: Macmillan.

Hopkins, T. K. and Wallerstein, I. (1996) *The Age of Transition: Trajectory of the World-System, 1945–2025*. London: Zed Books.

Hutton, W. (1995) 'The thirty, thirty, forty society', in *The State We're In*. London: Jonathan Cape, 105–10.

ILO (2004) *World Employment Report*. Geneva: International Labour Organisation.

ILO (2005) *A Global Alliance Against Forced Labour*. Geneva: International Labour Organisation.

Jencks, C. (1993) *Rethinking Social Policy: Race, Poverty and the Underclass*. New York: HarperCollins.

Jessop, B. (1990a) *State Theory: Putting the Capitalist State in its Place*. Cambridge: Polity.

Jessop, B. (1990b) 'Regulation theories in retrospect and prospect', *Economy and Society* 19/2: 153–216.

Jessop, B. (1992) 'Fordism and post-Fordism: a critical reformulation', in M. Storper and A. J. Scott (eds) *Pathways to Industrialization and Regional Development*. London and New York: Routledge, 46–69.

Jessop, B. (1994) 'Post-Fordism and the state', in A. Amin (ed.) *Post-Fordism: A Reader*, 251–79.

Jessop, B. (2002) *The Future of the Capitalist State*. Cambridge: Polity.

Jessop, B. (2003) 'Cultural political economy, the knowledge-based economy, and the state', in A. Barry and D. Slater (eds) *The Technological Economy*. London and New York: Routledge.

Johnston, R. J., Taylor, P. J. and Watts, M. J. (2002) 'Introduction to part 1: the reconfiguration of late twentieth-century capitalism', in R. J. Johnston, P. J. Taylor and M. J. Watts (eds) *Geographies of Global Change: Remapping the World*. Malden and Oxford: Blackwell, 21–8.

Kaldor, M. (1999) 'Transnational civil society', in T. Dunne and N. Wheeler (eds) *Human Rights in Global Politics*. Cambridge: Cambridge University Press, 195–213.

Kaldor, M. (2000) 'Civilizing globalization: the implication of the Battle in Seattle', *Millennium: Journal of International Studies* 29/1: 105–14.

Keohane, R. O. and Nye, J. S. Jr (2000) 'Globalization: What's new? What's not? (And so what?)', *Foreign Policy*, Spring: 104–19.

Kilmister, A. (2000) 'Restructuring', in G. Browning, A. Halcli and F. Webster (eds) *Understanding Contemporary Society: Theories of the Present*. London: Sage, 252–65.

King, A. (1990a) *Urbanism, Colonialism and the World Economy: Colonial and Spatial Foundations of the World Urban System*. London and New York: Routledge.

King, A. (1990b) *Global Cities: Post-Imperialism and the Internationalization of London*. London and New York: Routledge.

King, A. (1990c) 'Architecture, capital and the globalization of culture', in M. Featherstone (ed.) *Global Culture: Nationalism, Globalization and Modernity*. London: Sage, 397–411.

King, A. (ed.) (1991) *Culture, Globalisation and the World System*. London: Macmillan.

Klare, M. T. (2003) 'The empire's new frontiers', *Current History* 102/667: 383–7.

Klein, N. (2000) *No Logo*. New York: Picador.

Klein, N. (2002) *Fences and Windows: Dispatches from the Front Lines of the Globalization Debate*. New York: Picador.

Knowles, S. (2001) 'Inequality and economic growth: the empirical relation reconsidered in the light of comparable data', UN/Wider Discussion Paper 2001/128. United Nations University, World Institute for Development Economics Research, Helsinki. *http://www.wider.unu.edu/publications*.

Koenig-Archibugi, M. (2002) 'Mapping global governance', in D. Held and A. McGrew (eds) *Governing Globalization: Power, Authority and Global Governance*. Cambridge: Polity, 46–69.

Krugman, P. (1994) 'The myth of Asia's miracle', *Foreign Affairs* 73/6: 62–78.

Laclau, E. and Mouffe, C. (1987) *Hegemony and Socialist Strategy*. London: Verso.

Lai, H. H. (2001) 'Behind China's World Trade Organization agreement with the USA', *Third World Quarterly*, 22/2: 237–55.

Lash, S. and Urry, J. (1987) *The End of Organized Capitalism*. Cambridge: Polity.

Lash, S. and Urry, J. (1994) *Economies of Signs and Space*. London: Sage.

Leadbeater, C. (1999) *Living on Thin Air: The New Economy*. Harmondsworth: Viking.

Lechner, F. and Boli, J. (eds) (2003) *The Globalization Reader* (second edition). Oxford: Blackwell.

Lee, D. J. and Turner, B. S. (1996a) 'Introduction: myths of classlessness and the "death" of class analysis', in D. J. Lee and B. S. Turner (eds) *Conflicts about Class: Debating Inequality in Late Industrialism*. London: Longman, 1–22.

Lee, D. J. and Turner, B. S. (eds) (1996b) *Conflicts about Class: Debating Inequality in Late Industrialism*. London: Longman.

Leicht, K. T. (ed.) (2005) *Research in Social Stratification and Mobility*, Volume 23. Oxford: Elsevier.

Lemire, B., Pearson, R. and Campbell, G. (eds) (2002) *Women and Credit*. New York: Berg.

Lenin, V. I. (1982) [1916] *Imperialism: The Highest Stage of Capitalism*. Moscow: Progress Publishers.

Lewis, O. (1959) *Five Families: Mexican Case Studies in the Culture of Poverty*. New York: Basic Books.

Lewis, O. (1966) *La Vida: A Puerto Rican Family in the Culture of Poverty – San Juan and New York*. New York: Random House.

Lewis, O. (1996) [1966] 'The culture of poverty', in R. T. Le Gates and F. Stout (eds) *The City Reader*. London and New York: Routledge, 218–24.

Lipietz, A. (1986) 'New tendencies in the international division of labour: regimes of accumulation and modes of regulation', in A. J. Scott and M. Storper (eds) *Production, Work, Territory: The Geographical Anatomy of Industrial Capitalism*. London: Allen and Unwin, 16–40.

Lipietz, A. (1987) *Mirages and Miracles: The Crisis in Global Fordism*. London: Verso.

Lipietz, A. (1994) 'Post-Fordism and democracy', in A. Amin (ed.) *Post-Fordism: A Reader*. Oxford: Blackwell, 338–57.

Lockwood, D. (1958) *The Blackcoated Worker: A Study in Class Consciousness*. London: Allen and Unwin.

Lury, C. (1996) *Consumer Culture*. Cambridge: Polity.

Luxemburg, R. (1968) [1913] *The Accumulation of Capital*. New York: Monthly Review Press.

McGrew, A. (2003) 'Models of transnational democracy', in D. Held and A. McGrew (eds) *The Global Transformations Reader* (second edition). Cambridge: Polity, 500–13.

McRobbie, A. (1998) *British Fashion Design: Rag Trade or Image Industry?* London: Routledge.

McRobbie, A. (1999) *In the Culture Society*. London and New York: Routledge.

McRobbie, A. (2002a) 'From Holloway to Hollywood: happiness at work in the new cultural economy?', in P. du Gay and M. Pryke (eds) *Cultural Economy*. London: Sage, 97–114.

McRobbie, A. (2002b) 'Club to company: notes on the decline of political culture in speeded-up creative worlds', *Cultural Studies* 16/4: 516–31.

Maddison, A. (2001) *The World Economy: A Millennial Perspective*. Paris: OECD.

Mair, A. (1997) 'Strategic localization: the myth of the postnational enterprise', in K. R. Cox (ed.) *Spaces of Globalization: Reasserting the Power of the Local*. New York: The Guilford Press, 64–88.

Mallet, S. (1975) *The New Working Class*. Nottingham: Spokesman Books.

Mann, M. (1997) 'Has globalization ended the rise of the nation-state?', *Review of International Political Economy* 4/3: 472–96.

Mann, M. (2003) *Incoherent Empire*. London: Verso.

Marcuse, P. (2002) 'Depoliticizing globalization: from neo-Marxism to the network society of Manuel Castells', in J. Eade and C. Mele (eds) *Understanding the City: Contemporary and Future Perspectives*. Oxford: Blackwell, 131–58.

Marshall, T. H. (1950) *Citizenship and Social Class*. Cambridge: Cambridge University Press.

Marx, K. and Engels, F. (1977) [1848] 'The Communist Manifesto', in D. McLellan (ed.) *Karl Marx: Selected Writings*. Oxford: Oxford University Press, 221–47.

Massey, D. S. and Denton, N. (1993) *American Apartheid: Segregation and the Making of an Underclass*. Cambridge, MA: Harvard University Press.

Mathews, J. T. (1997) 'Power shift', *Foreign Affairs* 76/1 (January/February): 50–66.

Mead, L. (1992) *The New Politics of Poverty: The Non-Working Poor in America*. New York: Basic Books.

Mies, M. (1998) *Patriarchy and Accumulation on a World Scale: Women in the International Division of Labour*. London: Zed Books.

Miller, P. and Rose, N. (1990) 'Governing economic life', *Economy and Society* 19/1: 1–31.

Mills, C. W. (1951) *White Collar: The American Middle Classes*. Oxford: Oxford University Press.

Milner, A. (1999) *Class*. London: Sage.

Mingeone, E. (ed.) (1996) *Urban Poverty and the 'Underclass'*. Oxford: Blackwell.

Mittelman, J. (2000) *The Globalization Syndrome: Transformation and Resistance*. Princeton, NJ: Princeton University Press.

Moody, K. (1997) *Workers in a Lean World: Unions in the International Economy*. London: Verso.

Moynihan, D. P. (ed.) (1969) *On Understanding Poverty: Perspectives from the Social Sciences*. New York: Basic Books.

Muirhead, R. (2004) *Just Work*. Cambridge, MA: Harvard University Press.

Munck, R. (2002) *Globalisation and Labour: The New 'Great Transformation'*. London: Zed Books.

Munck, R. and Waterman, P. (eds) (1999) *Labour Worldwide in the Era of Globalization*. London: Macmillan.

Murray, C. (1995) *Losing Ground: American Social Policy, 1950–1980* (second edition). New York: Basic Books.

Nash, J. (2001) *Mayan Visions: The Quest for Autonomy in an Age of Globalization*. London and New York: Routledge.

Nike (2005) *FY04 Corporate Responsibility Report*. *www.nike.com/nikebiz*.

Nugent, E. (2005) 'Building a creative persona', PhD thesis, Goldsmiths College, University of London.

Nye, J. S. Jr (2002) *The Paradox of American Power*. Oxford: Oxford University Press.

O'Brien, R., Goetz, A. M., Scholte, J. A. and Williams, M. (2000) *Contesting Global Governance: Multilateral Economic Institutions and Global Social Movements*. Cambridge: Cambridge University Press.

Offe, C. (1984) *Arbeitsgesellschaft*. Frankfurt/Main: Campus-Verlag.

Offe, C. (1985a) *Disorganized Capitalism*. Cambridge: Polity.

Offe, C. (1985b) 'Work: the key sociological category?', in *Disorganized Capitalism*. Cambridge: Polity, 129–50.

Ohmae, K. (1989) *Borderless World: Power and Strategy in the Interlinked Economy*. London: HarperCollins.

Ohmae, K. (1995) *The End of the Nation State: The Rise of Regional Economies*. New York: Free Press.

Oxfam (2002) *Rigged Rules and Double Standards*. Oxford: Oxfam Advocacy.

Oxfam (2003) 'Growth with equity is good for the poor', in F. Lechner and J. Boli (eds) *The Globalization Reader* (second edition). Oxford: Blackwell, 183–9.

Pakulksi, J. and Waters, M. (1996) *The Death of Class*. London: Sage.

Palloix, C. (1977) 'The self-expansion of capital on a world scale', *Review of Radical Political Economics* 9: 1–28.

Parkin, F. (ed.) (1974) *The Social Analysis of Class Structure*. London: Tavistock.

Parkin, F. (1979) *Marxism and Class Theory: A Bourgeois Critique*. London: Tavistock.

Parsons, T. (1949) *The Structure of Social Action*. New York: Free Press.

Parsons, T. and Smelser, N. (1956) *Economy and Society: A Study in the Integration of Economic and Social Theory*. Glencoe, Ill: Free Press.

Peck, J. and Tickell, A. (2002) 'Neoliberalizing space', *Antipode* 34/3: 380–404.

Perotti, R. (1996) 'Growth, income distribution, and democracy: what the data say', *Journal of Economic Growth* 1/1: 149–87.

Perrucci, R. and Wysong, E. (2003) *The New Class Society: Goodbye American Dream?* Lanham, MD: Rowman and Littlefield.

Petras, J. (2003) *The New Development Politics: The Age of Empire Building and New Social Movements*. Aldershot: Ashgate.

Petras, J. and Veltmeyer, H. (2001) *Globalization Unmasked: Imperialism in the Twenty-first Century*. London: Zed Books.

Phillips, A. (1999a) *Which Equalities Matter?* Cambridge: Polity.

Phillips, A. (1999b) 'Does economic inequality matter?', in *Which Equalities Matter?* Cambridge: Polity, 44–73.

Piore, M. J. and Sabel, C. F. (1984) *The Second Industrial Divide*. New York: Basic Books.

Piven, F. F. (1995) 'Is it global economics or neo-laissez-faire?', *New Left Review* 213: 107–15.

Polanyi, K. (1992) 'The economy as an instituted process', in M. Granovetter and R. Swedberg (eds) *The Sociology of Economic Life*. Boulder: Westview Press, 29–51.

Poster, M. (1990) *The Mode of Information*. Cambridge: Polity.

Poulantzas, N. (1973) *Political Power and Social Classes*. London: New Left Books.

Poulantzas, N. (1975) *Classes in Contemporary Capitalism*. London: New Left Books.

Power, M. (1997) *The Audit Society: Rituals of Verification*. Oxford: Oxford University Press.

Ray, L. and Sayer, A. (eds) (1999) *Culture and Economy after the Cultural Turn.* London: Sage.

Reich, R. (1991) *The Work of Nations: Preparing Ourselves for Twenty-first Century Capitalism.* New York: Alfred A. Knopf.

Ritzer, G. (1993) *The McDonaldization of Society.* Thousand Oaks, CA: Pine Forge Press.

Ritzer, G. (ed.) (2002a) *McDonaldization: The Reader.* London: Sage.

Ritzer, G. (2002b) 'McJobs: McDonaldization and its relationship to the labor process', in G. Ritzer (ed.) *McDonaldization: The Reader.* London: Sage, 141–7.

Ritzer, G. (2004) *The Globalization of Nothing.* London: Sage.

Robertson, R. (1990) 'Mapping the global condition: globalization as the central concept', in M. Featherstone (ed.) *Global Culture: Nationalism, Globalization and Modernity.* London: Sage, 15–30.

Robertson, R. (1995) 'Globalization: time–space and homogeneity–heterogeneity', in M. Featherstone, S. Lash and R. Robertson (eds) *Global Modernities.* London: Sage, 25–44.

Robinson, W. I. and Harris, J. (2000) 'Towards a global ruling class? Globalization and the transnational capitalist class', *Science and Society* 64/1: 11–54.

Rose, N. (1991) 'Governing the enterprising self', in R. Keat and N. Abercrombie (eds) *Enterprise Culture.* London and New York: Routledge, 141–64.

Rosenau, J. N. and Czempiel, E. (eds) (1991) *Governance without Government: Order and Change in World Politics.* Cambridge: Cambridge University Press.

Rosenberg, J. (2000) *The Follies of Globalization Theory.* London and New York: Verso.

Ross, A. (1997) *No Sweat: Fashion, Free Trade and the Rights of Garment Workers.* New York: W. W. Norton.

Ross, A. (1998) 'Jobs in cyberspace', in *Real Love: In Pursuit of Cultural Justice.* New York: New York University Press, 7–34.

Roy, A. (2000) *Power Politics.* Cambridge, MA: South End Press.

Royle, T. (2002) 'McWork in Europe', in G. Ritzer (ed.) *McDonaldization: The Reader.* London: Sage, 148–50.

Ruggiero, V. (2002) ' "ATTAC": A global social movement?', *Social Justice* 29/1–2: 48–60.

Sabel, C. (1994) 'Flexible specialisation and the re-emergence of regional economies', in A. Amin (ed.) *Post-Fordism: A Reader.* Oxford: Blackwell, 101–56.

Sahlins, M. (1972) *Stone Age Economics.* Chicago: Aldine-Atherton.

Sahlins, M. (1984) *Culture and Practical Reason.* Berkeley: University of California Press.

Said, Y. and Desai, M. (2001) 'The new anti-capitalist movement: money and global civil society', in H. Anheier, M. Glasius and M. Kaldor (eds) *Global Civil Society 2001.* Oxford: Oxford University Press, 51–78.

Said, Y. and Desai, M. (2003) 'Trade and global civil society: the anti-capitalist movement revisited', in H. Anheier, M. Glasius and M. Kaldor (eds) *Global Civil Society 2003.* Oxford: Oxford University Press, 59–85.

Sassen, S. (1994) 'A new geography of centres and margins: summary and implications', in *Cities in a World Economy.* Thousand Oaks: Pine Forge Press, 208–15.

Sassen, S. (1998) *Globalization and its Discontents.* New York: New Press.

Sassen, S. (1999) 'Digital networks and power', in M. Featherstone and S. Lash (eds) *Spaces of Cultures: City, Nation, World.* London: Sage, 48–63.

Sassen, S. (2001) *The Global City* (second edition). Princeton, NJ: Princeton University Press.

Saunders, P. (1990) *Social Class and Stratification*. London: Routledge.

Schwengel, H. (1991) 'British enterprise culture and German *Kulturgesellschaft*', in R. Keat and N. Abercrombie (eds) *Enterprise Culture*. London and New York: Routledge, 136–50.

Scott, A. (1997) 'Introduction – globalization: social process or political rhetoric?', in A. Scott (ed.) *The Limits of Globalization*. London and New York: Routledge, 1–22.

Scott, A. J. (1988) *New Industrial Spaces: Flexible Production, Organisation and Regional Development in North America and Western Europe*. London: Pion.

Seager, A. (2005) 'Europe sends the most jobs offshore', *Guardian*, 15 January: 24.

Sen, A. (1992) *Inequality Re-examined*. Oxford: Clarendon Press.

Sen, A. (1999) *Development as Freedom*. New York: Alfred A. Knopf.

Sen, A. (2002) 'How to judge globalism', *The American Prospect* 13/1: 2–6.

Sennett, R. (1998) *The Corrosion of Character: The Personal Consequences of Work in the New Capitalism*. New York: Norton.

Shiva, V. (1997) *Biopiracy: The Plunder of Nature and Knowledge*. Boston: South End Press.

Shiva, V. (2001) *Protect or Plunder? Understanding Intellectual Property*. London: Zed Books.

Shiva, V. (2002) *Water Wars: Privatization, Pollution and Profit*. London: Zed Books.

Sklair, L. (ed.) (1994) *Capitalism and Development*. London and New York: Routledge.

Sklair, L. (1998) 'Social movements and global capitalism', in F. Jameson and M. Miyoshi (eds) *The Cultures of Globalization*. Durham and London: Duke University Press, 291–308.

Sklair, L. (1999) 'Competing conceptions of globalization', *Journal of World-Systems Research* 5/2: 143–62.

Sklair, L. (2001) *The Transnational Capitalist Class*. Oxford: Blackwell.

Sklair, L. (2002) *Globalization: Capitalism and its Alternatives*. Oxford: Oxford University Press.

Slater, D. (1997) *Consumer Culture and Modernity*. Cambridge: Polity.

Slater, D. (2002) 'Capturing markets from the economists', in P. du Gay and M. Pryke (eds) *Cultural Economy: Cultural Analysis and Commercial Life*. London: Sage.

Slater, D. and Tonkiss, F. (2001) *Market Society*. Cambridge: Polity.

Smelser, N. J. and Swedberg, R. (eds) (2005) *The Handbook of Economic Sociology* (second edition). Princeton, NJ: Princeton University Press.

Smith, J. and Johnson, H. (eds) (2002) *Globalization and Resistance: Transnational Dimensions of Social Movements*. Lanham, MD: Rowman and Littlefield.

Smith, M. P. (2001) 'Transnationalizing the grassroots', in *Transnational Urbanism: Locating Globalization*. Oxford: Blackwell, 145–62.

Smith, M. P. and Guarnizo, L. (1998) *Transnationalism from Below*. New Brunswick, NJ: Transaction.

Smith, N. (2005) *The Endgame of Globalization*. New York: Routledge.

So, A. (1990) *Social Change and Development: Modernization, Dependency, and World-System Theory.* Newbury Park, CA: Sage.

Starr, A. (2000) *Naming the Enemy: Anti-Corporate Movements Confront Globalization.* London: Zed Books.

Stiglitz, J. E. (2002) *Globalization and its Discontents.* New York: Norton.

Stiglitz, J. E. and Yusuf, S. (eds) (2001) *Rethinking the East Asian Miracle.* New York: Oxford University Press/The World Bank.

Storper, M. and Scott, A. J. (eds) (1992) *Pathways to Industrialization and Regional Development.* London: Routledge.

Strange, S. (1996) *The Retreat of the State: The Diffusion of Power in the World Economy.* Cambridge: Cambridge University Press.

Swedberg, R. (1991) 'Major traditions of economic sociology', *Annual Review of Sociology* 17: 251–76.

Taylor, F. (1911) *The Principles of Scientific Management.* New York: Harper Brothers.

Taylor, L. (1997) 'The revival of the liberal creed: the IMF and the World Bank in a globalized economy', *World Development* 25/2: 145–52.

Thrift, N. (2002a) 'A hyperactive world', in R. Johnston, P. J. Taylor and M. J. Watts (eds) *Geographies of Global Changes: Remapping the World.* Malden and Oxford: Blackwell, 29–42.

Thrift, N. (2002b) 'Performing cultures in the new economy', in P. du Gay and M. Pryke (eds) *Cultural Economy: Cultural Analysis and Commercial Life.* London: Sage, 201–33.

Tickell, A. and Peck, J. (2003) 'Making global rules: globalisation or neoliberalisation?' in J. Peck and H. Yeung (eds) *Remaking the Global Economy: Economic-Geographical Perspectives.* London: Sage, 163–81.

Titmuss, R. (1968) *Commitment to Welfare.* London: Allen and Unwin.

Tobin, J. (1978) 'A proposal for international monetary reform', *Eastern Economic Journal* 4/3: 153–59.

Tomaney, J. (1994) 'A new paradigm of work organization and technology?' in A. Amin (ed.) *Post-Fordism: A Reader.* Oxford: Blackwell, 157–94.

Tomlinson, J. (1991) *Cultural Imperialism: A Critical Introduction.* London: Pinter.

Tonkiss, F. (2002) 'Markets against states: neoliberalism', in K. Nash and A. Scott (eds) *Companion to Contemporary Political Sociology.* Oxford: Blackwell, 250–60.

Touraine, A. (1971) *The Post-Industrial Society.* New York: Random House.

Townsend, I. (2004) *Income, Wealth and Inequality.* Research Paper 04/70. London: House of Commons Library Economic Policy and Statistics Section. *www.parliament.uk/commons/lib/research/rp2004/rp04–70.pdf.*

Trigilia, C. (2002) *Economic Sociology: State, Market and Society in Modern Capitalism.* Oxford: Blackwell.

Turner, B. S. (1988) *Status.* Milton Keynes: Open University Press.

UNCTAD (2002) *World Investment Report.* Geneva: United Nations Conference on Trade and Development.

UNDP (1999) *Human Development Report 1999: Globalization with a Human Face.* New York: Oxford University Press.

UNDP (2003) *Human Development Report 2003: Millennium Development Goals – A Compact Among Nations to End Poverty.* New York: Oxford University Press.

UNDP (2004) *Human Development Report 2004: Cultural Liberty in Today's Changing World*. New York: United Nations Development Programme.

Van der Pijl, K. (1998) *Transnational Classes and International Relations*. London: Routledge.

Veblen, T. (1934) [1899] *The Theory of the Leisure Class: An Economic Study of the Evolution of Institutions*. New York: Modern Library.

Wade, R. and Veneroso, F. (1998) 'The Asian crisis: the high debt model versus the Wall Street-Treasury-IMF complex', *New Left Review* 228: 3–23.

Waldinger, R. and Lichter, M. I. (2003) *How the Other Half Works: Immigration and the Social Organization of Labor*. Berkeley: University of California Press.

Wallerstein, I. (1974) *The Modern World-System: Capitalist Agriculture and the Origins of European World-Economy in the Sixteenth Century*. New York: Academic Press.

Wallerstein, I. (1979) *The Capitalist World-Economy*. Cambridge: Cambridge University Press.

Wallerstein, I. (1982) 'Crisis as transition', in S. Amin (ed.) *Dynamics of Global Crisis*. New York: Monthly Review Press, 11–54.

Wallerstein, I. (1984) *The Politics of the World-Economy: The States, the Movements, and the Civilisations*. Cambridge: Cambridge University Press.

Wallerstein, I. (1987) 'World-systems analysis', in A. Giddens and J. Turner (eds) *Social Theory Today*. Stanford: Stanford University Press, 309–24.

Wallerstein, I. (1990) 'Culture as the ideological battleground of the modern world-system', in M. Featherstone (ed.) *Global Culture: Nationalism, Globalization and Modernity*. London: Sage, 31–56.

Wallerstein, I. (1991) *Geopolitics and Geoculture: Essays on the Changing World-System*. Cambridge: Cambridge University Press.

Wallerstein, I. (2002) 'New revolts against the system', *New Left Review*, November–December: 29–39.

Wallerstein, I. (2003) [1974] 'The rise and future demise of the world capitalist system', in F. Lechner and J. Boli (eds) *The Globalization Reader* (second edition). Oxford: Blackwell, 63–9.

Walton, J. (1987) 'Urban protest and the global political economy: the IMF riots', in M. P. Smith and J. R. Feagin (eds) *The Capitalist City*. Oxford: Blackwell, 354–86.

Walton, J. (1998) 'Urban conflict and social movements in poor countries', *International Journal of Urban and Regional Studies* 22: 460–81.

Warde, A. (2002) 'Production, consumption and "cultural economy"', in P. du Gay and M. Pryke (eds) *Cultural Economy: Cultural Analysis and Commercial Life*. London: Sage, 185–200.

Waterman, P. and Wills, J. (eds) (2001) *Place, Space and the New Labour Internationalisms*. Oxford: Blackwell.

Waters, M. (2000) 'Inequality after class', in K. Nash (ed.) *Readings in Contemporary Political Sociology*. Oxford: Blackwell, 43–62.

Weber, M. (1978) [1922] 'Class, status and party', in W. G. Runciman (ed.) *Max Weber: Selections in Translation*. Cambridge: Cambridge University Press, 43–56.

Weber, M. (1982) [1922] 'Status groups and classes', in A. Giddens and D. Held (eds) *Classes, Power and Conflict: Classical and Contemporary Debates*. Basingstoke: Macmillan, 69–73.

Weiss, L. (1998) *The Myth of the Powerless State*. Cambridge: Polity.

Westergaard, J. H. (1995) *Who Gets What? The Hardening of Class Inequality in the Late Twentieth Century*. Cambridge: Polity.

Westergaard, J. H. and Resler, H. (1975) *Class in a Capitalist Society*. London: Heinemann.

Williams, R. (1980) [1960] 'Advertising: the magic system', in *Problems in Materialism and Culture*. London: Verso, 170–95.

Williamson, O. E. (1985) *The Economic Institutions of Capitalism: Firms, Markets, Relational Contracting*. New York: Free Press.

Wilson, W. J. (1987) *The Truly Disadvantaged: The Inner City, the Underclass, and Public Policy*. Chicago: University of Chicago Press.

Wilson, W. J. (1996) *When Work Disappears*. New York: Alfred A. Knopf.

Wolf, M. (2004) *Why Globalization Works: The Case for the Global Market Economy*. New Haven: Yale University Press.

Wood, E. M. (2005) *Empire of Capital*. London: Verso.

World Bank (2005) *Global Monitoring Report 2005*. Washington: World Bank.

World Social Forum (2003) 'Porto Alegre call for mobilization', in F. Lechner and J. Boli (eds) *The Globalization Reader* (second edition). Oxford: Blackwell, 435–7.

Wright, A. (2005) *Ripped and Torn: Levi's, Latin America and the Blue Jean Dream*. London: Ebury.

Wright, E. O. (1978) *Class, Crisis and the State*. London: New Left Books.

Wright, E. O. (1985) *Classes*. London: Verso.

Wright, E. O. (1997) *Class Counts: Comparative Studies in Class Analysis*. Cambridge: Cambridge University Press.

Wright, R. (2002) 'Transnational corporations and global divisions of labor', in R. J. Johnston, P. J. Taylor and M. J. Watts (eds) *Geographies of Global Change: Remapping the World*. Malden and Oxford: Blackwell, 68–77.

Yuen, E., Katsiaficas, G. and Burton Rose, D. (2001) *The Battle of Seattle: The New Challenge to Capitalist Globalization*. New York: Soft Skull Press.

Zelizer, V. A. (1997) *The Social Meaning of Money*. Princeton, NJ: Princeton University Press.

Zukin, S. and DiMaggio, P. (eds) (1990) *Structures of Capital: The Social Organization of the Economy*. Cambridge: Cambridge University Press.

Index

Economy and Society

MANAGING EDITOR: Grahame Thompson,
London School of Economics and Political Science, UK

This radical interdisciplinary journal of theory and politics continues to be one of the most exciting and influential resources for scholars in the social sciences worldwide.

As one of the fields leading scholarly refereed journals, *Economy and Society* plays a key role in promoting new debates and currents of social thought. For over 25 years, the journal has explored the social sciences in the broadest interdisciplinary sense, in innovative articles from some of the world's leading sociologists and anthropologists, political scientists, legal theorists, philosophers, economists and other renowned scholars.

In regular issues, and through issues devoted to special themes, *Economy and Society* covers questions ranging from economic governance to developments in the life sciences and beyond, and publishes major new work on current issues confronting progressive politics throughout Europe and North America, Australasia and the Pacific Rim.

**The journal is abstracted and indexed within the ISI® Science Citation Index.
Current impact factor is 1.069.**

For further information, please visit the website at: **www.tandf.co.uk/journals**